READING
LESSONS

READING LESSONS

■ ■ ■

An Introduction to Theory

Scott Carpenter
Carleton College

PRENTICE-HALL
Upper Saddle River, New Jersey 07458

Library of Congress Cataloging-in-Publication Data

Carpenter, Scott,
    Reading lessons : an introduction to theory / Scott Carpenter.
        p.   cm.
    Includes bibliographical references (p.) and index
    ISBN 0-13-021100-1
    1. Literature—History and criticism—Theory, etc.   2. Books and
    reading.   3. Criticism.   I. Title.
    PN81.034 1999
    801'.95—dc21   99-13133
                                                                  CIP

Editor-in-Chief: Leah Jewell
Acquisitions Editor: Carrie Brandon
Editorial Assistant: Gianna Caradonna
AVP/Director of Production and Manufacturing: Barbara Kittle
Manufacturing Manager: Nick Sklitsis
Prepress and Manufacturing Buyer: Mary Ann Gloriande
Cover Design: Kiwi Design
Cover Art: "Adiago" © 1998 by Mimi Jensen
        oil on canvas, 48 × 36
        Courtesy Hespe Gallery, San Francisco
Marketing Manager: Sue Brekka

This book was set in 10.5/12 Goudy by Pub-Set, Inc.
and was printed and bound by Courier Companies, Inc.
The cover was printed by Phoenix Color Corp.

© 2000 by Prentice-Hall, Inc.
Upper Saddle River, NJ 07458

Printed in the United States of America
10 9 8 7 6 5 4 3 2 1

ISBN 0-13-021100-1

Prentice-Hall International (UK) Limited, London
Prentice-Hall of Australia Pty. Limited, Sydney
Prentice-Hall Canada, Inc., Toronto
Prentice-Hall Hispanoamericana, S.A., Mexico
Prentice-Hall of India Private Limited, New Delhi
Prentice-Hall of Japan, Inc., Tokyo
Pearson Education Asia Pte. Ltd., Singapore
Editora Prentice-Hall do Brasil, Ltda., Rio de Janeiro

For Paul and Muriel,
whose sense of play
is an inspiration.

CONTENTS

■ ■ ■

FOREWORD

■ ■ ■

This book aims to make reading hard again, to restore some of the impenetrability of texts, while rekindling the delight we took in discovery. It is meant to furrow your brow.

—Scott Carpenter, "Introduction"

Professor Scott Carpenter's *Reading Lessons: An Introduction to Theory*, like the popular novel *Sophie's World*, written by the Norwegian Professor of Philosophy and the History of Ideas, Jostein Gaarder, raises questions about the presentation of sophisticated, often difficult theories to a broader group of readers than the group to whom these theories are usually addressed. This is always a risky venture, but when it succeeds, as I think it does in Scott Carpenter's book on literary theory, then one should be, as I will, lavish in one's praise.

In this engaging book on how to perform close readings and informed readings of literary and filmic texts, Scott Carpenter pleads for a slowing down in our reading habits and concomitantly for our greater tolerance of ambiguity and uncertainty in the texts we read and the films we view. The intended audience for *Reading Lessons* is those undergraduate students (with poor reading habits) who are beginning to study literature, as well as a general reading public (also perhaps with poor reading habits) that would probably not read the works of some of the major names in contemporary literary theory with whom Scott Carpenter engages—Jacques Lacan, Jacques Derrida, Judith Butler, Steven Greenblatt—or more conventionally written academic books and articles about them. Buoyed by his success in presenting literary theory in the classroom during the past eight or more years, Scott Carpenter is convinced, and so are his editors, that these groups would be seduced by the sprightly, sometimes impudent tone of *Reading Lessons*, by Carpenter's punning and his range of references from high and popular cultures, and by his deep commitment to this project.

The sentence from the "Introduction" that I have used as an epigraph may be taken as a microcosm of Carpenter's intentions and his style. It is direct, punchy, and slightly irreverent. Carpenter is afraid neither of declaring his intentions "aims," nor of troubling his intended reader by suggesting that hard work lies ahead, for this book is about matters with which the reader is most likely unfamiliar. But it would be a mistake to consider this book as uniquely for the noninitiated. Indeed, professors, scholars, critics, advanced students of literature as well as the "cultivated" lay reader will take great pleasure in and will learn from the innovative ways in which Scott Carpenter has organized his material. The chapter titles are all inviting: "Monkeys at the Typewriter: Signs/Meaning/Communication," "Rounding Up Some Unusual Suspects: Formalism and Structuralism," "Mssng Lttrs: Poststructuralism and Deconstruction," "The Remembrance of Things Past: Psychoanalysis," "Gender Gaps: Feminism and Gender Studies," "The Importance of Context: New Historicism and Cultural Studies," "Click _Here_: Hypertexts, and Reader Response," "For Eclecticism: The Role of Theory." Scott Carpenter, as exegete, has the ability to move quickly to the heart of the matter. Scott Carpenter, as scholar, has read widely and presents an impressive range of examples. This range means that readers carrying diverse kinds of intellectual and cultural baggage will find allusions to some texts with which they are familiar. This is perhaps one of the major strengths of Scott Carpenter's offering, and what distinguishes it from most other books on literary and filmic criticism that draw their examples from the masterpieces of national literatures. To "furrow" the reader's brow, one must begin with some elements that the reader considers familiar and clear before proceeding to make the familiar strange and ambiguous.

Reading Lessons is a superb defense of the important role played by theory in literary studies as well as a plea for understanding the importance of storytelling in all of our lives. Thus Scott Carpenter, without ever attacking academic writing per se, offers his readers a book that is an elegant vulgarization of high theory in a form that is at the same time accessible and arduous. His accomplishment in maintaining the integrity of the theories he discusses and in sustaining the reader's excitement is remarkable.

Elaine Marks
Germaine Brée Professor of French and Women's Studies,
University of Wisconsin—Madison

Former president of the Modern Language Association of America

PREFACE

The User's Guide

Reading Lessons is an introduction to literary theory imagined differently. Rather than presenting key terms, names, and definitions in a traditional, expository fashion, I have tried to engage readers by highlighting the playfulness of theory and the way it can enhance the pleasure of reading. This has meant setting aside, as least provisionally, much of the technical jargon used by some theoreticians in hopes of bringing students into direct contact with the compelling issues evoked by such movements as post-structuralism or gender studies.

In its presentation of ideas *Reading Lessons* draws on a wide variety of media, including film, literature, advertising, puzzles, and more. These examples, many of which are para-literary, should help readers make connections between theory and everyday life—a difficult but important task. The book approaches reading as a series of questions: What is the role of the author? How can one understand the relationship between texts and historical contexts? How does gender influence the practices of reading and writing? How, in the encounter between text and reader, does *meaning* arise? The theoretical schools introduced—namely, structuralism, post-structuralism, deconstruction, psychoanalysis, feminism, gender studies, new historicism, cultural studies, reader response—do not answer these questions in any definitive fashion, but they hint at ways in which such questions may illuminate our reading of any given text. The goal of *Reading Lessons*, then, is to put readers in touch with important questions, and to equip them with the tools they need to formulate questions of their own.

Reading Lessons is not comprehensive, and it cannot replace the rich theoretical writings which have inspired it. This volume may be useful in courses where students are just beginning to ask literary questions; it may also have a place in more advanced courses, as a way of easing students into more technical readings. (Many such readings are recommended at the end of each chapter.) The book works especially well as a whole, and I have taken pains to interweave the chapters, showing how various schools relate to each other. However, *Reading Lessons* can also be segmented, and its segments may be re-ordered or used selectively. There is no royal road to theory; as it turns out, theory is not a destination.

ACKNOWLEDGMENTS

This book has multiple, perhaps innumerable authors, and I can only begin to cite them. I refer not merely to the obvious cases—the Derridas and Lacans, the Butlers and Greenblatts whose work I condense, distort, and represent here. Much of what appears in *Reading Lessons* comes from friends, colleagues, teachers, and students.

In a hopelessly inadequate recognition of their contributions, let me at least list the names of a very few special cases. Anne Maple believed in this book more than I did, and without her relentless encouragement and her sharp eye, I would never have finished it. Carleton College has offered support in many ways, and college funds have helped provide the time and resources necessary for the completion of this project. Many friends served as readers and offered invaluable advice, especially Anne Ulmer, Dana Strand, Clara Hardy, Sigi Leonhard, James Winchell, John Greene, Karen Cherewatuk, and Doug Northrop. Thanks also to Terry Geesken, of the Film Stills Archive at the Museum of Modern Art, who was extraordinarily accommodating, and to Abram H. Boulding and Katrina Petersen for their artistry in the line drawings. I have an unending intellectual debt to Maria Paganini. And thanks to six years worth of Carleton students who have suffered—cheerily, with good spirit—through Literary Studies 245. I would also like to thank the following reviewers for their thoughtful suggestions: James Winchell, University of Alabama, Huntsville; Timothy Spurgin, Lawrence University; Seth Lerer, Stanford University.

Finally, thanks to my student assistants: Meg Collins, Sarah Kleb, Kristin Knudson, and Julia Steinmetz. You proved indefatigable in the painful, tedious tasks I assigned you, and someday you will forgive me.

—Scott Carpenter

READING LESSONS

An Introduction

■ ■ ■

Life being very short, and the quiet hours of it few, we ought to waste none of them in reading valueless books.

— John Ruskin, 1865

Remember when reading pained you?

A child's first encounters with the written word are not always friendly. The alphabet travels with a song, but as kids come in contact with print, when they make the transition from repeating stories they have learned by heart to actually deciphering the letters on a page, a struggle ensues. Visit a kindergarten class, or a first or second grade: at reading time, the rooms are full of lightly furrowed brows. When put before a book, these tykes, taking their first, hesitant steps into literacy, pour over the printed page with incomparable intensity. Fingers press upon the paper as if to pin the words in place. Lips move as kids strive to breathe life into dead print, as they labor to get their tongues around strange clumps of consonants. Reading is hard, and yet not without the reward of difficulties conquered: faces light with surprise and sudden satisfaction as a sentence falls into place.

But the delight is not enduring. Sometime between these early years and our entrance into adolescence, print lost its secrets. The opacity of those strangely shaped marks faded, and we began to see through them. One day we fumbled with the simplest of phrases; the next we were rocketing through storybooks, children's magazines, and more. The activity we once found so cumbersome became automatic, seemingly effortless, and suddenly we were doing it unconsciously and incessantly: from the back of the Rice Krispies box in the morning, to the lyrics of songs, to the messages from Mom stuck on the fridge, and to the *TV Guide*, reading found us at every turn of our daily lives. After suffering through our painful initiation to the written word years earlier, we had finally got what we thought we wanted: *we could read without thinking about it.* Since then, many of us have known periods of real readerly voracity, devouring novels, histories, mysteries, or romances. And reading became flexible. When faced in school with more pages than we could stomach, we accelerated the process, and speed-reading or skimming turned into an academic survival tactic. Reading became so fast and so easy that it almost felt as if we hadn't even done it—which often was more or less true.

This book aims to make reading hard again, to restore some of the impenetrability of texts, while rekindling the delight we took in discovery. It is meant to furrow your brow.

The endeavor I propose here differs, of course, from our first introduction to letters. We have already mastered vocalization, and we are expert at following stories or deciphering VCR manuals. Like Alexander the Great before the Gordian knot, we slash through complications mercilessly, getting to the core of what things mean. This practice is not surprising, for it reflects our training, which has focused on the rapid distillation of meaning. When we stepped up to literacy so many years ago, ambiguity was our nemesis. Nothing slows down a six-year-old like a word that waffles: in a story about a young detective, does the child read, in any given sentence, "sùs-pect," the noun, or "sus-pèct," the verb? Polysyllabic words can bring minor panic attacks upon a first grader, and young readers regularly transform unknown words into their more familiar cousins: "wandered" may roam off to become "wanted," while "lunge" is dished up as "lunch." With age (we say this more every year) comes wisdom, and as we grow in years, when neither teacher nor parent spies over our shoulder, we refine our tactics, often learning simply to ignore words, passages, or even whole books we don't understand. As a rule, we never abandon these strategies for hacking our way through the wilderness of texts. In fact, as we accelerate our lives, learning how to speed-live, many of us shed all tolerance for anything that slows us down. At the rate we travel, an encounter with ambiguity or uncertainty in reading can be like sticking a metal bar in the spokes of a passing motorcycle.

To make matters more difficult, ambiguity has received a lot of bad press. Whole fields of intellectual inquiry—and ones that tend to be in the national limelight, ranging from the natural sciences to statistical analysis, from computer science to economics—strive quite systematically to eradicate the very ambiguity championed by literary analysis. To these fields ambiguity is like a roach infestation, so many "bugs" in the operation of an otherwise happy, stable system. De-bugging amounts to disambiguating (yes, that is a word, though not a very pleasant one) the world around us. Nothing opposes more the revelry of a literary approach like Deconstruction than the De-Con spray of much scientific scrutiny, used to exterminate those am-bug-uities scurrying in the dark.

Disambiguating is what allows us to read, think, live, and conclude *quickly*. This book, however, means to be an initiation to a different kind of reading; it attempts to reintroduce the allure of slowness. In many ways it works against the grain of the lessons of our early years, laying out the *attractions* of ambiguity rather than its dangers.

Perhaps "ambiguity" is still too limiting a term, for it implies two-ness, mere binarity—as if literature were simply ambidextrous, pointing in two directions at once. The richness of language lies in its ability to point in many directions. Unlike a *code* (you might think, for example, of the relative ease with which one can transcribe the dots and dashes of Morse into letters), the meanings we detect in language are multiple and in constant evolution. Some see this as a frustration, for it precludes our ever uttering the final word or nailing down "the" meaning of a text. Instead, reading leads us to various understandings, including multiple (and sometimes mutually exclusive) interpretations or meanings, ideas about how a text functions or is structured, or an awareness of how a given work is entangled with the time of its production (writing) or consumption (reading).

We have strong institutional and social pressures to avoid investigating this multiplicity, for it threatens to slow us down—and slowing down is tantamount to a cardinal sin in turn-of-the-millennium America. Ambiguity represents a bifurcation, a branching off of directions offered to the reader: the text is always a possible, and possibly dangerous, maze. Like the mythical king Theseus, who entered mazes only to conquer their dangers and escape unscathed, readers cling to their own versions of Ariadne's thread, following it toward the light.

It is most likely impossible to read without a thread or guiding principle. But it can be useful to release the threads one already knows, even if only provisionally, and to grope in the darkness. There is a certain amount of pleasure to be had from losing oneself in a maze, and from discovering new passageways.

Such discoveries, however, are rarely serendipitous, and in literary study they rely on two principle elements. The first of these goes by the name of *close reading.* Although it sounds like something you might need corrective lenses for, it refers simply to a slow, studied reading of a text (often focusing on brief passages), one in which the reader attempts to develop an awareness of technical branchings and entanglements. The second element has to do with the sense one makes of these entanglements, which is largely a question of *method.*

Discussions about method come under the heading of *theory*—a word that often has people scrambling for cover. And yet, *theory* comes from an old Greek word meaning only "to look at." To theorize about reading suggests nothing more than adjusting our sights, lifting our gaze from the book in our hands and taking a gander at just what it is we *do* when we read. Why should we bother to reflect on reading? Because if we don't understand how we read, we will be condemned to read everything the same way. For the fact is that everyone *already* has some kind of literary approach. So-called casual readers are *not* free of method, despite what we might assume. But their methods—the judgments they make about what is important in a book and what is not, about what something means, about how much attention they need to pay to themes, historical background, puzzling inconsistencies—are largely *implicit*; they make decisions according to guidelines they have "a feel for." Nothing is wrong with such an intuitive approach—and who among us does not indulge in the pleasure of losing himself or herself in a good story? Nevertheless, there is a trade-off, and the way we read largely determines what we are looking for in a book, which, consequently, prescribes what we can find. Thus, our way of reading may blind us to aspects of a work we have never thought to consider. Whence the methodological double bind: method arms us with a beam of light, yet the way we point it determines not just the field of our vision, but also the much vaster steppes of our blindness.

Talking about ways of reading forces us to make our assumptions and prejudices explicit. Then, when we have laid our cards on the table, we can look them over, see how we like them, and think about how we might wish to play our hand. Better yet, it helps us to see that different readers read differently. If various approaches enhance our reading pleasure in particular ways, perhaps it will do us some good to get inside another way of thinking, even if just for a short span of time. We can try these other methods on for size, walk around in them for a while, and see how they feel.

The present volume is meant neither to decry various trends in literary analysis nor to champion them, but rather simply to introduce them. Drawing on a variety of national literatures (mostly from the Western tradition), as well as on nonliterary genres (films, advertisements, current events), I have attempted to lay out many of the major issues and concerns of critical reading today. Although *Reading Lessons* provides some scant history of the development of various schools of thought and of their major players, emphasis is placed on outlining the kinds of questions various approaches ask, and why. Moreover, special care is taken to demonstrate what might be the implications of such movements as structuralism, deconstruction, and gender studies beyond the confines of literature. Perhaps the greatest challenge, and the most important, consists of learning to use these "tools for thinking" in arenas broader than literary analysis, and beyond the walls of academe.

That said, this book is not a "how-to" manual. It does not present recipes for producing, for example, poststructuralist or psychoanalytic reading. Instead, it provides a survey of just what kind of theories underpin various forms of literary and cultural reading in the humanities today. Some of the discussions may strike you initially as extreme, but bear with them; taking assumptions to their logical extremes is often the best way to discover their limits and implications.

Reading Lessons is an initiation to the complex and often difficult thought of contemporary theorists, but it should not be considered a substitute for the writings it explains. This book engages, necessarily, in a certain amount of simplification, which is always a kind of distortion. To appreciate the richness and texture of this thought, one must confront, eventually, some of the theoretical texts directly. To this end, each chapter concludes with a list of suggestions for further reading. If something piques your interest, follow up on it.

Who knows? Maybe you will shelve these ideas at the end and stick with what you have; with luck, you will at least know more about what drives your own reading. On the other hand, you may be opening a kind of Pandora's box: as we found when we were children, learning to read is tough enough; *unlearning* it is well-nigh impossible.

1

MONKEYS
AT THE TYPEWRITER
■■■
Signs/Meaning/Communication

How else to begin a book about reading other than with a story—a story about reading?

One year, when I was a college student spending a year in England, relatives invited me to spend spring break with them in Belgium. I leapt at the chance. Equipped with a small bag and an even smaller understanding of French, I began an odyssey of hitchhiked rides, subway travel, a ferry crossing on a choppy channel, followed by various rail segments. Sometime around midnight I arrived in the smallish train station of Liège, in central Belgium, where I immediately phoned my uncle, who lived twenty minutes away. His phone was out. After loitering for some time in the station, attempting without success to enlist the aid of a grumpy clerk who seemed incapable of enunciating clearly enough for my untrained ear, and after making repeated attempts to contact my hosts, I set out in hopes of locating lodging for the night.

Liège is not a large city. And yet, unknown as it was to me, at night it seemed immense. Strangely, I failed to locate anything resembling a hotel district, a business district, or even a restaurant district (although I did stray into the red-light district). It was with considerable relief that I eventually spotted a sober little sign pointing me in the direction of the *Hôtel de Ville*, the "City Hotel." Its rather grand name and classy, understated advertising suggested it would outstrip my usual lodgings, as well as my budget, but the hour was late, and I was in no position to be picky. Following these diminutive black and white signs up and down streets, turning right here, left there, I finally emerged on a broad square facing a sumptuous palace surrounded by wrought iron fencing. Worked in metal above the broad, locked gate were the words "*Hôtel de Ville*." A series of plaques bolted to the gate provided information ranging from the location of administrative offices to the hours of service.

Hôtel de Ville, I learned then and there, meant "City Hall," and they were not about to put me up for the night.

Ten years later I would be teaching French in a small liberal arts college; I never told anyone of my inauspicious beginnings.

I have often thought of this incident as a parable about reading, about the way we try to make sense of the signs we deal with on a daily basis, about how misreadings occur, and about how we correct them.

For me, this brief adventure raises compelling questions. How, as readers, do we ascertain which things are signs? More important, how do we know what they *represent*—that is, just what they are signs *of*? The questions are elementary, to be sure—even childlike—but they underpin vast expanses of human activity, ranging from sophisticated scientific inquiries to the most mundane of tasks. Usually we ask these questions practically, automatically, and in the most ordinary aspects of daily life. On your way to the supermarket, for example, you stop obediently at a red light, continuing on your way when it turns green. In the dairy aisle you pick up a tub of cream cheese announcing itself as "lite." In the checkout lane you spy a headline reporting alien abductions. All of these items you may passively identify as signs, and rightly or wrongly you attribute meanings to them: red means stop; "lite" suggests "liter" than the other stuff; the *National Enquirer* headlines you may decipher as signs of utter nonsense. Most such interpretations of commonplace signs occur routinely, even unconsciously.

However, it is precisely in such cases as the *National Enquirer* that our questioning of meaning may cross the threshold into conscious inquiry: we inquire into the *Enquirer*. Assuming we acknowledge that the headline is indeed a sign, it is not at all clear what it might be a sign *of*. Reading naively, we may accept it as reporting unusually aggressive behavior by extraterrestrials; alternatively we could see in it a commentary on the state of the American imagination, or on the financial status of certain sectors of the mass media. In any case, the *National Enquirer* may strike us as far more interesting than the stoplight precisely because we don't quite know *what* it means. In general, the headline holds more interest than the traffic light because, although both the light and the tabloid are signs of sorts, the stoplight is entirely unambiguous—*obviously* a sign, and one of *obvious* meaning.

What seems to command our attention, then, is ambiguity: the uncertainty of meaning, or the possibility of multiple meanings.

One might say that ambiguity is the diet of literary studies. This is not to imply that literature programs in colleges and universities across the country are busily scrutinizing the *National Enquirer*. At least, not necessarily. But the fundamental questions one asks in literature programs are the same everywhere, and they generally spring from the basic reflections about signs articulated above. What does image X in book Y mean, and how does it mean it? How does one determine which words, verses, images, themes, sections, books, authors, traditions are significant, and what they signify? How is meaning produced? How is one to read? Indeed, *what* is one to read—what is literature, and what is not?

These are the questions we need to address, not so much to answer them once and for all, but rather to show the various ways they have been approached—and *why*.

WHAT *IS* LITERATURE, ANYWAY?

It may appear easier to answer some questions negatively. For example, rather than defining literature by, say, amassing an exhaustive list of authors or works that "count" (Austen, Dickens, Balzac, Tolstoy, the Bible), we may find it simpler to begin by providing counterexamples, a list of the kinds of writings that do *not* count (technical manuals, legal documents, scurrilous journalism, shopping lists). By most tallies, the *National Enquirer* doesn't make the grade. Few would rank it among commonly acknowledged literary masterpieces. However, just where one draws the line between literature and nonliterature is subject to a good deal of dispute: does one include in the literary canon detective novels? Movie scripts? Casual verse? Dirty limericks? Ghost stories? And what if the ghost story is penned by a consecrated author, such as Edgar Allan Poe or Henry James?[1] What if the limericks are found in James Joyce's personal diaries, or are attributed to Joyce by Tom Stoppard?[2] What if the detective story is called *Oedipus Rex*? It quickly becomes apparent that what one includes among the ranks of literature is largely a matter of personal or collective preference, and that no essential, absolute distinctions can be made to separate the literary wheat from the chaff of hack writers. For this reason, critics have largely abandoned the notion of Literature with a capital L, often replacing it with the more elementary notion of *text*. In general, in literary studies, a text consists of any object (usually comprised of language) that might be considered to be "readable" in some sense. The term *text* is value neutral; it implies no qualitative judgment. "Literature" remains as the somewhat arbitrary category of those texts we find especially interesting, particularly in their creative use of language.

Given this definition, the *National Enquirer* I find in the checkout lane qualifies not only as a text, but as a relatively sophisticated (although not necessarily compelling) one. To find something more closely approximating a text reduced to its barest essentials, one needs to stoop even lower, so to speak.

Stooping lower in my supermarket I find, on the same rack as the *Enquirer*, but well below it, a cheap collection of word games, printed on pulpy newsprint, bound with staples, entitled *Super Word Circle*.[3] Everyone knows this kind of word game. Each page consists of a grid of apparently random letters, yet within this alphabetic chaos is nested a hidden order. Experienced

---

[1] Edgar Allan Poe, "The Tell-Tale Heart," in *The Complete Works of Edgar Allan Poe*, ed. James A. Harrison (New York: AMS Press, 1965); Henry James, *The Turn of the Screw* (New York: Dover Publications, 1991).

[2] Tom Stoppard has insane limericks tripping off Joyce's tongue in *Travesties* (New York: Grove Press, 1975).

[3] *Super Word Circle: Over 80 Fast Fun Games* (New York: Modern Day Periodicals, February, 1993).

readers detect words encrypted within the grid, and in the most unlikely patterns: horizontally, vertically, diagonally, forwards, and backwards. From the jumble of words more order emerges as the terms in each individual puzzle reveal themselves to be united by a particular theme (for example, citing from the copy I have on hand: "Delicious Pizza," "Art Supplies," "Buried Treasure," "At the Mall").

They look like Figure 1.1 below. This puzzle is a basic text: written, it invites us to read. Just *how* we are to read, though, is a complicated issue.

The initial separation of the meaningful from the meaningless is generally a two-step process. First, we need to identify patterns. Patterns are the sign of order and organization: if we look at the stars in the night sky as a random smattering of twinkles, we are unlikely to attribute much meaning to them. However, if we stretch our imagination a bit and connect the dots, constellations appear, and our clustering of these flecks of light can turn them into celestial writing pregnant with meaning. As this example shows, the recognition of a pattern can be a bit of a judgment call. Nevertheless, it exudes objectivity in comparison to the second step in the process of winnowing meaning from nonsense. Patterns, even (or especially) imaginary ones, are relatively easy to identify: a ten-year-old child can listen to a sequence of Morse code and begin to recognize repetitions. However, determining just what the code *means*, what it *represents*, is another matter altogether. The sun rises every morning: is this just a phenomenon that recurs—a pattern—or does it *mean* something as well?

Figure 1.1   Super Word Circle 75.   *Courtesy of Modern Day Periodicals.*

S	H	T	U	R	T	C	U	N	K	P	O	W
T	Z	G	N	O	L	B	H	C	R	A	E	S
C	R	D	U	U	N	K	N	O	W	N	S	E
A	E	E	E	O	X	G	B	O	Z	L	U	T
F	V	T	S	P	R	E	C	I	S	E	N	O
A	I	E	M	U	C	O	L	D	K	A	C	N
N	D	R	P	N	L	O	H	E	S	R	E	Z
A	E	M	E	U	C	T	L	T	R	N	V	R
D	N	I	F	A	R	A	N	A	L	Y	Z	E
Y	C	N	T	D	K	P	G	I	O	E	C	K
S	E	E	L	Y	N	B	O	L	P	I	B	A
Z	Y	N	I	T	U	R	C	S	M	Y	A	E
E	U	N	C	U	N	C	O	V	E	R	K	B

Our "reading" of the Super Word Circle will be guided by the same principles of repetition and representation. As we peruse the puzzle, we check various clusters of letters against our internal dictionaries, hoping to discover overlap, repetition. For example, the S H of the first line seems promising at first blush, for sh- is a possible cluster in initial position in English. However, when added to the subsequent letters, T U R T, the jumble matches no terms in memory, and may thus be discarded as meaningless filler—until, that is, we read backwards, and find that the apparently nonsensical S H T U R T gives rise to nothing less than the grandest of ideals: T R U T H S. In the final line we may more readily uncover the word U N C O V E R, although our reading initially stutters with the repetition of the first three letters of the word (U N C U N C O V E R). Cursory examination of this text presses it to reveal more of its secrets, and most readers will match such words as *unknowns*, *analyze*, and *precise*; more diligent readers will discover *evidence*, *notes*, *result*, and others. Finally, as more words appear (*mice*, *facts*, etc.) we may note a certain commonality; the mass of repetitions gives us some clue as to what the text represents. If puzzles can have topics, if they can *mean* something, then this one is in some sense "about" scientific experimentation: a *theme* has emerged.

Lingering over such a document as a Super Word Circle may seem absurd. Although it serves as a model for some simple reading practices, one can argue persuasively that puzzles are a special case, and that most texts

Figure 1.2 Super Word Circle 75. The puzzle partially completed. *Courtesy of Modern Day Periodicals.*

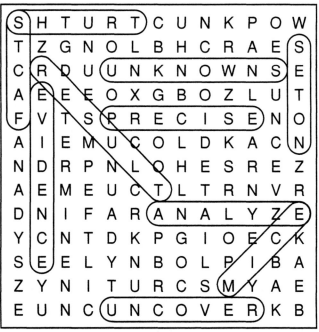

are not written as puzzles. Before rejecting the model out of hand, however, one should note that there is, in fact, a tradition of writing—and reading— in this way. A simple example is the medieval and Renaissance genre of acrostics, poems in which the first letter of each line can be read vertically to spell a name or phrase. Thus begins Ben Jonson's play, *The Alchemist*, dating from 1610:[4]

> **T**he sickness hot, a master quit, for fear,
> **H**is house in town: and left one servant there.
> **E**ase him corrupted, and gave means to know
> **A** cheater and his punk; who, now brought low,
> **L**eaving their narrow practice, were become
> **C**ozeners at large: and only wanting some
> **H**ouse to set up, with him they here contract,
> **E**ach for a share, and all begin to act.
> **M**uch company they draw, and much abuse,
> **I**n casting figures, telling fortunes, news,
> **S**elling of flies, flat bawdry, with the stone:
> **T**ill it, and they, and all in fume are gone.

A quick glance will suffice to show how the initial letter of each line spells out the title of the play. But more unusual instances are not wanting, and many acrostics and other devices have been used to encode names, verses, or other information. The fifteenth-century French poet Charles d'Orléans once used acrostics and allegories in ballads he sent home while imprisoned by the British: he encrypted information about British military plans and even about his own incarceration.[5] (Neither the guards reading his letters nor those receiving them deciphered all the codes; d'Orléans rotted in London for 25 years.) Centuries later, the marquis de Sade, locked in the Bastille while he scribbled away about philosophy and libertinism, became convinced that his wife's letters contained encrypted alpha-numeric references, and he even teased out some imaginative readings.[6]

Paul Zumthor, a scholar of medieval and Renaissance literature, spent his career unraveling rather puzzling texts and has presented some curious examples. One of the documents he rescued from obscurity is a religious poem written in Latin by the monk Rabanus Maurus (also called Ramus), dating from the ninth century. Entitled "On the Adoration of the Cross by an Artisan" ("De Adoratione Crucis ab Opifice"), the poem is printed in block letters in a gridlike pattern rather resembling a word puzzle. Although it can be read "normally" (that is, it makes sense to read the lines of the poem from left to right, and to read each line in sequence), this poetic praise of God has

---

[4]Ben Jonson, *The Alchemist*, ed. F. H. Mares (Manchester: Manchester University Press, 1997), 9.

[5]Norma Lore Goodrich, *Charles Duke of Orléans: A Literary Biography* (New York: Macmillan, 1963), 167–171.

[6]Maurice Lever, *Donatien Alphonse François, marquis de Sade* (Paris: Fayard, 1991), 348–351.

other meanings enfolded within it. Zumthor, in fact, reads "On the Adoration of the Cross" *as if* it were a Super Word Circle. He discovers that one of the key lines of the poem—the middle verse, in fact, of the first block of text—is repeated vertically in the middle column of letters, a mid-verse acrostic. In addition to being repeated in this manner, this line "*oro te Ramus aram ara sumar et oro*" ("I, Ramus, pray at your foot, altar, that I may be consumed upon the altar as I pray") is also a *palindrome*, which is to say that it reads the same forwards as backwards (like "Madam, I'm Adam," or "Lepers repel"). In the second block of text, Zumthor ingeniously discovers a more carefully encrypted message, one that is not a palindrome, but a kind of *palimpsest* (palimpsests are ancient parchments that, when re-used, continued to show traces of earlier inscriptions), where one text overlays another: in an oddly shaped cluster Zumthor finds the phrase "*Rabanum memet clemens rogo Christe tuere o pie judicio*" ("I beseech thee, O Christ, in thy mercy and goodness, to forgive me, Raban"). The poem, as read by Zumthor, is reproduced on the next page.[7]

It is with the discovery of encrypted lines that Zumthor's reading takes a crucial turn: he notes not only that the poem has multiple, overlapping messages, but also that the encrypted phrases cross the line between word and image to depict the sense of the poem *visually*: the intersecting lines of the central palindrome, in fact, form the shape of the very cross the poem and the line itself are about; likewise, he contends, the oddly distorted sentence regarding the poet's prayer for forgiveness bears an uncanny resemblance to a monk (presumably the poet himself) kneeling in adoration at the foot of the cross in the text above.

Has Zumthor unlocked this poem? Or is his reading in some sense insane? Has he read this text the way other people play Boggle or try to read alphabet soup? Is his interpretation just one more piece of evidence showing that literary critics have a dangerous amount of time on their hands? Unlike the Super Word Circle, Rabanus's poetry contains no appendix of solutions, and it is hard to know when one has surpassed intended meanings. When, we might very well ask ourselves, are we reading a text, and when are we reading *into* it?

This question is the focus of a story by the famous Argentinean writer Jorge Luis Borges (1899–1986). Celebrated for his tales about books and reading, Borges often drew on his experience as head of the National Library of Argentina. In fact, his depiction of libraries earned him an homage by Umberto Eco in the Italian author's novel *The Name of the Rose* (1983).[8] In Eco's book (and the film made after it), the mazelike library is inspired by Borges—and the blind chief librarian is a stand-in for Borges himself, who also went blind later in life. The source for Eco's images is Borges's "The Library of Babel" (1956),[9] which tells the fantastic tale of a man—the

---

[7]Paul Zumthor, *Langue, Texte, Enigme* (Paris: Editions du Seuil, 1975), 28–35.

[8]Umberto Eco, *The Name of the Rose*, trans. William Weaver, 1st Harvard ed. (San Diego: Harcourt Brace, 1994).

[9]Jorge Luis Borges, *Ficciones*, ed. Anthony Kerrigan (New York: Grove Press, 1963).

```
o m n i p o t e n s v i r t u s m a i e s t a s a l t a s a b a o t h
e s c e l s u s d o m i n u s v i r t u t u m s u m m e c r e a t o r
f o r m a t o r m u n d i h o m i n u m t u v e r e r e d e m p t o r
t u m e a l a u s v i r t t u g s o r i a e u n c t a s a l u s q r e
t u r e x t u d o c t o r t u e r r e c t o r c a r e m a g i s t e r
t u p a s t o r p a s c e n s p r o t e c t o r v e r u s o u i l i s
p o r t i o t u q e m e a s a n c t e s a l u a t o r e t a u c t o r
d u x v i a l u x v i t a m e r c e s b o n a i a n u a r e g n i e s
v o x s e n s u s v e r b u m v i r t u t u m l a e t a p r o p a g o
a d t e d i r e x i e t c u m u l a n s n u n c d i r i g o v e r b a
m e n s m e a t e l o q u i t u r m e n t i s i n t e n t i o t o t a
q u i c q u i d l i n g u a m a n u s o r a t e t b u c c a b e a t e
c o r h u m i l e e t v i t a i u s t a s a c r a t a v o l u n t a s
o m n i a t e l a u d a n t e t c a n t a n t c r i s t o s e r e n e
n a m q e g o t e d o m i n u m p r o n u s e t l a e t u s a d o r o
a t q e c r u c i d e m i s e t u a e h i n c d i c o s a l u t a n s
s p e m o r o t e r a m u s a r a m a r a s u m a r e t o r o h i n c
h o c m e u s e s t a r d o r c l a r u s h o c i g n i s a m o r i s
h o c m e a m e n s p o s c i t p r i m u m h o c f a m e n e t o r a
h o c s i t i s e s t a n i m i m a n d e n d i m a g n a c u p i d o
v t m e t u p i e s u s c i p i a s b o n e c r i s t e p e r a r a m
o b l a t u m f a m u l u m q o d u i c t i m a s i m t u a i e s u s
h o s t i a q o d t u a s i m m e m e t c r u c i f i x i o t o t u m
i a m t u a c o n s u m a t e t p a s s i o m i t i g e t a e s t u m
c a r n a l e m v i t i a c o n f r i n g a t d e p r i m a t i r a m
r e f r e n e t l i n n u a m p i e t a t i s v e r b a r e p o n a t
m e n t e m p a c i f c c e t v i t a m d e d u c a t h o n e s t a m
n a m q u e t u u s q u a n d o t o t o f u l g e s c e t o l y m p o
i g n e u s a d u e n i u s t o r r e b i t e t a r d o r i n i q o s
t e m p e s t a s s t r i d e t c o r n u i a m m u g i t e t o r b e
a n t e a p p a r e b i t q u a n d o c r u c i s a e r e s i g n u m
t u m r o g o m e e r i p i a t f l a m m i s v l t r i c i b i p s a
a t q e p o e t a m a g n i p r o p r i u m d e f e n d a t a b i r a

c u i c a n o i u r e c a n a m h r a b a n u s v e r s i b u s o r e
c o r d e m a n u s e m p e r d o n u m m e m o r a b i l e c a n t u
q u o d d e d e r a t v i t a e m c m e t c l e m e n t e r l n a r a
q a n d o i p s a i e s u s c l e m e n s r o g o a b e r u : t i m o
i n t e r n i r e q i e m n u n c o c r i s t e a r c e p o l o r u m
d a m i h i h o c p o s c o s p e r o e t u e r a o m n i a c r e d o
q u a e p r o m i s i s t i h o c t e n l e o p i e t a t e f i d e q e
q u o d v e r a x f a c i s o r d i n e i u d i c i o m n i a v e r o
i n u n c a d s u p e r o s i n c a e l i s r i t e t r i u m p h o s
o l a u s a l m a c r u c i s s e m p e r s i n e t i n e v a l e t o
```

Figure 1.3

narrator of the story—who spends his life within the walkways and galleries of an immense and labyrinthine library, so vast, in fact, that some confuse it with the universe itself. The narrator and his compatriots while away their days wandering through this bookish maze, dedicating their lives to a search for meaning. The task would not be so daunting in a library, one would think, where answers are always within arm's reach. The problem, however, is that the majority of books are entirely illegible, consisting apparently of gibberish; to make matters worse, they are shelved randomly, with no reliable catalog.

The scope of the problem becomes apparent as the narrator explains the physical layout of his world: each gallery consists of six walls lined with five shelves apiece; each shelf contains thirty-two books of identical format; each book contains four hundred and ten pages, each page forty lines, each line eighty black characters, limited to combinations of twenty-five letters. When one "librarian of genius" adduced that the library consisted of all possible books, that is, of all the possible permutations of letters allowed by the four hundred and ten page format, the initial response was one of "extravagant joy," for it implied that the library contained *all meaning*. On some shelf could be found not only the true catalog of the entire collection, but also, for instance, an accurate biography of the narrator's life, as well as an equally accurate prediction of his future. Somewhere within this imaginary library sits *your* biography, as well as my own, along with the very book, *Reading Lessons*, that you are in the midst of reading. Of course, because the collection contains *all* possible books, it would also hold false catalogs and inaccurate biographies and prophecies; it would contain not only the explanation of the Library itself, but also copies of that explanation varying only by a single letter, by several letters, by several words, by whole chapters . . . and how would one ever know *which* was the *true* one? For if the Library contained all meaning, it also contained much vaster amounts of nonsense: mathematically inclined readers can quickly calculate that the Library holds $10^{1,834,097}$ (that is, ten followed by 1,834,097 zeros) volumes—if there are no duplicates.

In Borges's story, then, most books end up bearing an eerie resemblance to . . . Super Word Circles: pages of alphabetic chaos. Not surprisingly, obsessive readers in the Library, when confronted with one of the many volumes of gibberish, employ creative, if desperate, techniques, ones that make the diagonal or backward reading of word puzzles seem like child's play. For example, one volume appears to be an unfathomable and chaotic stream of letters, with the phrase "O Time your pyramids" surfacing perversely in the middle of the penultimate page. But even texts such as these need not be entirely meaningless: it is speculated that one book consisting only of the letters MVC repeated from start to finish may be legible according to a certain code: if the value of the letters were to change with each repetition (perhaps the second M is to be read as an A; the third as an E, etc.), then sense may yet be rescued from apparent nonsense.

Such a technique of reading, one where the reader essentially *rewrites* the text in part or in whole, changing words or ignoring letters in order to uncover a secret, encoded meaning, may strike many people as patently insane. But what happens if we step out of Borges's library for a moment and read his own text in such a cryptic way? The piece begins with an architectural description: "The universe (which others call the Library) is composed of an indefinite, perhaps infinite, number of hexagonal galleries, with enormous ventilation shafts in the middle, encircled by very low railings. From any hexagon the upper or lower stories are visible, interminably." Taking Borges's text in the original Spanish, and following the perverse reading practices he later describes, we might read thus:

El universo (que otros llaman la **B**iblioteca)
se **c**ompone de un
nú**m**ero indefinido, y tal
vez infinito, de **g**al
erías
hexágonale**s** . . .

Reading once again according to the logic of a Super Word Circle, we are surprised, and perhaps delighted, to find a kind of authorial signature—"Borges" (complete with the capitalized initial B)—encrypted within the text. This kind of linguistic legerdemain is entirely consonant with the games Borges plays in his stories and the kinds of interpretation his characters must accomplish. Yet how do we judge when a reading has gone too far, when it reveals what we expect to find—or want to find—rather than what the text actually contains? For example, the same passage from "The Library of Babel" can give rise to other, even more astonishing readings:

El univer**s**o (que otros llaman la
Biblio**t**ec**a**
se **c**ompone de un número indefinido,
y t**a**l vez
infi**n**ito, de galerías hexágonales
con
vastos pozos de ventilación en el médio,
cercad**o**
por barandas ba**j**ismismas.
Desde cualquier
hex**á**ga**no**, se ven los pisos inferiores y superiores
int
e
rminablemente.

Indeed, if we're not careful, Borges's own story can *become* the Library of Babel, a text containing *all possible meanings*, depending only on how we read. Caution is advised. As we looked at the Super Word Circle, it became evident that reading entails in part an exercise in the recognition of patterns: repetition and representation. To this we should now add the criterion of *specificity*: if our methods of reading prove so general as to apply to all parts of all texts indiscriminately, then their value is considerably diminished. Although Borges's story does *contain* the author's name (as well as my own, and probably yours), it is less than clear that this is what the text actually *communicates*, and most approaches to literature assume some kind of communication to be fundamental to reading.

Of course, all this talk of acrostics, word circles, and Babel is beside the point, for *nobody* would ever read this way. Or would they? In the spring of 1997 a book entitled *The Bible Code*[10] made headlines by reading in precisely the way I have described above. Using a specially designed computer program (it always seems to lend credibility to an enterprise when computers are used), three Israeli mathematicians searched the Hebrew Bible by "skip code," a device allowing them to "read" every other letter of the text, then every third letter, every fourth, every twentieth, every thousandth, etc. The vast majority of these readings—like most of the readings in Borges's Library of Babel—were utter gibberish. A few, however, made sense. And ominous sense it sometimes was: encrypted within pages of the Torah, in vertical, horizontal, and diagonal patterns extremely reminiscent of Super Word Circles, they found references to past, present, and future events (for example, the Kennedy and Rabin assassinations, as well as a California earthquake scheduled for 2010). The argument in favor of reading the Torah this way is based on statistical probability: it is, in fact, highly unlikely (tens of thousands to one) that such patterns would appear in random configurations of letters—a fact that makes at least some readers suspect that they are *not* random, but instead meaningful utterances.

The Bible Code is probably a case of a few scholars who have gone off the deep end, and it certainly does nothing to endear mathematics to literary scholars. Nevertheless, it is an interesting exercise in reading because it hovers right at the limit of what people are willing to believe. Moreover,

Figure 1.4   *The Bible Code;* a case of finding what you're looking for?

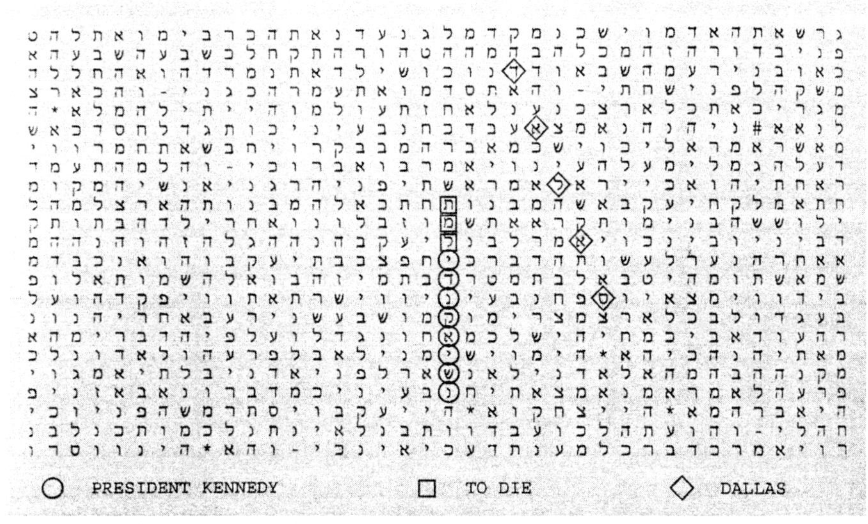

| ○ PRESIDENT KENNEDY | □ TO DIE | ◇ DALLAS |

[10]Michael Drosnin, *The Bible Code* (New York: Simon & Schuster, 1997).

it demonstrates that the determination of meaning is almost never cut and dried; it is nearly always the result of what we, the readers, determine to be *probable*. Most of our reading gives us better "odds" than *The Bible Code*; nevertheless, the same principle is at work. If we choose our interpretation by the throw of the dice, we may be entertained by the results, but we will probably not feel that any real communication has taken place.

WORDS AND COMMUNICATION

We began the last section by attempting to define literature, falling back on the broader notion of text. "The Library of Babel" moves the notion of text itself onto shaky ground, asking how we can even tell when something is "legible." Borges has clearly taken things to an extreme, poking fun at the kind of intellectual gymnastics in which some readers are willing to participate in order to satisfy their curiosity. Yet within his playfulness lie serious questions, especially this: even when words seem to make *sense*, how do we determine whether they are *meaningful*? That is to say, when we find the phrase "O Time your pyramids" on a page otherwise filled with the letters MVC, how do we know when these intelligible words are the result of chance or are instead present to *express* something?

Most readers, I suspect, would find the Library of Babel a decidedly dissatisfying place to read. The books contained therein are more or less the product of a simian secretarial pool—the proverbial monkeys at a typewriter. When sensible text *does* appear in such settings, we know it is the product of happenstance. The untrained monkey, one with no understanding of typing, writing, or English, may indeed generate words, and although they may be words we *mistake* as meaningful (the way a pre-Pavlovian might have thought trained horses could understand language, instead of simply producing a learned response), not much *communication* has taken place.

Yet the notion of communication has been central to most understandings of literary analysis. The assertion may seem unsurprising, as it is implicit in questions commonly asked in the most casual conversations about books: "What does this story *tell* us?" we ask a child about a fairy tale; "What is the author trying to *say* here?" a teacher may ask pointedly in a class; "I don't see what this book is *getting at*," someone may remark in a reading group. In general, we assume in our reading of a text that *something* is being said by *someone* to *someone* else in *some* way and for *some* reason. The trick, it would appear, is to determine who is saying what to whom, how, and why.

Understanding texts, then, requires understanding how communication operates generally, and literary study today is indebted to work done in the 1950s on the mechanics of communication. A figure of particular import was Roman Jakobson (1896–1982), a Russian ex-patriot whose influential and often highly technical work in linguistics served as a cornerstone in the development of structuralism, a movement about which we will hear more later.

In a well-known essay on linguistics and poetics Jakobson took pains to map out what he understood to be the components necessary for any verbal communication.[11] In short (and I replace here Jakobson's technical vocabulary with more common terms), a *sender* sends a *message* to a *receiver* by way of a *medium*; the message can be understood because it is part of a *language* (or *code*) understood by both sender and receiver, and the message transmits *information*; that is, it means something. This simple operation can be presented schematically in a hypothetical example recalling the laboratory theme of our Super Word Circle: Picking up the phone (*medium*), Peter (*sender*) calls Mary (*receiver*) to tell her, in English (*language*), "Get over to the lab right away! We've got rat trouble again," (*message*), which alerts her to the fact that some number of rodents are currently relishing their freedom (*information*).

The schematical for this example is shown in Figure 1.5.

Jakobson contends that if any one of these components is absent or fails to function properly, communication misfires. Obviously, if Peter sends no message, communication does not occur; nor is it any more successful if Mary fails to pick up her phone, or again if the phone lines are down. Likewise, if, in his panic, Peter lapses into his native German, thus introducing problems of code or language, Mary may not understand; furthermore, had Peter uttered, instead of screaming about rats, "O Time your pyramids," it seems at least likely that, although a message may have been transmitted, its information will have eluded the receiver.

Figure 1.5

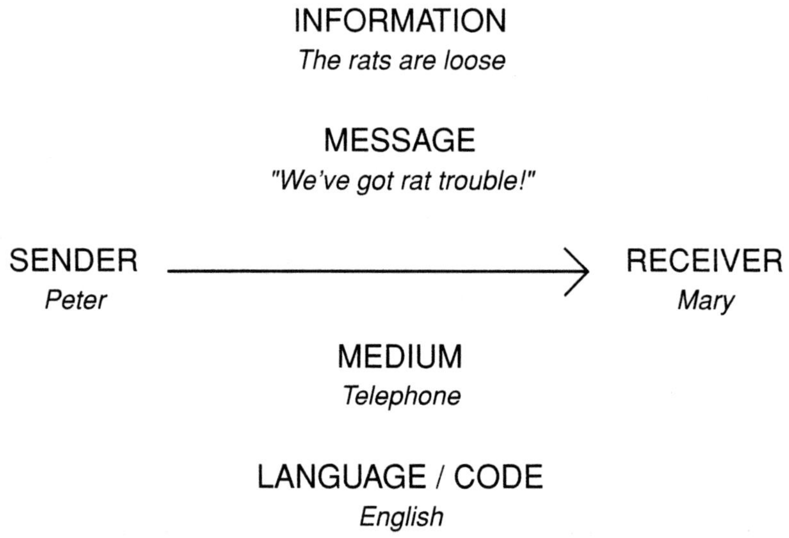

INFORMATION
The rats are loose

MESSAGE
"We've got rat trouble!"

SENDER ————————————⟶ RECEIVER
Peter   *Mary*

MEDIUM
Telephone

LANGUAGE / CODE
English

---

[11]Roman Jakobson, "Linguistics and Poetics," in *Style in Language*, ed. T. Sebeok (Massachusetts: Technology Press of the Massachusetts Institute of Technology, 1960).

In a further refinement of his model, Jakobson points out not only that the success of communication depends on these six components, but also that every act of communication is "weighted" in favor of at least one of these functions. That is, when Peter introduces himself over the phone ("This is Peter"), his utterance refers to the sender; when he cries "Get over to the lab right away!" the imperative form points to the receiver. Mary's stunned silence, her failure to respond to the news, may elicit Peter's desperate, "Are you there?" as he checks on the medium, making sure the line hasn't gone dead. Should Peter fall into German, Mary may tell him to speak English (focus on language), whereas the words "O Time your pyramids" will probably leave her asking, "What the hell do you mean?" (focus on information). Finally, if Peter garbles his report as he mumbles in terror, Mary will instruct him to clarify the *message*.

Let us assume for the time being that texts—including what we call "literary" texts—are instances of communication. We can add to this the fact that interpretations of texts, be they formal and academic, or casual and conversational, are themselves acts of communication. As such, according to Jakobson's considerations, they too are weighted toward one or more of the elements of communication. In fact, Jakobson's model can serve as a convenient illustration of the various tacks textual criticism can take today: interpretations focusing on the sender tend toward *biographical criticism* (study of the author); those emphasizing the receiver fall in the category of *reader response criticism*. Similarly, focus on the message invites formal and stylistic analyses (including *structuralism*), stress on the medium forms part of *historical* approaches (practices of publishing, etc.), concentration on language or code tends to lead to *poststructuralist* and *deconstructionist* readings; and focus on information belongs to the field of *hermeneutics*.

Of course, these categories are not entirely discrete, and many have considerable overlap. Biographical criticism is certainly related to historical studies; deconstructive approaches often pay heed to both message and information (often pointing out the tension between them). Moreover, some schools of thought (such as feminism/gender studies or cultural studies) are so broadly defined that individual interpretations may focus on any one of the above components. Psychoanalytic criticism, which originally focused on the author/sender, has also been brought to bear on the reader/receiver, on information, and on language itself. Still, a given reading or interpretation will generally gravitate toward one of Jakobson's linguistic functions.

In the coming chapters we will look at a few of the most influential schools of thought, following a rough chronology of their entrance into literary study. The presentation, which will include structuralism, poststructuralism, psychoanalysis, gender studies/feminism, cultural studies, and reader response, is skewed in at least two respects. First, by the unavoidable division into separate chapters, it creates the illusion that these approaches exist independently of one another, that they have no overlap; in fact, nothing could be further from the truth, and we will endeavor to entwine approaches as appropriate.

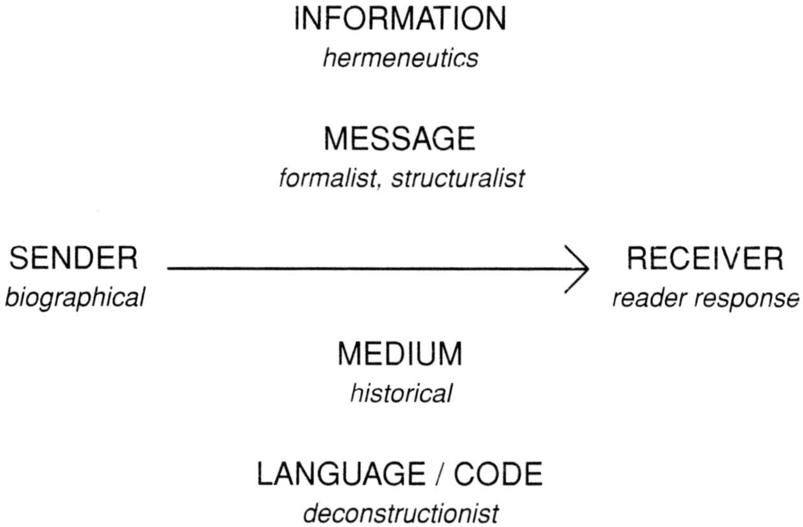

INFORMATION
hermeneutics

MESSAGE
formalist, structuralist

SENDER ────────────────⟶ RECEIVER
biographical   *reader response*

MEDIUM
historical

LANGUAGE / CODE
deconstructionist

Figure 1.6

Second, the focus on particular approaches can lead certain readers to feel that interpretations deal incompletely with the texts they address. "Sure," one might say of a feminist interpretation of *Hamlet*, "there's something to be said for Ophelia. But the play is hardly about gender issues *alone*." Such a complaint is certainly valid; however, it is important to recall that individual interpretative approaches almost never do more than illuminate a single facet of a given text (the psychology of characters, the life of the author, the role of desire, etc.). The collection of theoretical approaches resembles a kind of toolbox, with each approach serving to accomplish certain kinds of tasks. Deconstructive criticism, for example, is designed to ask a particular sort of question of texts (often questions of logic), and we can hardly fault it for not producing answers to questions it does not ask. Of course, texts present the reader with many issues; thankfully, most readers—both "professional" and casual—read eclectically, paying heed to many different aspects of a book simultaneously. To keep sight of this "well-roundedness" of texts, we will try to be "ecological" in our references to particular texts, literary and otherwise, by "recycling" them from chapter to chapter.

The discussions are deliberately nontechnical. Although I provide some background on the major players in particular movements, what follows is less the story of individuals than that of the development of certain trains of thought, and the sets of questions that drive them. More important than these movements are the texts themselves. What good is literary study if, at some level, it doesn't enhance our readerly pleasures and satisfactions? To that end, the stories we shall deal with will often occupy center stage. In some cases the "texts" come from supposedly nonliterary genres (as in the case of *Casablanca* and *Invasion of the Body Snatchers*, or, in chapter 7, the World Wide Web), in part because they help expand or challenge our notion of text, and in part because they have worked themselves so deeply into the American imagination. Other tales (by Poe, Kaschnitz, and others) are actually included in this book so that you may revel in them. You don't *have* to read these stories to follow most of the discussion, but why deprive yourself of that pleasure?

FURTHER READING

Interpretation in General:

Eco, Umberto. *The Limits of Interpretation*. Bloomington: Indiana University Press, 1990.

Eco, Umberto, with R. Rorty, J. Culler, C. Brooke-Rose. *Interpretation and Overinterpretation*. Edited by Stefan Collini. Cambridge: Cambridge University Press, 1992.

The Johns Hopkins Guide to Literary Theory and Criticism. Edited by Michael Groden and Martin Kreiswirth. Baltimore: Johns Hopkins University Press, 1994.

Voice of the Shuttle Web links on semiotics (including links regarding Roman Jakobson): http://humanitas.ucsb.edu/shuttle/theory.html#semiotics

Communication:

Jakobson, Roman. "Linguistics and Poetics." In *Style in Language*, edited by Thomas Sebeok. Cambridge: Technology Press of the Massachusetts Institute of Technology, 1960.

The Nature of Signs:

de Saussure, Ferdinand. *Course in General Linguistics*. Edited by Charles Bally and Albert Sechehaye, translated by Wade Baskin. London: Fontana, 1974. (See esp. "The Nature of the Linguistic Sign.")

Peirce, Charles Sanders. *Peirce on Signs: Writings on Semiotics*. Edited by James Hoopes. Chapel Hill: University of North Carolina Press, 1991.

2

ROUNDING UP SOME UNUSUAL SUSPECTS

■ ■ ■

Formalism and Structuralism

On a crowded train platform, as rain begins to fall, a poker-faced man wrapped in a trench coat tears open an envelope. He scans a few lines penned in an elegant, feminine hand. A whistle blows in the background. As the words dissolve under the impact of raindrops, the man's fist gnarls the paper into a ball, which he discards as he swings himself up onto one of the last cars of the departing train. He stares bitterly into the void.

Fade.

The same man, somewhat worn, sits in a deserted café, a drained bottle of bourbon on the table before him. He drops his head into his hands, knocking over his drink in the process. A large black man emerges from the shadows behind him, touches him on the shoulder, and rights the overturned glass. A door opens; a woman appears in a halo of light.

Who doesn't remember these scenes from *Casablanca*, where Bogey rues the loss of Ingrid Bergman? As one critic has noted, people remember sequences like this even if they haven't seen the movie.[1] Abandoned by Ilsa (Bergman) on the platform of the gare de Lyon in Paris, Rick Blaine (that's Bogart, and not Ronald Reagan, as originally cast) begins a journey that is as figurative as it is literal, one that drives him just outside the reach of the Third Reich, into Casablanca in French Morocco, and into the bittersweet oblivion of drink. The scene reaches its peak of pathos as Rick knocks over his glass.

What does this overturned lowball *mean* in *Casablanca*? In one sense, it operates quite trivially, drawing on our general knowledge of everyday life and commonplace alcohol abuse.[2] The glass serves to indicate the degree of Rick's

---

[1] Umberto Eco, "*Casablanca*: Cult Movies and Intertextual Collage," in *Philosophy and Film*, ed. Cynthia A. Freeland and Thomas E. Wartenberg (New York: Routledge, 1995).

[2] Eco refers to this setting of a scene as a "common frame." The use of stock characters or cliché motifs constitutes an "intertextual frame" ("*Casablanca*: Cult Movies").

intoxication, the extent of his distress: drunkards barely know up from down, and rebuffed lovers don't even care. However, the glass can take on other shades of meaning when placed in a context broader than this single scene. In fact, glasses are overturned on more than one occasion in *Casablanca*; the film is in some sense marked by rather unsteady tableware.

But we are getting ahead of ourselves. To understand the role of such minutiae as lowballs, we need to freshen our memory of the general context. So, with apologies to those readers who can recite *Casablanca* line by line, let's review the action.

The film takes place in French Morocco in 1942. The city of Casablanca has become a magnet for French and other refugees fleeing the growing reach of the Third Reich. Yet Casablanca is the end of the line: few manage to escape from this sweltering purgatory where the fear and anticipation rapidly give way to boredom and booze, the second of which is used to combat the first, preferably in Rick's Café Américain. The café is an oasis of sorts, where camaraderie, conspiracy, even love, can flourish in the otherwise arid surroundings of the French collaboration with the Nazis, incarnated in the movie by the suave and self-interested Prefect of Police, Louis Renaud (Claude Rains). The monotony of Casablanca is interrupted at the very beginning of the movie by a news bulletin (*news* is antithetical to Casablanca, where, supposedly, nothing ever happens): two German couriers carrying precious letters of transit (letters granting the bearers safe passage out of Casablanca to the Free World) have been murdered, and the letters have vanished. To recover them Major Strasser (Conrad Veidt), of the German S.S., has arrived on the scene, with the added mission of heading off the elusive resistance leader Victor Laszlo (Paul Henreid). Laszlo is known to be traveling with a "lady friend"—who will be none other than Ilsa (women in this film have only first names), the dame who had stood Rick up years earlier at the gare de Lyon.

Of course, all roads lead to Casablanca, and all roads in Casablanca lead to Rick's. Rick, Strasser, Renaud, Laszlo, and Ilsa all eventually find themselves staring at one another over drinks in the nightclub, lulled by the soulful tunes of Sam (Dooley Wilson). It is in the café that the sleazy Ugarte (Peter Lorre) asks Rick to hide those letters of transit (we don't know how he got them): it is in the café that Renaud's men shoot it out with Ugarte when he tries to run for it; and it is again in the café that Rick and Ilsa meet secretly to talk about their troubled past, that Rick drinks himself into flashbacks of Paris, that Laszlo tries to negotiate for the letters. Repeatedly the café serves as the commonplace *par excellence*, the meeting point. This lasts until the very end, when something actually *happens*, and the main players (Strasser, Rick, Renaud, Victor, and Ilsa) all convene at the Casablanca airstrip. A similar encounter, though a very different dynamic: Strasser will bleed to death on the tarmac, Ilsa and Victor leave victorious, Rick and Renaud, redeemed, head for the *maquis*.

"READING" A FILM

Is it fair to read a film like a text? I don't see why not; an image is a collection of meaningful signs, much like a printed page; a series of images may not be that different from the leaves of a book. Toward the beginning of *Casablanca*, for example, when the camera zooms in from above the rooftops of the city down into the chaotic marketplace, the screen is full of meaningful emblems. My personal favorite is the parrot perched on a stand in the market. The camera glides past it rapidly, but a second is all it takes. In a single instant that bird has communicated vast amounts of information, and much more efficiently than dialog ever could: he acts like a little, ornithological neon sign flashing the idea: "I am Exotic." Little does it matter whether polly is an African or a South American species; the parrot is one of a few fetishistic signs of exoticism dutifully trotted out in the film.[3]

In any case, films are stories, and in this respect *Casablanca* (whether you like the film or loathe it) is undeniably literary. This movie is a mixed bag of themes: love, politics, intrigue all wriggle together in a delightfully kitsch way. Yet, what is *missing* from the list of themes, and from the schematic summary of the action, is precisely that detail I highlighted at the beginning of this chapter: the overturned glass. No matter how you look at it, glassware plays an inconspicuous role in this movie, which—let's admit it—was never praised for its subtlety. When, at the end of the flashback, a thoroughly soused Rick knocks over his lowball, who even notices? The action seems only to impart realism or common sense: don't entrust your fine crystal to drunkards. Certainly the role of glassware pales in comparison to those big-ticket themes, like Man versus Society, Boy meets Girl, and so forth. But the relative invisibility of the role of glassware stems from the fact that this role is *not* purely thematic; it is *structural*.

This would be a tough argument to make without more evidence. But, happily, cups, glasses, and tumblers take a fall on a regular basis in *Casablanca*. Let's consider the pattern. Devotees of the movie may recall the two other key occasions. First, after Ugarte is shot by the police in the Café Américain, Rick walks between the tables, calming the guests, assuring them that order has been restored. He pauses in midstride to right an overturned wineglass. The second scene occurs during the central flashback presenting Rick and Ilsa's Parisian romance. When the news breaks that the Nazis are on the threshold of the city, and as Rick plans their departure between gulps of champagne, Ilsa utters her prophetic, lightly accented, "Kiss me. Kiss me, as if it were for the last time." As the couple embraces, a wayward elbow sends stemware tumbling.

---

[3]This technique is related to what Roland Barthes called the "reality effect": certain signs serve to communicate a general mood ("exoticism," "the supernatural," "objectivity," etc.) rather than a specific meaning. See Barthes, "The Reality Effect," in *French Literary Theory Today: A Reader*, ed. Tzvetan Todorov, trans. R. Carter (Cambridge: Cambridge University Press, 1982), 11–17.

Figure 2.1 Shots of such "banal" elements as overturned glasses are not commercially available. But here, when Ilsa returns to the café to find Rick thoroughly inebriated, we see the puddle of spilled liquor on the table. Sam righted the glass a few moments earlier. *Courtesy of Warner Brothers Studios.*

The scenes present remarkable similarities. The cascade of glassware always involves alcohol (first wine, then champagne, then bourbon; no one drinks milk in the Café Américain). Alcohol itself is associated with forgetfulness—first in the café, where people come to forget that they are stranded in Casablanca; then in Paris, where one drinks to forget the arrival of the Germans (and to make sure the Krauts don't get ahold of the good stuff); finally, again, in the café, where Rick drinks to forget Paris. Moreover, the overturned glass comes to emblematize the eruption of *disorder* in an already unstable world: the café shoot-out, the invasion of the Germans, the resurfacing of Ilsa into Rick's protected world. The scenes also underscore just *who* is in control: after Ugarte's arrest, it is Rick—cool, collected—who restores order and rights the glass; in the flashback Rick and Ilsa embrace carelessly, and the glass remains overturned, as a sign of impending doom (*nobody* is in control, unless it's the Nazis, which is just as bad); and when Rick, in his stupor, knocks over his bourbon, it is lowly Sam

Figure 2.2 When Rick meets Ilsa in the Café Américain, we see how elegant glassware adds to the sense of order and decorum. A few minutes earlier, when Renaud's men arrested Ugarte, the decorum—and some glassware—was upset. Rick righted a glass as he reassured the guests: "It's all over now. Everything's all right." *Courtesy of Warner Brothers Studios.*

who plays the role of the boss, picking up the glass as he helps Rick pick up the pieces of his life.

These three scenes lead to a fourth, similar yet different. At the end of the film, Ilsa leaves with Victor Laszlo, Major Strasser lies dead on the tarmac, and the French official, Louis Renaud (Claude Rains), is about to denounce Rick to the authorities. As Renaud starts to pour himself a glass of Vichy water (reminiscent of the French collaboration with the Germans, headquartered at Vichy), he stares at the label and suddenly recoils in disgust, dropping the whole bottle into the trash and giving the basket a swift kick. Another image of disorder? Or rather, the rejection of a corrupt, distasteful order, tossed aside in favor of something new. "You know, Louis," Rick growls as they head into the fog toward the underground forces of the Resistance, "I think this is the beginning of a beautiful friendship."

Figure 2.3   "Kiss me, as if it were for the last time." A few frames later, the glass goes over, with the din of the Nazi invasion audible in the background *Courtesy of Warner Brothers Studios.*

AUTHORS

Is it possible for an overturned glass to mean all this? Is it excessive, or even ludicrous, to read politics, love, and the battle between order and chaos into minor accidents at the table? When, exactly, does one overstep the boundaries of meaningfulness into the nonsense of the Library of Babel?[4]

The answer to this question depends on one's point of view. That is, what a text "means" requires that we decide *who* we think is authorized to assign meaning. For a long time the ultimate authority was taken for granted, and for many people it still is. Thus, when someone makes an apparently outlandish claim about a text, the interpretation is often countered by a somewhat indignant "harrumph!", followed by the suggestion that a given author was unlikely to have had *that* in mind. Nothing kills discussion faster than

---

[4]See the discussion of Borges in chapter 1.

invoking the disapproval of an almost always absent (and usually conveniently dead) author. In the history of literature, authors have been a useful invention: they have served as the guardrails of meaning. Our reliance on the concept of authorship helps anchor texts to a kind of unity (even when a single name, such as Homer, covers multiple writers), and allows us to imagine that works are extensions of a particular, consistent psychology.[5]

But when we watch a film, just who is the author? For *Casablanca*, is it Michael Curtiz, the director? Or Joan Alison and Murray Burnett, the authors of the play, *Everybody Comes to Rick's*, on which the movie is based? Or Arthur Edeson, the director of photography, who framed what we see and what we don't? Or the actors themselves, who by all accounts improvised key sequences in the movie?[6]

Movies are a useful place to examine notions of authorship because they are frequently such collective, collaborative projects that in the end nobody really knows who is responsible for what. However, this does not mean that authorship shrinks in importance just because it is so difficult to attribute. For many approaches—many of which are associated with a movement called *structuralism*—the question of authorship is simply not germane.[7]

Structuralism is a multifaceted group of theories with varied and disparate goals. As mentioned in chapter 1, it tends not to focus on the author or reader, but rather on the construction of the "message," or text, itself. The movement is primarily the legacy of two independent schools of thought, both emerging shortly after the turn of the century: modern linguistics, under the guidance of the Swiss linguist Ferdinand de Saussure,[8] and Russian formalism, as represented by such figures as Vladimir Propp and Victor Shklovsky.[9] The essence of early structuralism was remarkably simple, proposing only that the forms and structures of language or literature could be studied independently of their content. Thus, to take a pedestrian example, it is

---

[5]On the uses to which we put author's names, see Michel Foucault's discussion of the author function in "What Is an Author?" in *Textual Strategies: Perspectives in Post-Structuralist Criticism*, ed. Josué Harari (Ithaca, N.Y.: Cornell University Press, 1979), 141–160.

[6]For background on the movie, and anecdotes connected with its production, see Jeff Siegel, *The Casablanca Companion: The Movie and More* (Dallas: Taylor Publishing, 1992), and Aljean Harmetz, *Round Up the Usual Suspects: The Making of Casablanca—Bogart, Bergman, and World War II* (New York: Hyperion, 1992).

[7]The primacy of the author was challenged implicitly by the early Russian formalists (see Victor Shklovsky, "Art as Technique," in *Russian Formalist Criticism: Four Essays* (Lincoln: University of Nebraska Press, 1965). The structuralists, in the 1960s, dethroned the author more explicitly. See Roland Barthes, "The Death of the Author" in *Image, Music, Text*, trans. Stephen Heath (New York: Hill and Wang, 1977); and Gérard Genette, "Structuralism and Literary Criticism," in *Figures of Literary Discourse*, trans. Alan Sheridan (New York: Columbia University Press, 1982). In the Anglo-American tradition, a somewhat similar impulse resulted in M. C. Beardsley and W. K. Whimsatt's essay, "The Intentional Fallacy," in *On Literary Intention: Critical Essays*, ed. David Newton-de Molina (Edinburgh: University Press, 1976), 1–13.

[8]Ferdinand de Saussure, *Course in General Linguistics*, ed. Charles Bally and Albert Sechehaye, trans. Wade Baskin (London: Fontana, 1974).

[9]Vladimir Propp, *Morphology of the Folktale* (Austin: University of Texas Press, 1968); Shklovsky, "Art as Technique."

entirely possible to hum the rhythmic pattern of a limerick, and to have it be recognized as such, without ever attaching the usual scabrous verses. Or, one could undertake to show that a great number of stories—certain fairy tales, for instance—conform to a general pattern: a child is abandoned, encounters danger, and is magically rescued.[10] These kinds of patterns can be studied even when abstracted from the particulars of a given story. Certain kinds of literature (pulp romances are a favorite example) can be extremely formulaic; more sophisticated texts develop more sophisticated, though equally "abstractable," conventions.

Whether an author *meant* to follow certain patterns is rarely, if ever, the issue for structuralists. Later structuralists attempted to dismantle the function of the author even further, insisting that, in the first place, it is nearly impossible to determine what most authors intended to do in their works; in the second, even if the author's intent were *knowable*, there is no guarantee that this intent was *realized*. A practical example may help to illustrate this. If I tear out this page, crumple it into a ball, and toss it toward the end of my desk, I may be *aiming* for my wastebasket, but there is no guarantee I will *hit* it. All sorts of factors—physical (am I throwing right- or left-handed?), psychological (am I feeling uptight?), even meteorological (has the wind blown my shot to the side?)—may intervene. Now, as Jakobson's model of communication showed in chapter 1, language is considerably more complicated than shooting hoops with paper balls, and so, while I may *hope* that in this book I will explain certain aspects of modern literary study, what is the likelihood that this hope will fully *succeed*—or at least succeed in the way I had originally planned? In short, just because an author *meant* to communicate something in a book, poem, or film, does not ensure that she or he will have done so.

When one hears that some forms of literary study preach that "the author is dead," all that claim really means is that for some readers the author is no longer the ultimate arbiter for determining the usefulness or validity of an interpretation.[11] Thus, when the incredulous discussant blurts out, "But did the author really *mean* that?" the structuralist may reply, "Who cares?" This does not suggest that for structuralists all interpretations are equally valid, only that they test ideas against different criteria.

---

[10]It is precisely this kind of structural study Propp undertakes in *Morphology of the Folktale*. The compendium of fairy-tale types known as the Aarne/Thompson index works in the same vein: Antti Amatus Aarne, *The Types of the Folktale: A Classification and Bibliography*, trans. Stith Thompson (Helsinki: Academia Scientarum Fennica, 1961).

[11]Actually, the now infamous proclamation that "the author is dead" derives largely from a compelling conundrum regarding authorial intention. The notion is generally attributed to Michel Foucault in his essay "What Is an Author?" where one reads that the author "must assume the role of the dead man in the game of writing" (p. 143 in *Textual Strategies*). This is an error of translation, for the expression Foucault uses in French, putting the author "à la place du mort" refers to a role in a particular game: bridge. In bridge, the "mort" is the "dummy," the player who sits passively while others play off his hand. See Michel Foucault, "Qu'est-ce qu'un auteur?" *Bulletin de la Société française de Philosophie* 63 (1969): 73–104

STRUCTURES

What does all this have to do, as they say, with the price of tea in China, or for that matter, with the price of bourbon in Casablanca? For one thing, it invites us to consider meanings without succumbing to the urge to refer to intentions. Was the motif of the overturned glass *planned* by Curtiz, by Alison and Burnett, by Edeson, or by Bogey himself—or was it simply haphazard? I don't know the answer to that question, but it doesn't necessarily matter. Regardless of what motivated it, the overturned glass takes on meaning for at least some viewers because it seems to fit into a certain kind of logic, because it appears to be part of a pattern.

However, this single image, that of a glass turned on its side, does not suffice for the creation of meaning. A single point does not make for a structure any more than a single beat can establish a rhythm, or a single note a melody. Patterns are established by *repetition and differentiation.* When Ilsa spies Sam (Dooley Wilson) in Rick's café and begs him to play "As Time Goes By," Sam could stall by playing nothing more than the initial E natural of the melody, for this note by itself means nothing. But as he moves from note to note, the particular spread separating one note from the next (the intervals) creates a pattern that is immediately recognizable to both Ilsa and Rick. Likewise, the spilled drinks become significant only because they mark a difference: overturned glasses are different from upright glasses.

This is, of course, a trivial observation, but one that is nevertheless key to understanding structuralist approaches to literature. For the smallest structural unit is not, in fact, a "unit" at all; it is a *pair,* an opposition between two things, a "binary" opposition.[12]

Anyone who has had much to do with computers has probably come across references to binarity. Digital computers (along with compact discs, digital tapes, etc.) all operate according to the principle of binarity. Computer chips are nothing but masses of switches that can be in one of two positions: on or off. The famous computer "bit" (not the same as a "byte") is the smallest unit of digital information; it can be registered only as a 1 or 0. However, binary oppositions are not the invention of the technological age. Indeed, they exist everywhere (though in less digitized format) in daily life and are used to organize, in very practical ways, our understanding of the world around us. What is "up"? It's whatever is not "down." What is "big"? The opposite of "small." What is "life"? That which is not "death." These are all terms that have no intrinsic, absolute definition: a mouse may be small in relation to an elephant, but it is monstrous next to a flea. The terms, then, are relative; they are defined by the fact of their difference from something else.

---

[12]Binary opposition is key to most strains of structuralist thought, and is fundamental to structuralist anthropology. See Claude Lévi-Strauss, for example, in *The Raw and the Cooked,* trans. John and Doreen Weightman (New York: Harper & Row, 1970). In poetics, Roman Jakobson provides an excellent example of the use of oppositions in "Linguistics and Poetics," in *Style in Language,* ed. Thomas A. Sebeok (Cambridge: Technology Press of the Massachusetts Institute of Technology, 1960).

Thus, a glass lying horizontally can only be recognized as "overturned" when we are aware that the "normal" position for a glass is vertical. In *Casablanca* we are taught again and again that this normalcy is being challenged.

Glassware is only the smallest of players in the film, and in *Casablanca* binary oppositions appear everywhere: there are the good guys (the Laszlos) and the bad guys (the Nazis); those who are dressed in white (the Laszlos again), and those dressed in black (more Nazis); those who are innocent (Ilsa, and the Bulgarian lovers) and those who are corrupt (Ferrari, Ugarte, Renaud). It is a movie about the Allies versus the Germans, about the past (Paris) versus the present (Casablanca), and about cowardice versus heroism. As in so many stories, the movie pits these conflicting forces against each other and culminates in their resolution. One side of each opposition emerges as triumphant, and because this is a Hollywood movie from the forties, all the oppositions are resolved in a happy, compatible way: the pure—or recently purified—forces of Resistance conquer the corrupt. Even the idyllic past, which one might have thought irretrievably lost, manages to overshadow the dreary dangers of the present, for the past is transformed into the eternal: "We'll always have Paris."

The development of these binary oppositions is pretty conventional in *Casablanca* and holds very few surprises. Thus the analysis of these thematic tensions (good versus evil, innocence versus corruption, etc.) is simple and simultaneously—or even consequently—relatively uninteresting. Luckily, there is more. Structuralists tend to look at texts as games. The text is not a game one can play oneself, but is rather one that plays itself out in front of the reader as she reads. Moreover, it is a *new* game, one the reader does not yet know, the rules of which she must attempt to deduce. The situation is not unlike that of a novice following the games of chess or bridge published in many newspapers, where only a single move occurs every day: even if one has no prior knowledge of the game, with time and attention, one could eventually divine the rules. With a bit more time, one could even start to understand strategies and appreciate particularly elegant tricks. For the structuralist reader, the text is a compilation of "moves" in a game we do not know. It is, in fact, a game that, as often as not, *nobody* knows, including the author, who may have organized things a certain way because they "felt" right, or because certain patterns were an unconscious part of the way he or she thinks. The goal of structuralist reading is to make the rules and strategies of this game explicit.

In *Casablanca* it was not enough to jumble together a certain number of thematic oppositions. You can't just mix together a few Nazis with a few good guys and expect to produce a cult movie. What makes *Casablanca* interesting from a structuralist perspective is the way in which these various oppositions are orchestrated.

Remember Jakobson's model of communication from chapter 1? There are plenty of scenes where it would be a handy tool of analysis: when Berger identifies himself to Laszlo by showing his secret ring, when the French drown out the Nazi anthem with the *Marseillaise*, or when Rick reads Ilsa's enigmatic letter on the train platform. However, the model has broader implications than in these select instances. Ilsa's Dear Rick letter is not the only letter of consequence in the film; there is another act of communication that encompasses and motivates the others. In the opening scene of the film we hear a military radio dispatcher reporting the murder of two German couriers, and the theft of their letters of transit (signed by De Gaulle himself), so freshly issued that the courier's names had not even been entered as the bearers. These two letters trigger nearly all the action in the movie. They structure the plot, without actually being a part of the structure themselves. In a sense, we witness in *Casablanca* the long, tortuous delivery of these letters, the delayed—though ultimately realized—connection between "sender" and "receiver." We have the sense that these letters, although not originally addressed to Laszlo, have finally reached their destination when put into Ilsa's hands. Let's look at the function of these letters blow by blow:

1. They trigger, by their disappearance, the rounding up of the "usual suspects" (those poor souls regularly picked up and released) by Renaud and his men.

2. They motivate, by their disappearance, the arrival of Major Strasser.

3. They focus attention on Rick's café. Renaud invites Strasser to witness the arrest, assuring him that the thief "will be at Rick's tonight. Everyone comes to Rick's."

4. Renaud is right: Strasser comes to Rick's to recover the letters; Ugarte comes to Rick's to sell the letters; Laszlo comes to Rick's to buy the letters.

5. Rick becomes the depository of the letters; he hides them "in the open," placing them in Sam's piano in front of the crowd.

6. After Ugarte's death, Rick becomes the focus of attention because of the letters: Renaud questions him, Laszlo befriends him, Ilsa returns to him, Ferrari bargains with him.

7. Ilsa's return to the café in search of the letters triggers the flashback to Paris, which ends with another kind of letter of transit—the "walking papers" Ilsa sent to Rick on the train platform.

8. Rick delivers the letters to Ilsa and Laszlo. As with each transmission of the letters (the couriers, Ugarte), there is a death; this time it is Strasser, gunned down by Rick himself.

9. When the letters disappear, there is a return to the status of the beginning of the film: Renaud orders another rounding up of suspects; Strasser is gone, Ilsa is gone, Laszlo is gone.

Of course, the parallelism between the opening of the movie and the conclusion is illusory. The situation is nearly the same, and yet radically different: Ilsa has redeemed herself, Renaud has joined Rick in the fight against the Germans, the Germans have actually suffered a loss.

What are the rules of this game? There are many possible answers to this question. Early on in the film we are brought to think of Casablanca as the social equivalent of a stalemate: people arrive there after painful pilgrimages across Europe and North Africa, after which they "wait . . . and wait . . . and wait. . . ." Casablanca is marked by monotony, where people endlessly engage in the same moves (they drink, they hock a few gems, they check on the status of their exit visas, after which they are driven again to drink . . .), without ever making progress. Clearly the film could not sustain itself if left in this kind of endgame. However, the arrival of the letters corresponds to the introduction of a new piece, to the turning over of a new card—and this new card is a joker, bearing very different values for those who desire it: money for Ugarte, freedom for Ilsa, return to the "cause" for Laszlo, a dangerous unknown for Strasser. For the viewer, the letters of transit represent nothing short of *surprise*; they are the eruption of the unexpected in this world of extraordinary monotony. Once the letters arrive, all our expectations are called into question; with luck, they will be frustrated.

Yes, frustrated. One of the greatest discoveries of structuralist thought has been that of the limitations of primitive notions of structure. For, although stories may operate according to certain *patterns*, they are not textual machines, endlessly cranking through the same motions. The notion of a literary pattern requires that there be *simultaneously* an element of repetition *and* one of variation.[13] Thus, even in the rigorously structured world of formal poetry, an element such as rhyme entails an element of sameness (*cat* and *rat* share certain sounds), but also one of difference (and this difference is essential: in formal poetry a word may not be rhymed with *itself*). These conventions require a constantly evolving pattern, one in which the reader is always anticipating the text, formulating expectations of the twists and surprises that lie beyond the turn of the next phrase. If the function of the poem (or story, or film) proves entirely predictable, it falls into monotony (Casablanca *before* the letters); if it proves entirely *un*predictable, even in retrospect, then it appears gratuitous or illogical. The "trick," so to speak, is to vary the pattern so that it seems always surprising, yet always inevitable. When our expectations are "frustrated" in this way, the experience often proves immensely satisfying.

This is the realm in which *Casablanca* truly excels. The film is, so to speak, ambidextrous: with one hand it works hard to create certain expectations on the part of the viewer, while the other hand prepares to pull the rug out from beneath his feet. These moments—when the viewer is tumbling— are the ones when we feel a shiver of pleasure race through the audience.

One of the key examples of this underhandedness brings us back to the problem Rick has around glassware: his drunkenness is surprising in the light of what we are "trained" to expect early in the film. When a self-important guest at the café tells Karl, the head waiter, to invite Rick over for a drink,

---

[13]Jakobson, "Linguistics and Poetics."

Karl throws his hands up in the air and exclaims, "Oh, he never drinks with customers!" When Ugarte talks Rick into concealing the letters of transit for him, he offers the big guy a drink, quickly correcting himself: "Oh, I forgot, you never drink. . . ." But when Laszlo invites Rick to join them for a drink, and Renaud begins to trot out his excuse on behalf of his American friend, Rick interrupts him: "Thanks, I will." There is astonishment on the part of Renaud, and Rick has fallen off the wagon for good.

Other patterns in the film follow this lead. In the film Renaud is an incorrigible skirt-chaser, and he has an unsavory habit of selling exit visas for sex. Time and again we see him gallantly offer to rescue damsels in distress. He assigns a tryst, and then issues a visa the morning after. But Rick takes pity on a young Bulgarian woman, torn between betraying her husband and insuring their safe passage to America, and when he fixes the roulette wheel to allow her to buy the visa with cash rather than favors, it is Renaud whose expectations are frustrated.

This last example is linked to a third. On two separate occasions Rick makes it clear that he doesn't "stick [his] neck out for nobody." But gradually, after the arrival of the letters and of Ilsa, Rick's neck begins to emerge. He helps the Bulgarian woman, he lets the band play the *Marseillaise*, and he gives away the invaluable letters of transit. In a world rigorously structured by theft and exchange, Rick's selflessness is unexpected, unthinkable. Yet his apparent unpredictability is felt by the audience as inevitable.

Thus on a number of occasions certain patterns are clearly established, only to be overturned in the most delightful of ways. However, this strategy itself poses a problem for the end of the film—a problem that was at some level intuited by the director and the actors who, up until the last moment, were not sure with whom—Rick or Victor?—Ilsa was actually going to leave Casablanca. The problem is, in a sense, that the early patterns in the film train the viewer to *expect* a frustration of expectations, to be prepared for the unexpected.

For we have seen enough of Rick and Ilsa in the movie to recognize the pattern of their relationship: when they meet in the café there is mention of Ilsa having abandoned Rick in Paris; we see this confirmed in the flashback, and we see it repeated when Ilsa leaves Rick drunk in the bar. The pattern might lead us to think that, in the final scene, Rick will again be abandoned by Ilsa. But there have been so many surprises in other parts of the film; might he not leave *with* her this time? However, this expectation itself is hardly surprising, because it fits with the larger pattern of reversals within the film, not to mention how it conforms to the broader tradition of happy Hollywood endings.

What actually happens at the end of *Casablanca* is a stroke of genius— or at least of luck. Rick is neither abandoned by Ilsa, nor does he leave with her. Instead, although he is indeed left at the airport (thus, *structurally* identical to his abandonment at the train station in Paris), in this case *he* is the one to have sent Ilsa packing, which is *thematically* the opposite of their first parting. Expectations are frustrated, but in a way that is entirely compatible with the pattern established throughout the film.

OTHER DIRECTIONS

So what has been done in the preceding pages that might be qualified as structuralist? Well, first and foremost, the author has been let off the hook for guaranteeing a particular meaning for the text. This frees us, as readers, to examine what really *happens* in a text, rather than struggling to identify what someone might have hoped to achieve. Second, setting the author aside encourages us to focus less on *what* a text means, and more on *how* it means it. That is, our reading of *Casablanca* doesn't linger over the moral of the story (which is likely, after all, to be fairly banal); nor does it discuss the psychological consistency of characters; nor again does it worry about the image the film presents of gender roles or social classes. The fact that the structuralist analysis steers clear of these topics does not suggest that they are unworthy of discussion (the presentation of women in Hollywood films, for example, is almost guaranteed to engender considerable debate), only that this kind of analysis has set itself a different sort of task, and asks a particular set of questions. These questions will focus less on meaning than on structure—although structure and meaning will always be interrelated. How, then, is the text organized? What patterns (in plot, images, vocabulary, rhythm, etc.) does it establish, and how does it vary them? What is the hidden logic, what are the secret rules of the text?

Text, text, text. And yet this chapter has dealt almost exclusively with . . . a *film*. I could defend this choice by reminding you that the film was originally a play, and that most people don't mind reading plays in a literature class. Or I could point out that the discussion of a film was a strategically useful choice, because readers are less predisposed to worry about authorship in movies than in novels. Both points are, in fact, true. However, one of the aspects of modern literary theory is that it generally takes a broad view of what constitutes an object of study. Is it not possible to "read" a film as one reads a book? Can they not both be pressed to reveal the subtleties of their organization, their skeletal structure?

There is nothing sacred about the particular patterns we identified in *Casablanca*, and structural readings in literary texts can head off in a number of different directions. If we were reading Shakespeare's *Hamlet*, we might investigate the pattern of alternations between main plot and subplots, or the function of ghosts, or—if we were strong in versification—in the irregularities in iambic pentameter. In Mary Shelley's *Frankenstein* we might be tempted to look at parallels between the personal story of the narrator and the story of the monster. Toni Morrison's *Beloved* might prompt us to reflect on the strange operation of *time* in the novel, time being a key structural element.

However, organizing the present discussion around *Casablanca* is also useful in that it helps demonstrate how structuralism has implications that reach well beyond the printed page. In fact, the movement has been of considerable influence in fields other than literary studies, especially in anthropology, where various thinkers have used structuralism as a lever to change our understanding of human behavior. In this broad perspective, literature and art become but particular examples of human expression, all of which can be revealed to conform to certain structural patterns. Probably the most obvious of these structured "behaviors" come in the form of rituals, where rules of conduct and deportment can be more or less explicit. But we see the same things in many other activities, ranging from the apparently banal (for instance, sports spectatorship, which in many ways has evolved structures akin to those of religion), to the supposedly grand (say, political campaigns, where as often as not the heavy reliance on certain patterns serves to create the illusion of content, to camouflage the fact that, in reality, very little is being said). Moreover, Western societies have found binary oppositions such a convenient organizational principle that our lives are dominated by them, especially as they are realized in the pressing, sometimes volatile topics of American public discourse: Republicans versus Democrats, Rich versus Poor, White versus Black, North versus South, Women versus Men. These polarizations are sometimes useful, sometimes questionable, and often dangerous; but in any case they help us to simplify, and thus understand and manipulate, the world around us.

In many different walks of life one may be able to identify tacit structures. However, as so often in the humanities, there is a potential problem of objectivity: how can we be sure that the patterns we identify are ones we have *discovered*, and not ones that we have *projected?* The problem relates back to the Super Word Circles of chapter 1: how many repetitions do we need before concluding that we have hit upon a pattern? How do we know that we have not simply found what we were looking for, that the "rules" we have uncovered are more revealing of the "text" we have read than they are of our own habits and structures of reading?

Some readers shrug their shoulders at these questions and assert that objectivity is simply a matter of conscience and attentiveness: one does the best one can to remain "faithful" to the text. Those who are truly bothered by the implications of these concerns, however, have clear and certain recourse: they become poststructuralists. For more on that, move on to the next chapter.

FURTHER READING

Authors:

Barthes, Roland. "The Death of the Author." In *Image, Music, Text*, translated by Stephen Heath. New York: Hill and Wang, 1977.

Beardsley, M. C., and W. K. Whimsatt. "The Intentional Fallacy." In *On Literary Intention: Critical Essays*, edited by David Newton-de Molina. Edinburgh: University Press, 1976.

Foucault, Michel. "What Is an Author?" In *Textual Strategies: Perspectives in Post-Structuralist Criticism*, edited by Josué Harari. Ithaca, N.Y.: Cornell University Press, 1979.

Structuralism, Formalism, Semiotics:

Culler, Jonathan. *Structuralist Poetics: Structuralism, Linguistics, and the Study of Literature.* Ithaca, N.Y.: Cornell University Press, 1975.
Eco, Umberto. "*Casablanca*: Cult Movies and Intertextual Collage." In *Philosophy and Film*, edited by Cynthia A. Freeland and Thomas E. Wartenberg. New York: Routledge, 1995.
Lye, John. "Some Elements of Structuralism and its Application to Literary Theory." Available on the World Wide Web at: http://www.brocku.ca/english/courses/4F70/struct.html
Voice of the Shuttle Web links on structuralism: http://humanitas.ucsb.edu/shuttle/theory.html#structuralism

Patterns and Readerly Expectations:

Jakobson, Roman. "Linguistics and Poetics." In *Style in Language*, edited by Thomas Sebeok. Cambridge: Technology Press of the Massachusetts Institute of Technology, 1960.

Structuralism and Literature:

Genette, Gérard. "Structuralism and Literary Criticism." In *Figures of Literary Discourse*, translated by Alan Sheridan. New York: Columbia University Press, 1982.

3

"Mssng Lttrs"

Poststructuralism and Deconstruction

Nothing succeeds like excess.

—Oscar Wilde

Have you ever read Edgar Allan Poe's "The Purloined Letter"? It's a brilliant story. If you haven't had the pleasure, read it now. We'll wait for you.

The Purloined Letter[1]

Nil sapientiae odiosius acumine nimio.

—Seneca.

At Paris, just after dark one gusty evening in the autumn of 18——, I was enjoying the twofold luxury of meditation and a meerschaum, in company with my friend C. Auguste Dupin, in his little back library, or book-closet *au troisième*, No. 33, Rue Dunot, Faubourg St. Germain. For one hour at least we had maintained a profound silence; while each, to any casual observer, might have seemed intently and exclusively occupied with the curling eddies of smoke that oppressed the atmosphere of the chamber. For myself, however, I was mentally discussing certain topics which had formed matter for conversation between us at an earlier period of the evening; I mean the affair of the Rue Morgue, and the mystery

---

[1] The text reprinted here is from Edgar Allan Poe, *Complete Stories* (New York: Doubleday, 1966), 125–138.

attending the murder of Marie Rogêt. I looked upon it, therefore, as something of a coincidence, when the door of our apartment was thrown open and admitted our old acquaintance, Monsieur G——, the Prefect of the Parisian police.

We gave him a hearty welcome; for there was nearly half as much of the entertaining as of the contemptible about the man, and we had not seen him for several years. We had been sitting in the dark, and Dupin now arose for the purpose of lighting a lamp, but sat down again, without doing so, upon G.'s saying that he had called to consult us, or rather to ask the opinion of my friend, about some official business which had occasioned a great deal of trouble.

"If it is any point requiring reflection," observed Dupin, as he forbore to enkindle the wick, "we shall examine it to better purpose in the dark."

"That is another of your odd notions," said the Prefect, who had a fashion of calling every thing "odd" that was beyond his comprehension, and thus lived amid an absolute legion of "oddities."

"Very true," said Dupin, as he supplied his visitor with a pipe, and rolled towards him a comfortable chair.

"And what is the difficulty now?" I asked. "Nothing more in the assassination way, I hope?"

"Oh no; nothing of that nature. The fact is, the business is *very* simple indeed, and I make no doubt that we can manage it sufficiently well ourselves; but then I thought Dupin would like to hear the details of it, because it is so excessively *odd*."

"Simple and odd," said Dupin.

"Why, yes; and not exactly that, either. The fact is, we have all been a good deal puzzled because the affair *is* so simple, and yet baffles us altogether."

"Perhaps it is the very simplicity of the thing which puts you at fault," said my friend.

"What nonsense you *do* talk!" replied the Prefect, laughing heartily.

"Perhaps the mystery is a little *too* plain," said Dupin.

"Oh, good heavens! who ever heard of such an idea?"

"A little *too* self-evident."

"Ha! ha! ha!—ha! ha ha!—ho! ho! ho!"—roared our visitor profoundly amused, "oh, Dupin, you will be the death of me yet!"

"And what, after all, *is* the matter on hand?" I asked.

"Why, I will tell you," replied the Prefect, as he gave a long, steady, and contemplative puff, and settled himself in his chair. "I will tell you in a few words; but, before I begin, let me caution you that this is an affair demanding the greatest secrecy, and that I should most probably lose the position I now hold, were it known that I confided it to any one."

"Proceed," said I.

"Or not," said Dupin.

"Well, then; I have received personal information, from a very high quarter, that a certain document of the last importance, has been purloined from the royal apartments. The individual who purloined it is known; this beyond a doubt; he was seen to take it. It is known, also, that it still remains in his possession."

"How is this known?" asked Dupin.

"It is clearly inferred," replied the Prefect, "from the nature of the document, and from the non-appearance of certain results which would at once arise from its passing *out* of the robber's possession;—that is to say, from his employing it as he must design in the end to employ it."

"Be a little more explicit," I said.

"Well, I may venture so far as to say that the paper gives its holder a certain power in a certain quarter where such power is immensely valuable." The Prefect was fond of the cant of diplomacy.

"Still I do not quite understand," said Dupin.

"No? Well; the disclosure of the document to a third person, who shall be nameless, would bring in question the honor of a personage of most exalted station; and this fact gives the holder of the document an ascendancy over the illustrious personage whose honor and peace are so jeopardized."

"But this ascendancy," I interposed, "would depend upon the robber's knowledge of the loser's knowledge of the robber. Who would dare——"

"The thief," said G., "is the Minister D——, who dares all things, those unbecoming as well as those becoming a man. The method of the theft was not less ingenious than bold. The document in question—a letter, to be frank—had been received by the personage robbed while alone in the royal *boudoir*. During its perusal she was suddenly interrupted by the entrance of the other exalted personage from whom especially it was her wish to conceal it. After a hurried and vain endeavor to thrust it in a drawer, she was forced to place it, open as it was, upon a table. The address, however, was uppermost, and, the contents thus unexposed, the letter escaped notice. At this juncture enters the Minister D——. His lynx eye immediately perceives the paper, recognizes the handwriting of the address, observes the confusion of the personage addressed, and fathoms her secret. After some business transactions, hurried through in his ordinary manner, he produces a letter somewhat similar to the one in question, opens it, pretends to read it, and then places it in close juxtaposition to the other. Again he converses, for some fifteen minutes, upon the public affairs. At length, in taking leave, he takes also from the table the letter to which he had no claim. Its rightful owner saw, but, of course, dared not call attention to the act, in the presence of the third personage who stood at her elbow. The minister decamped; leaving his own letter—one of no importance—upon the table."

"Here, then," said Dupin to me, "you have precisely what you demand to make the ascendancy complete—the robber's knowledge of the loser's knowledge of the robber."

"Yes," replied the Prefect; "and the power thus attained has, for some months past, been wielded, for political purposes, to a very dangerous extent. The personage robbed is more thoroughly convinced, every day, of the necessity of reclaiming her letter. But this, of course, cannot be done openly. In fine, driven to despair, she has committed the matter to me."

"Than whom," said Dupin, amid a perfect whirlwind of smoke, "no more sagacious agent could, I suppose, be desired, or even imagined."

"You flatter me," replied the Prefect; "but it is possible that some such opinion may have been entertained."

"It is clear," said I, "as you observe, that the letter is still in possession of the minister; since it is this possession and not any employment of the letter, which bestows the power. With the employment the power departs."

"True," said G.; "and upon this conviction I proceeded. My first care was to make thorough search of the minister's hotel; and here my chief embarrassment lay in the necessity of searching without his knowledge. Beyond all things, I have been warned of the danger which would result from giving him reason to suspect our design."

"But," said I, "you are quite *au fait* in these investigations. The Parisian police have done this thing often before."

"O yes; and for this reason I did not despair. The habits of the minister gave me, too, a great advantage. He is frequently absent from home all night. His servants are by no means numerous. They sleep at a distance from their master's apartment, and, being chiefly Neapolitans, are readily made drunk. I have keys, as you know, with which I can open any chamber or cabinet in Paris. For three months a night has not passed, during the greater part of which I have not been engaged, personally, in ransacking the D—— Hôtel. My honor is interested, and, to mention a great secret, the reward is enormous. So I did not abandon the search until I had become fully satisfied that the thief is a more astute man than myself. I fancy that I have investigated every nook and corner of the premises in which it is possible that the paper can be concealed."

"But is it not possible," I suggested, "that although the letter may be in possession of the minister, as it unquestionably is, he may have concealed it elsewhere than upon his own premises?"

"This is barely possible," said Dupin. "The present peculiar condition of affairs at court, and especially of those intrigues in which D—— is known to be involved, would render the instant availability of the document—its susceptibility of being produced at a moment's notice—a point of nearly equal importance with its possession."

"Its susceptibility of being produced?" said I.

"That is to say, of being *destroyed*," said Dupin.

"True," I observed; "the paper is clearly then upon the premises. As for its being upon the person of the minister, we may consider that as out of the question."

"Entirely," said the Prefect. "He has been twice waylaid, as if by footpads, and his person rigorously searched under my own inspection."

"You might have spared yourself this trouble," said Dupin. "D——, I presume, is not altogether a fool, and, if not, must have anticipated these waylayings, as a matter of course."

"Not *altogether* a fool," said G., "but then he's a poet, which I take to be only one remove from a fool."

"True," said Dupin, after a long and thoughtful whiff from his meer-schaum, "although I have been guilty of certain doggerel myself."

"Suppose you detail," said I, "the particulars of your search."

"Why the fact is, we took our time, and we searched *every where*. I have had long experience in these affairs. I took the entire building, room by room; devoting the nights of a whole week to each. We examined, first, the furniture of each apartment. We opened every possible drawer; and I presume you know that, to a properly trained police agent, such a thing as a *secret* drawer is impossible. Any man is a dolt who permits a 'secret' drawer to escape him in a search of this kind. The thing is *so* plain. There is a certain amount of bulk—of space—to be accounted for in every cabinet. Then we have accurate rules. The fiftieth part of a line could not escape us. After the cabinets we took the chairs. The cushions we probed with the fine long needles you have seen me employ. From the tables we removed the tops."

"Why so?"

"Sometimes the top of a table, or other similarly arranged piece of furniture, is removed by the person wishing to conceal an article; then the leg is excavated, the article deposited within the cavity, and the top replaced. The bottoms and tops of bed-posts are employed in the same way."

"But could not the cavity be detected by sounding?" I asked.

"By no means, if, when the article is deposited, a sufficient wadding of cotton be placed around it. Besides, in our case, we were obliged to proceed without noise."

"But you could not have removed—you could not have taken to pieces *all* articles of furniture in which it would have been possible to make a deposit in the manner you mention. A letter may be compressed into a thin spiral roll, not differing much in shape or bulk from a large knitting-needle, and in this form it might be inserted into the rung of a chair, for example. You did not take to pieces all the chairs?"

"Certainly not; but we did better—we examined the rungs of every chair in the hotel, and, indeed, the jointings of every description of fur-niture, by the aid of a most powerful microscope. Had there been any obvious as an apple. Any disorder in the gluing—any unusual gaping in the joints—would have sufficed to insure detection."

"I presume you looked to the mirrors, between the boards and the plates, and you probed the beds and the bed-clothes, as well as the curtains and carpets."

"That of course; and when we had absolutely completed every particle of the furniture in this way, then we examined the house itself. We divided its entire surface into compartments, which we numbered, so that none might be missed; then we scrutinized each individual square inch throughout the premises, including the two houses immediately adjoining, with the microscope, as before."

"The two houses adjoining!" I exclaimed; "you must have had a great deal of trouble."

"We had; but the reward offered is prodigious."

"You include the *grounds* about the houses?"

"All the grounds are paved with brick. They gave us comparatively little trouble. We examined the moss between the bricks, and found it undisturbed."

"You looked among D——'s papers, of course, and into the books of the library?"

"Certainly; we opened every package and parcel; we not only opened every book, but we turned over every leaf in each volume, not contenting ourselves with a mere shake, according to the fashion of some of our police officers. We also measured the thickness of every book-*cover*, with the most accurate admeasurement, and applied to each the most jealous scrutiny of the microscope. Had any of the bindings been recently meddled with, it would have been utterly impossible that the fact should have escaped observation. Some five or six volumes, just from the hands of the binder, we carefully probed, longitudinally, with the needles."

"You explored the floors beneath the carpets?"

"Beyond doubt. We removed every carpet, and examined the boards with the microscope."

"And the paper on the walls?"

"Yes."

"You looked into the cellars?"

"We did."

"Then," I said, "you have been making a miscalculation, and the letter is *not* upon the premises, as you suppose."

"I fear you are right there," said the Prefect. "And now, Dupin, what would you advise me to do?"

"To make a thorough re-search of the premises."

"That is absolutely needless," replied G——. "I am not more sure that I breathe than I am that the letter is not at the Hôtel."

"I have no better advice to give you," said Dupin. "You have, of course, an accurate description of the letter?"

"Oh yes!"—And here the Prefect, producing a memorandum-book, proceeded to read aloud a minute account of the internal, and especially of the external appearance of the missing document. Soon after finishing the perusal of this description, he took his departure, more entirely depressed in spirits than I had ever known the good gentleman before.

In about a month afterwards he paid us another visit, and found us occupied very nearly as before. He took a pipe and a chair and entered into some ordinary conversation. At length I said,—

"Well, but G——, what of the purloined letter? I presume you have at last made up your mind that there is no such thing as overreaching the Minister?"

"Confound him, say I—yes; I made the re-examination, however, as Dupin suggested—but it was all labor lost, as I knew it would be."

"How much was the reward offered, did you say?" asked Dupin.

"Why, a very great deal—a *very* liberal reward—I don't like to say how much, precisely; but one thing I *will* say, that I wouldn't mind giving my individual check for fifty thousand francs to any one who could obtain me that letter. The fact is, it is becoming of more and more importance every day; and the reward has been lately doubled. If it were trebled, however, I could do no more than I have done."

"Why, yes," said Dupin, drawlingly, between the whiffs of his meerschaum, "I really—think, G——, you have not exerted yourself—to the utmost in this matter. You might—do a little more, I think, eh?"

"How?—in what way?"

"Why—puff, puff—you might—puff, puff—employ counsel in the matter, eh?—puff, puff, puff. Do you remember the story they tell of Abernethy?"

"No; hang Abernethy!"

"To be sure! hang him and welcome. But, once upon a time, a certain rich miser conceived the design of sponging upon this Abernethy for a medical opinion. Getting up, for this purpose, an ordinary conversation in a private company, he insinuated his case to the physician, as that of an imaginary individual.

" 'We will suppose,' said the miser, 'that his symptoms are such and such; now, doctor, what would *you* have directed him to take?'

" 'Take!' said Abernethy, 'why, take *advice*, to be sure.' "

"But," said the Prefect, a little discomposed, "I am *perfectly* willing to take advice, and to pay for it. I would *really* give fifty thousand francs to any one who would aid me in the matter."

"In that case," replied Dupin, opening a drawer, and producing a checkbook, "you may as well fill me up a check for the amount mentioned. When you have signed it, I will hand you the letter."

I was astounded. The Prefect appeared absolutely thunderstricken. For some minutes he remained speechless and motionless, looking incredulously at my friend with open mouth, and eyes that seemed starting from their sockets; then, apparently recovering himself in some measure, he seized a pen, and after several pauses and vacant stares, finally filled up and signed a check for fifty thousand francs, and handed it across the table to Dupin. The latter examined it carefully and deposited it in his pocket-book; then, unlocking an *escritoire*, took thence a letter and gave it to the Prefect. This functionary grasped it in a perfect agony of joy, opened it with a trembling hand, cast a rapid glance at its contents, and then, scrambling and struggling to the door, rushed at length unceremoniously from the room and from the house without having uttered a syllable since Dupin had requested him to fill up the check.

When he had gone, my friend entered into some explanations.

"The Parisian police," he said, "are exceedingly able in their way. They are persevering, ingenious, cunning, and thoroughly versed in the knowledge which their duties seem chiefly to demand. Thus, when G——detailed to us his mode of searching the premises at the Hôtel D——, I felt entire confidence in his having made a satisfactory investigation—so far as his labors extended."

"So far as his labors extended?" said I.

"Yes," said Dupin. "The measures adopted were not only the best of their kind, but carried out to absolute perfection. Had the letter been deposited within the range of their search, these fellows would, beyond a question, have found it."

I merely laughed—but he seemed quite serious in all that he said.

"The measures, then," he continued, "were good in their kind, and well executed; their defect lay in their being inapplicable to the case, and to the man. A certain set of highly ingenious resources are, with the Prefect, a sort of Procrustean bed, to which he forcibly adapts his designs. But he perpetually errs by being too deep or too shallow, for the matter in hand; and many a schoolboy is a better reasoner than he. I knew one about eight years of age, whose success at guessing in the game of 'even and odd' attracted universal admiration. This game is simple, and is played with marbles. One player holds in his hand a number of these toys, and demands of another whether that number is even or odd. If the guess is right, the guesser wins one; if wrong, he loses one. The boy to whom I allude won all the marbles of the school. Of course he had some principle of guessing; and this lay in mere observation and admeasurement of the astuteness of his opponents. For example, an arrent simpleton is his opponent, and, holding up his closed hand, asks, 'are they even or odd?' Our schoolboy replies, 'odd,' and loses; but upon the second trial he wins, for he then says to himself, 'the simpleton had them even upon the first trial, and his amount of cunning is just sufficient to make him have them odd upon the second; I will therefore guess odd;'—and he guesses odd, and wins. Now, with a simpleton a degree above the first, he would have reasoned thus: 'This fellow finds that in the first instance I guessed odd, and, in the second, he will propose to himself upon the first impulse, a simple variation from even to odd, as did the first simpleton; but then a second thought will suggest that this is too simple a variation, and finally he will decide upon putting it even as before. I will therefore guess even;'—he guesses even, and wins. Now this mode of reasoning in the schoolboy, whom his fellows termed 'lucky,'—what, in its last analysis, is it?"

"It is merely," I said, "an identification of the reasoner's intellect with that of his opponent."

"It is," said Dupin; "and, upon inquiring of the boy by what means he effected the *thorough* identification in which his success consisted, I received answer as follows: 'When I wish to find out how wise, or how stupid, or how good, or how wicked is any one, or what are his thoughts at the moment, I fashion the expression of my face, as accurately as possible, in accordance with the expression of his, and then wait to see what thoughts or sentiments arise in my mind or heart, as if to match or correspond with the expression.' This response of the schoolboy lies at the bottom of all the spurious profundity which has been attributed to Rochefoucauld, to La Bougive, to Machiavelli, and to Campanella."

"And the identification," I said, "of the reasoner's intellect with that of his opponent, depends, if I understand you aright, upon the accuracy with which the opponent's intellect is admeasured."

"For its practical value it depends upon this," replied Dupin; "and the Prefect and his cohort fail so frequently, first, by default of this identification, and, secondly, by ill-admeasurement, or rather through non-admeasurement of the intellect with which they are engaged. They consider only their *own* ideas of ingenuity; and, in searching for anything hidden, advert only to the modes in which *they* would have hidden it. They are right in this much—that their own ingenuity is a faithful representative of that of *the mass*; but when the cunning of the individual felon is diverse in character from their own, the felon foils them, of course. This always happens when it is above their own, and very usually when it is below. They have no variation of principle in their investigations; at best, when urged by some unusual emergency—by some extraordinary reward—they extend or exaggerate their old modes of *practice*, without touching their principles. What, for example, in this case of D——, has been done to vary the principle of action? What is all this boring, and probing, and sounding, and scrutinizing with the microscope, and dividing the surface of the building into registered square inches— what is it all but an exaggeration *of the application* of the one principle or set of principles of search, which are based upon the one set of notions regarding human ingenuity, to which the Prefect, in the long routine of his duty, has been accustomed? Do you not see he has taken it for granted that *all* men proceed to conceal a letter,—not exactly in a gimlet-hole bored in a chair-leg—but, at least, in *some* out-of-the-way hole or corner suggested by the same tenor of thought which would urge a man to secrete a letter in a gimlet-hole bored in a chair-leg? And do you not see also, that such *recherchés* nooks for concealment are adapted only for ordinary occasions, and would be adopted only by ordinary intellects;

for, in all cases of concealment, a disposal of the article concealed—a disposal of it in this *recherché* manner,—is, in the very first instance, presumable and presumed; and thus its discovery depends, not at all upon the acumen, but altogether upon the mere care, patience, and determination of the seekers; and where the case is of importance—or, what amounts to the same thing in the *policial* eyes, when the reward is of magnitude,—the qualities in question have *never* been known to fail. You will now understand what I meant in suggesting that, had the purloined letter been hidden any where within the limits of the Prefect's examination—in other words, had the principle of its concealment been comprehended within the principles of the Prefect—its discovery would have been a matter altogether beyond question. This functionary, however, has been thoroughly mystified; and the remote source of his defeat lies in the supposition that the Minister is a fool, because he has acquired renown as a poet. All fools are poets; this the Prefect *feels*; and he is merely guilty of a *non distributio medii* in thence inferring that all poets are fools."

"But is this really the poet?" I asked. "There are two brothers, I know; and both have attained reputation in letters. The Minister I believe has written learnedly on the Differential Calculus. He is a mathematician, and no poet."

"You are mistaken; I know him well; he is both. As poet *and* mathematician, he would reason well; as mere mathematician, he could not have reasoned at all, and thus would have been at the mercy of the Prefect."

"You surprise me," I said, "by these opinions, which have been contradicted by the voice of the world. You do not mean to set at naught the well-digested idea of centuries. The mathematical reason has long been regarded as *the* reason *par excellence*."

" '*Il y a à parier*,' " replied Dupin, quoting from Chamfort, " '*que toute idée publique, toute convention reçue, est une sottise, car elle a convenu au plus grand nombre.*' The mathematicians, I grant you, have done their best to promulgate the popular error to which you allude, and which is none the less an error for its promulgation as truth. With an art worthy a better cause, for example, they have insinuated the term 'analysis' into application to algebra. The French are the originators of this particular deception; but if a term is of any importance—if words derive any value from applicability—then 'analysis' conveys 'algebra' about as much as, in Latin, '*ambitus*' implies 'ambition,' '*religio*' 'religion,' or '*homines honesti*,' a set of *honorable* men."

"You have a quarrel on hand, I see," said I, "with some of the algebraists of Paris, but proceed."

"I dispute the availability, and thus the value, of that reason which is cultivated in any especial form other than the abstractly logical. I dispute, in particular, the reason educed by mathematical study. The mathematics are the science of form and quantity; mathematical reasoning is merely logic applied to observation upon form and quantity. The great error lies in supposing that even the truths of what is called *pure* algebra, are abstract or general truths. And this error is so egregious that I am confounded at the universality with which it has been received. Mathematical axioms are *not* axioms of general truth. What is true of *relation*—of form and quantity—is often grossly false in regard to morals, for example. In this latter science it is very usually *untrue* that the aggregated parts are equal to the whole. In chemistry also the axiom fails. In the consideration of motive it fails; for two motives, each of a given value, have not, necessarily, a value when united, equal to the sum of their values apart. There are numerous other mathematical truths which are only truths within the limits of *relation*. But the mathematician argues, from his *finite truths*, through habit, as if they were of an absolutely general applicability—as the world indeed imagines them to be. Bryant, in his very learned 'Mythology,' mentions an analogous source of error, when he says that 'although the Pagan fables are not believed, yet we forget ourselves continually, and make inferences from them as existing realities.' With the algebraists, however, who are Pagans themselves, the 'Pagan fables' *are* believed, and the inferences are made, not so much through lapse of memory, as through an unaccountable addling of the brains. In short, I never yet encountered the mere mathematician who could be trusted out of equal roots, or one who did not clandestinely hold it as a point of his faith that $x^2 + px$ was absolutely and unconditionally equal to q. Say to one of these gentlemen, by way of experiment, if you please, that you believe occasions may occur where $x^2 + px$ is *not* altogether equal to q, and, having made him understand what you mean, get out of his reach as speedily as convenient, for, beyond a doubt, he will endeavor to knock you down.

"I mean to say," continued Dupin, while I merely laughed at his last observations, "that if the Minister had been no more than a mathematician, the Prefect would have been under no necessity of giving me this check. I knew him, however, as both mathematician and poet, and my measures were adapted to his capacity, with reference to the circumstances by which he was surrounded. I knew him as a courtier, too, and as a bold *intriguant*. Such a man, I considered, could not fail to be aware of the ordinary *policial* modes of action. He could not have failed to anticipate—and events have proved that he did not fail to anticipate—the waylayings to which he was subjected. He must have foreseen, I reflected, the secret investigations of his premises. His frequent absences from home at night, which were hailed by the Prefect as certain aids to his success, I regarded only as *ruses*, to afford opportunity for thorough search to the police, and thus the sooner to impress them with the conviction to which G——, in fact, did finally arrive—the conviction that the letter was not upon the premises. I felt, also, that the whole train of thought, which I was at some pains in detailing to you just now, concerning the invariable principle of *policial* action in searches for articles concealed—I felt that this whole train of thought would necessarily pass through the mind of the Minister. It would imperatively lead him to despise all the ordinary *nooks* of concealment. *He* could not, I reflected, be so weak as not to see that the most intricate and remote recess of his hotel would be as open as his commonest closets to the eyes, to the probes, to the gimlets, and to the microscopes of the Prefect. I saw, in fine, that he would be driven, as a matter of course, to *simplicity*, if not deliberately induced to it as a matter of choice. You will remember, perhaps, how desperately the Prefect laughed when I suggested, upon our first interview, that it was just possible this mystery troubled him so much on account of its being so *very* self-evident."

"Yes," said I, "I remember his merriment well. I really thought he would have fallen into convulsions."

"The material world," continued Dupin, "abounds with very strict analogies to the immaterial; and thus some color of truth has been given to the rhetorical dogma, that metaphor, or simile, may be made to strengthen an argument, as well as to embellish a description. The principle of the *vis inertiæ*, for example, seems to be identical in physics and metaphysics. It is not more true in the former, that a large body is with more difficulty set in motion than a smaller one, and that its subsequent *momentum* is commensurate with this difficulty, than it is, in the latter, that intellects of the vaster capacity, while more forcible, more constant, and more eventful in their movements than those of inferior grade, are yet the less readily moved, and more embarrassed and full of hesitation in the first few steps of their progress. Again: have you ever noticed which of the street signs, over the shop doors, are the most attractive of attention?"

"I have never given the matter a thought," I said.

"There is a game of puzzles," he resumed, "which is played upon a map. One party playing requires another to find a given word—the name of town, river, state or empire—any word, in short, upon the motley and perplexed surface of the chart. A novice in the game generally seeks to embarrass his opponents by giving them the most minutely lettered names; but the adept selects such words as stretch, in large characters, from one end of the chart to the other. These, like the over-largely lettered signs and placards of the street, escape observation by dint of being excessively obvious; and here the physical oversight is precisely analogous with the moral inapprehension by which the intellect suffers to pass unnoticed those considerations which are too obtrusively and too palpably self-evident. But this is a point, it appears, somewhat above or beneath the understanding of the Prefect. He never once thought it probable, or possible, that the Minister had deposited the letter immediately beneath the nose of the whole world, by way of best preventing any portion of that world from perceiving it.

"But the more I reflected upon the daring, dashing, and discriminating ingenuity of D——; upon the fact that the document must always have been *at hand*, if he intended to use it to good purpose; and upon the decisive evidence, obtained by the Prefect, that it was not hidden within the limits of that dignitary's ordinary search—the more satisfied I became that, to conceal this letter, the Minister had resorted to the comprehensive and sagacious expedient of not attempting to conceal it at all.

"Full of these ideas, I prepared myself with a pair of green spectacles, and called one fine morning, quite by accident, at the Ministerial hotel. I found D—— at home, yawning, lounging, and dawdling, as usual, and pretending to be in the last extremity of *ennui*. He is, perhaps, the most really energetic human being now alive—but that is only when nobody sees him.

"To be even with him, I complained of my weak eyes, and lamented the necessity of the spectacles, under cover of which I cautiously and thoroughly surveyed the apartment, while seemingly intent only upon the conversation of my host.

"I paid special attention to a large writing-table, near which he sat, and upon which lay confusedly, some miscellaneous letters and other papers, with one or two musical instruments and a few books. Here, however, after a long and very deliberate scrutiny, I saw nothing to excite particular suspicion.

"At length my eyes, in going the circuit of the room, fell upon a trumpery filagree card-rack of paste-board, that hung dangling by a dirty blue ribbon, from a little brass knob just beneath the middle of the mantelpiece. In this rack, which had three or four compartments, were five or six visiting cards and a solitary letter. This last was much soiled and crumpled. It was torn nearly in two, across the middle—as if a design, in the first instance, to tear it entirely up as worthless, had been altered, or stayed, in the second. It had a large black seal, bearing the D—— cipher *very* conspicuously, and was addressed, in a diminutive female hand, to D——, the minister, himself. It was thrust carelessly, and even, as it seemed, contemptuously, into one of the upper divisions of the rack.

"No sooner had I glanced at this letter, than I concluded it to be that of which I was in search. To be sure, it was, to all appearances, radically different from the one of which the Prefect had read us so minute a description. Here the seal was large and black, with the D—— cipher; there it was small and red, with the ducal arms of the S—— family. Here, the address, to the Minister, was diminutive and feminine; there the superscription, to a certain royal personage, was markedly bold and decided; the size alone formed a point of correspondence. But, then, the *radicalness* of these differences, which was excessive; the dirt; the soiled and torn condition of the paper, so inconsistent with the *true* methodical habits of D——, and so suggestive of a design to delude the beholder into an idea of the worthlessness of the document; these things, together with the hyper-obtrusive situation of this document, full in the view of every visitor, and thus exactly in accordance with the conclusions to which I had previously arrived; these things, I say, were strongly corroborative of suspicion, in one who came with the intention to suspect.

"I protracted my visit as long as possible, and, while I maintained a most animated discussion with the Minister, on a topic which I knew well had never failed to interest and excite him, I kept my attention really riveted upon the letter. In this examination, I committed to memory its external appearance and arrangement in the rack; and also fell, at length, upon a discovery which set at rest whatever trivial doubt I might have entertained. In scrutinizing the edges of the paper, I observed them to be more *chafed* than seemed necessary. They presented the *broken* appearance which is manifested when a stiff paper, having been once folded and pressed with a folder, is refolded in a reversed direction, in the same creases or edges which had formed the original fold. This discovery was sufficient. It was clear to me that the letter had been turned, as a glove, inside out, re-directed, and re-sealed. I bade the minister good morning, and took my departure at once, leaving a gold snuff-box upon the table.

"The next morning I called for the snuff-box, when we resumed, quite eagerly, the conversation of the preceding day. While thus engaged, however, a loud report, as if of a pistol, was heard immediately beneath the windows of the hotel, and was succeeded by a series of fearful screams, and the shoutings of a mob. D—— rushed to a casement, threw it open, and looked out. In the meantime, I stepped to the card-rack, took the letter, put it in my pocket, and replaced it by a fac-simile (so far as regards externals) which I had carefully prepared at my lodgings; imitating the D—— cipher, very readily, by means of a seal formed of bread.

"The disturbance in the street had been occasioned by the frantic behavior of a man with a musket. He had fired it among a crowd of women and children. It proved, however, to have been without ball, and the fellow was suffered to go his way as a lunatic or a drunkard. When he had gone, D—— came from the window, whither I had followed him immediately upon securing the object in view. Soon afterwards I bade him farewell. The pretended lunatic was a man in my own pay."

"But what purpose had you," I asked, "in replacing the letter by a *fac-simile*? Would it not have been better, at the first visit, to have seized it openly, and departed?"

"D——-," replied Dupin, "is a desperate man, and a man of nerve. His hotel, too, is not without attendants devoted to his interests. Had I made the wild attempt you suggest, I might never have left the Ministerial presence alive. The good people of Paris might have heard of me no more. But I had an object apart from these considerations. You know my political prepossessions. In this matter, I act as a partisan of the lady concerned. For eighteen months the Minister has had her in his power. She has now him in hers; since, being unaware that the letter is not in his possession he will proceed with his exactions as if it was. Thus will he inevitably commit himself, at once, to his political destruction. His downfall, too, will not be more precipitate than awkward. It is all very well to talk about the *facilis descensus Averni*; but in all kinds of climbing, as Catalani said of singing, it is far more easy to get up than to come down. In the present instance I have no sympathy—at least no pity—for him who descends. He is that *monstrum horrendum*, an unprincipled man of genius. I confess, however, that I should like very well to know the precise character of his thoughts, when, being defied by her whom the Prefect terms 'a certain personage,' he is reduced to opening the letter which I left for him in the card rack."

"How? did you put any thing particular in it?"

"Why—it did not seem altogether right to leave the interior blank—that would have been insulting. D——, at Vienna once, did me an evil turn, which I told him, quite good-humoredly, that I should remember. So, as I knew he would feel some curiosity in regard to the identity of the person who had outwitted him, I thought it a pity not to give him a clue. He is well acquainted with my MS., and I just copied into the middle of the blank sheet the words—

> ——Un dessein si funeste,
> S'il n'est digne d'Atrée, est digne de Thyeste.

They are to be found in Crébillon's 'Atrée.' "

Quite a good read, don't you think? Let's review the main lines of the story before taking it on in detail. The whole thing unfolds in nineteenth-century Paris, and the tale is recounted by a friend of Auguste Dupin, a detective whom readers of Poe may know from two other stories ("The Murders in the Rue Morgue" and "The Mystery of Marie Rogêt"). The story consists of a mystery and its solution. One evening, as our narrator and his friend Dupin enjoy a quiet pipe in the latter's library, they are graced with a visit by the Prefect of Police, charged with an important mission. A letter has been purloined from the royal apartments, and under the most extraordinary of circumstances. According to the Prefect, an "exalted royal personage" (let's call her the Queen), received a letter, which she attempted to peruse in her boudoir. The reading is interrupted, however, by the arrival of another royal personage (whom we shall call the King). Wishing to conceal the letter from her royal consort, the Queen has time to do no more than cast the envelope on her writing table as if it were of no importance, in hopes that the King will thus overlook it. Her plan succeeds, until the two are joined by the canny Minister D——, who sizes up the situation, notices the letter, and manages to exchange the Queen's envelope for one of his own. He then leaves the chambers, bearing with him the mysterious missive that will give him considerable power over the Queen.

The Prefect has been engaged by the Queen to recover the letter while maintaining the utmost secrecy. Yet his most meticulous investigations of the person and premises of the Minister D—— have revealed nothing, and he has come to Dupin for advice.

Dupin, as clever as he is smug, regales the narrator and the reader with portraits of the Prefect's ineptness, accusing the Prefect of thinking too narrowly, of operating mathematically, of seeing things as entirely too simple. The

Minister D——, he insists, plays his games at a higher level altogether. He exhorts the police to look harder.

When the Prefect returns for a second visit some weeks later, having made no headway, and now offering Dupin a fantastic sum to assist him, Dupin suddenly, astonishingly, produces the letter. Then he recounts how he came into its possession: before paying a visit to Minister D——, the detective donned colored glasses, which allowed him to glance discretely about the Minister's apartment. There, above the fireplace, displayed on a card rack, he spotted a soiled, half-torn envelope, which he recognized at once as the object of his search. Returning the next day under another pretext, Dupin arranges for D—— to be distracted by an outside diversion, providing the few moments he needs to switch the envelope with a counterfeit. The original may thus be remitted to the Queen while leaving D—— convinced that he is still in possession of the tool of his blackmail. He will be surprised, Dupin remarks, when he is finally driven to open the letter, as it contains nothing more than a barbed quotation, designed to reveal to D—— just who it is who has outsmarted him.

This is an impoverishing synopsis, but it will have to suffice for the time being. It barely accounts for the interest the story generates, much of which derives from those delightfully eccentric, singularly Poe-esque characters: the Minister excites our loathing and admiration, the Prefect presents a comical mix of canine loyalty and excruciating fastidiousness, and Dupin leads us through a maze of the most improbable of discussions, ranging from mathematics to games to poetry.

Does the story remind you of *Casablanca?* The film, you may recall, also revolved around purloined letters (the letters of transit), which at one point were "hidden" in full view (in Sam's piano, before the crowd). As in the film, Poe's tale comes to an end when the letter—like the letters of transit—is finally "delivered." These similarities encourage us at least to begin our discussion in terms reminiscent of the previous chapter. Readers who look at Poe's text from a structuralist perspective may note that "The Purloined Letter" is an extraordinarily *orderly* story, one that surrenders some of its patterns fairly readily. The most obvious of these lies in the repeated thefts: first, the Queen's letter is lifted by the Minister; then, in the second installment, Dupin steals it back. The two thefts appear to be organized in the same triangular fashion: one character conceals the letter from a second (who fails to see it); in each case a third character arrives on the scene and spirits the envelope away, leaving a facsimile in its place. It is Jacques Lacan (1901–1981), the eminent French psychoanalyst, who first pointed out these repetitions.[2] Drawn schematically, they look like this:[3]

---

[2]Jacques Lacan, "Seminar on 'The Purloined Letter'," in *The Purloined Poe: Lacan, Derrida, and Psychoanalytic Reading*, ed. J. Muller and W. Richardson (Baltimore: The Johns Hopkins University Press, 1988), 28–54. Collected in the same volume are two excellent essays that help clarify the presentations made by Lacan and, later, by Derrida: Shoshana Felman's "On Reading Poetry: Reflections on the Limits and Possibilities of Psychoanalytic Approaches," and Barbara Johnson's "The Frame of Reference: Poe, Lacan, Derrida."

[3]This diagramming is based on that proposed by Shoshana Felman, in "On Reading Poetry," *The Purloined Poe*, 145.

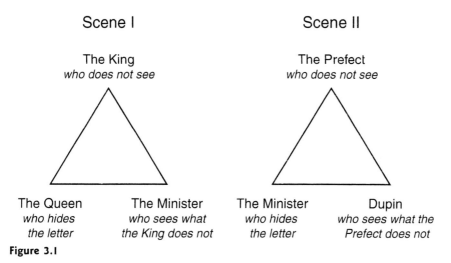

Figure 3.1

Scene I, we might be tempted to assert, "equals" Scene II; the repetition of the pattern establishes an equilibrium between the two events recounted in the story. The symmetry of this analysis has a certain appeal, and the mathematical precision of the equation would appear entirely consistent with the ruminations on mathematics and numbers that appear within the story itself. Furthermore, we could point to a third instance of this structure, one in which the reader herself participates. The reader is in a position not unlike that of the Prefect, puzzled before an unfathomable mystery. Yet, as we discover, the reason the Prefect finds the case so impenetrable is that the whole idea of impenetrability *itself* is misplaced. The Prefect need not penetrate *anything*, in fact, for the solution to the mystery lies *on the surface*: the letter is in the open. Like the Prefect, the reader is often guilty of a peculiar blindness, constantly overlooking that which the story states obviously and repeatedly. Dupin gives a hint ("Perhaps the mystery is a little *too* plain," he says to the scoffing Prefect) on the opening page. The statement warns the Prefect not to look too deeply, and Poe thus puts the key to the entire mystery in full view of both the Prefect and the reader. Like the letter itself, overlooked by the King and the Prefect, this hint generally escapes the reader's detection; the reader is *duped*, just like the Prefect and Dupin. So a third triangle could be drawn, looking something like Figure 3.2.

Might we not find within the story further examples of this structure? Dupin recounts other instances in which the obvious is overlooked. First, there is the game one plays with maps, in which one player challenges another to find the name of a town, river, or other geographical entity. "A novice," Dupin explains, "seeks to embarrass his opponents by giving them the most minutely lettered names; but the adept selects such words as stretch, in large characters, from one end of the chart to another. These, like the overlargely lettered signs and placards of the street, escape observation by dint of

Scene III

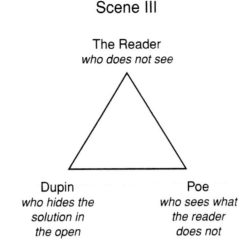

Figure 3.2

being excessively obvious." Moreover, Dupin points out that the principles of the map game are symptomatic of a general phenomenon, one by which the human mind tends to overlook "those considerations which are too obtrusively and too palpably self-evident." Are these two passages, the map game and the philosophical commentary, Scenes IV and V of the same pattern?

Perhaps. Such might be the structuralist impulse. Poststructuralists, though, are wary of rapid conclusions, and they like to pay a great deal of attention to detail. One may reduce the story to a series of equations (Scene I = Scene II = Scene III, etc.), but such a procedure entails a certain amount of violence. Moreover, it makes use of a kind of reasoning that the text itself criticizes: the methods of the Prefect. As he reflects on the methods employed by the police to locate the missing letter—methods that consisted of scrutinizing every inch of the Minister's apartment, plumbing the insides of furniture, leafing through every book, checking the moss between each of the paving stones in the grounds—Dupin criticizes the Prefect for employing "a sort of Procrustean bed." The reference is to Procrustes, a mythical bandit in ancient Greece who subjected his victims to an unusual torture. Laying them out on a bed of his own design, he made them fit it by hacking off their limbs if they proved too large, or by stretching them on a rack if they were too small. Dupin's allusion to Procrustes suggests that the Prefect can only see things one way, that he forcibly adapts the situation to fit his perspective. Anything that is not "equal" to the missing letter he will set aside.

Doesn't the establishment of a rigid pattern turn into a kind of Procrustean bed? That is, if we reduce the story to a repetition of triangular structures, we do so only by putting the story on the rack, distorting or amputating anything that differentiates the various scenes.[4] To be sure, a certain similarity *does* exist between the theft of the letter in the royal chambers and its recovery in D——'s apartment, but significant differences also exist. In the second scene, for example, the players are not all present at the same time: the Prefect is not present when Dupin steals back the letter, although the King was present at its initial disappearance. For that matter, one could demonstrate that the second half of the story involves a greater number of players, including the Queen (who is being blackmailed and who has engaged the Prefect), and, not insignificantly, the narrator himself. By what right— other than because they did not fit the triangular structure—have these actors been axed? And there is more: considerable differences in dynamics exist between Scene I and Scene II: it is true that neither the King nor the Prefect see the letter, but the former is not even aware of its existence, whereas the latter searches for it avidly; the Queen knows that D—— has seen and removed the letter, but in the second scene, D—— is unaware that Dupin has spotted it; and while D—— knows the Queen watched him take the letter in Scene I, Dupin knows that he is *not* seen when he takes the letter in Scene II. These are but a few of the differences that have had to be sacrificed in order to assert the structuralist reading, and Scene III (the one involving the reader) would stand up even less to this kind of scrutiny, to say nothing of Scenes IV and V. The structuralist reading, at least in this case, would appear to be a Procrustean act of carnage.

POSTSTRUCTURALISM

Poststructuralism often dismantles structuralist readings or structuralist thought. It accuses structuralism of conjuring away difficulties, of participating in what might be called the "Voom complex." You remember Voom—it was made famous by an American author at least as celebrated (though in different circles) as Poe: Dr. Seuss. In the juvenile classic *The Cat in the Hat Comes Back!*, Seuss tells a tale that works like a fable of Western philosophy.[5] A smart-aleck cat comes up with what seems to him to be a really good idea: he eats cakes while splashing and soaking in someone else's tub. Of course, this results in a problem—the cat leaves a stubborn bathtub ring, and the rest of the book will be spent by the cat trying, like a rather insouciant Lady MacBeth, to get that damn spot out. True, wiping it up with the mother's dress *does* remove the ring

---

[4]This is the criticism leveled by Jacques Derrida in "The Purveyor of Truth" (translated and abridged in *The Purloined Poe*, 173–212; the complete essay, "Le Facteur de la vérité" is to be found in Derrida's *The Post Card: From Socrates to Freud and Beyond*, trans. Alan Bass (Chicago: University of Chicago Press, 1987), in which he assails Lacan's reading of "The Purloined Letter." A similar argument against structuralist thinking more generally is to be found in his "Structure, Sign and Play in the Discourse of the Human Sciences" in *Writing and Difference*, trans. Alan Bass (Chicago: University of Chicago Press, 1978); there he shows how Lévi-Strauss's adherence to certain arbitrary structures both limits and predetermines the range of a structuralist anthropology.

[5]Dr. Seuss, *The Cat in the Hat Comes Back!* (New York: Random House. 1958).

from the tub, but it just displaces the problem. Each page brings the thought that just *one more step* will do the trick: from the dress the spot is smacked on the wall; from the wall it travels to shoes; from the shoes it is wiped on the rug. And so it travels from rug to bed, and finally to the yard. There the cat decides he needs just *a little more help*, and he lifts his hat to reveal "little cat A." Under little cat A's hat, we find littler cat B; and so it goes in a series of increasingly smaller supplements, all the way to itsy-bitsy cat Z ("Z is too small to see. So don't try."). But this entire feline alphabet proves to be of little assistance: the creatures succeed only in breaking the spot into smaller and smaller bits, spreading it around, never quite getting rid of it. This is when the Cat in the Hat calls in the big guns: under little cat Z's hat, one finds no more animals, only a mysterious, supplementary substance called "Voom," which whooshes out and cleans up the problem in no time.

That's a long way to get to this simple notion: Poststructuralists don't believe in Voom. Or rather, they really like seeing how Voom operates, how it is invoked by various philosophers who deftly sweep problems under the rug. But they want to recognize that, well, Voom is Voom—that there is a rhetorical sleight of hand that goes on in philosophy and in fiction in order to "clean things up" or make them simple.

Taking apart Voom, and bringing to the surface of texts various notions of complexity and contradiction, has led some people to conclude that this is an essentially negative movement. The connotations of the word *deconstruction*—which is variously claimed to be a subcategory of poststructuralism or a synonym for it—doesn't necessarily enhance the movement's image. However, from the movement's beginnings (it started in Europe and the United States in the seventies), adepts have been careful to point out that *deconstruction* does not mean *destruction*. Rather, the neologism refers to the idea that deconstruction "undoes"—or at least challenges—some of the ideas that have been artificially constructed by others; it de-*constructs* them.[6]

So, if it is not just a nihilistic, destructive movement, what exactly does deconstruction *do*? Frequently it calls into question commonsensical notions, notions that seem so obvious that they generally go untested. It was Voltaire, the wry eighteenth-century satirist, who pointed out that common sense is not so common;[7] it is theoreticians like Jacques Derrida (1930–   ) and Paul de Man (1919–1983) who sought to demonstrate that, as often as not, there is nothing less sensible.[8] As we saw in chapter 2, everyday life tends to be organized "commonsensically" in terms of oppositional pairs: good/evil, civilized/uncivilized, male/female, inside/outside . . . the list could go on forever. In this respect, everyday life is not so far removed from the supposedly "higher" realms

---

[6]The point is made by Barbara Johnson, in her book *The Critical Difference* (Baltimore: The Johns Hopkins University Press, 1980), 5.

[7]*Voltaire's Philosophical Dictionary* (New York: Knopf, 1924), 78.

[8]What might be called the founding documents of deconstructionist thought (and, more generally, of poststructuralism) are Jacques Derrida, *Of Grammatology*, trans. Gayatri Chakravorty Spivak (Baltimore: The Johns Hopkins University Press, 1976); and Paul de Man, *Blindness and Insight: Essays in the Rhetoric of Contemporary Criticism* (New York: Oxford University Press, 1971).

of human expression, such as art, literature, or philosophy, where binary oppositions can also play a major role. In "The Purloined Letter," for instance, it is relatively easy to list some of the oppositions that structure the narrative, oppositions that occur either between characters or between thematic strands:

Dupin	versus	Minister D——
obvious	versus	hidden
insight	versus	blindness
math	versus	poetry

This last opposition comes about explicitly in discussions within the story itself regarding reason: the Prefect, who is accused by Dupin of being mathematically minded, considers his opponent, the Minister D——, to be nearly a fool—"Not *altogether* a fool," he intones, "but then he's a poet, which I take to be only one remove from a fool." Supposedly superior mathematical reasoning is thus pitted against the foolish games of poetry.

Just what is meant by mathematics in "The Purloined Letter" becomes evident in Dupin's diatribes. He complains that mathematicians are hell-bent on arriving at *equations*, and that the error of many mathematicians is to assume that all realms of experience (such as morals or poetry) can be made to conform to the laws of algebra. "In short," he says, "I never yet encountered the mere mathematician ... who did not clandestinely hold it as a point of faith that $x^2 + px$ was absolutely and unconditionally equal to q. Say to one of these gentlemen, by way of experiment, if you please, that you believe occasions may occur where $x^2 + px$ is *not* altogether equal to q, and, having made him understand what you mean, get out of his reach as speedily as convenient, for, beyond doubt, he will endeavor to knock you down." The mathematical equation—that is, one on the order of $2 + 2 = 4$, one that "makes sense"—is opposed to poetic equations (such as similes, of the ilk of Burns's "My love is like a red, red rose"; that is, Love = Rose), which, from a mathematical point of view, make no sense at all.

There are also certain mathematical terms that appear in the story, terms that themselves operate according to a binary opposition. Such is the case with the game of "even and odd" that Dupin describes, the rules of which consist of one player guessing whether his opponent holds an even or odd number of marbles behind his back. Even/odd is thus appended to the list of binary oppositions at work within the story: Dupin/D——, math/poetry, hidden/obvious, insight/blindness. Poststructuralists, however, like to subject binary oppositions to scrutiny. How tight are these opposing categories? Are they natural, or are they artificially constructed? Even/odd is a good point of departure for this kind of inquiry in "The Purloined Letter," for the story of the game of marbles recalls another kind of oddness—*nonmathematical oddness*—which the Prefect evokes in the opening pages. He has come to Dupin in hopes the detective will shed some light on the mystery, but instead Dupin seems more interested in playing word games. Rather than illuminating the Prefect, he plunges the poor fellow further into darkness:

"If it is any point requiring reflection," observed Dupin, as he forbore to enkindle the wick, "we shall examine it to better purpose in the dark."

"That is another of your odd notions," said the Prefect, who had a fashion of calling every thing "odd" that was beyond his comprehension, and thus lived amid an absolute legion of "oddities."

"And what is the difficulty now?" I asked. "Nothing more in the assassination way, I hope?"

"Oh no; nothing of that nature. The fact is, the business is *very* simple indeed, and I make no doubt that we can manage it sufficiently well ourselves; but then I thought Dupin would like to hear the details of it, because it is so excessively *odd*."

"Simple and odd," said Dupin.

"Why, yes; and not exactly that, either. The fact is, we have all been a good deal puzzled because the affair *is* so simple, and yet baffles us altogether."

"Perhaps it is the very simplicity of the thing which puts you at fault," said my friend. "What nonsense you *do* talk!" replied the Prefect, laughing heartily.

"Perhaps the mystery is a little *too* plain," said Dupin.

"Oh, good heavens! who ever heard of such an idea?"

Excessively odd; *so* simple; *too* plain. As we have seen, Dupin later warns us against overlooking the "hyperobtrusive," so the sheer *abundance* of this oddness and simplicity demands that we pay heed to the terms. In the end it is the notion of "oddness" itself that ends up being odd in the story, for on the one hand, "oddness" bears a mathematical definition, which we know to be the opposite of "evenness"; on the other hand, oddness (as a synonym for strangeness and complexity) appears as the opposite of "simplicity" (which is why the Prefect breaks into gales of laughter when Dupin suggests that the matter is both simple *and* odd). Yet these two uses of the word are, appropriately enough, *at odds* with one another: *mathematical* oddness cannot, in some sense, be the opposite of simplicity, because it is defined *as* simplicity, as singularity. Mathematical oddness occurs when a number divided by two leaves a remainder of one. "One"—that is, singularity, simplicity ("single" and "simple" have the same linguistic root)—is the defining characteristic of oddness.

Already we can sense what might be called a "problematizing" of the opposition between even and odd: these "simple" terms are shown to harbor surprising ambiguities. Be careful, though: this does not necessarily suggest that there is no difference between evenness and oddness, especially as they are defined mathematically. It implies only that *in the construction of the story* "oddness" is a somewhat problematic term.

Poststructuralism likes these problems; it enjoys putting binary oppositions to the test. It does so, in part, by revealing that the oppositions are not really so binary after all: they in fact imply four different possible configurations. In chapter 2 we looked at the technological equivalent of binary thinking: digitalization. Digital machines proceed by examining small units of information, small "switches" called bits. In practical terms, bits can either be "on" (1) or "off" (0); it is the alternation between the terms of that primordial opposition of presence (1) versus absence (0). The distinction seems sensible enough: either you have something or you don't; you exist or you don't; this book is here or it isn't. However, in *theoretical* terms, presence and absence represent only two of the options allowed by a binary opposition, and one should recognize the theoretical *possibility*—even if one can imagine no practical applications—of something being *neither* present *nor* absent, or *both* present *and* absent. The simple binarity thus allows for a complication, which we could represent as shown in Figure 3.3. The bottom terms have been shaded because, for the most part, they belong to the realm of things that escape our attention, those things that, as Dupin would say, are best examined "in the dark."

Neither present nor absent? Both at once? Theoretical possibility is one thing, but in practical terms, does anything actually occupy the lower quadrants? Let us begin with neither/nor. In the last chapter we saw how the minimal terms for a structure are a pair: it takes two notes to begin a melody, two beats to initiate a rhythm, the alternation between stressed and unstressed syllables to make a poetic verse.[9] In short, it takes two to tango, structurally speaking. Now take the example of a computer processing its flow of ones and zeros, of presences and absences. If the flow of information is interrupted, the machine would be left without its alternation; even the absences would be missing; and in a context in which absences cannot be opposed to anything, the notion of absence ceases to make sense.

So, there may well be elements that fit the quadrant "neither/nor" simply because the opposition of presence and absence does not apply. But can

Figure 3.3

"Simple" Binarity

either: present	*or:* absent

Complication

neither: present *nor* absent	*both:* present *and* absent

[9]The discussion of rhythm is proposed by Jakobson in "Linguistics and Poetics" in *Style in Language* (Cambridge: Technology Press of the Massachusetts Institute of Technology, 1960).

anything be "both/and"? Well, what about a mirage? No, not necessarily the stereotypical vision of the oasis appearing amidst the dunes, but even its ordinary everyday counterpart: the word. A word on a page (Which word? *This* one. The word *word*? No, the word *this*. Which *this*—this one, or the last one? *This* one. Which one is that?) is a kind of a presence (a trace, a mark on the paper) that nevertheless always signals an absence: words "point" away from themselves, toward other words, toward ideas, toward the things they supposedly represent, toward the person (absent from the words themselves) who has spoken or written them. Words—and, for that matter, other forms of representation—hover at the frontier between presence and absence.[10]

All this is well beyond the bailiwick of computer science: there is no provision for computers to understand anything beyond the simple binarity. For better or worse, computers operate much like the Prefect: remaining faithful to a logic of either/or, they subject bits to their own kind of Procrustean bed, and anything that eludes the qualities of on-ness or off-ness will be discarded. In the best of cases computers ignore ambiguity; in the worst, ambiguity crashes the system.

One can hardly condemn computers for this intolerance, as they are simply more extreme examples of how society operates in general. For very practical (and often defensible) reasons, society likes to keep things simple. The complications of binary oppositions can be troublesome, even threatening. The category of neither/nor is often innocuous enough, for it can refer to objects that simply fall outside the purview of the simple opposition. Is the constant *pi* (3.1415 . . .) even or odd? Neither even nor odd, it would appear, first because no one knows how the number ends, and second because evenness and oddness only apply to whole numbers. Are apples even or odd? The terms simply do not apply. However, if the neither/nor category often escapes attention, figures that occupy the mixed category of both/and traditionally excite the fear and fascination of readers. Thus the intersection of such opposites as living/dead give rise to ghost stories (phantoms being both animate and inanimate), the blending of human and inhuman gives birth to such figures as Frankenstein's monster, and the intermingling of past and present becomes the stuff of science fiction. Historically, elements corresponding to the logic of both/and are regarded by society as exceptional, scandalous, and even monstrous. Often efforts are made to repress or at least to neutralize these representations of "in-between-ness."

Discovering that certain "crossover" terms do exist—that is, that some elements might indeed occupy the paradoxical quadrant of both/and—does little or nothing to deconstruct a binary opposition all on its own. In fact, to the extent that the crossover is recognized as *exceptional* (after all, ghosts, monsters, madness, and mirages are hardly regarded as *standards*), its very monstrosity may serve to reinforce our belief that opposites do not—or should not—mix. However, deconstruction generally goes farther: it suggests and tries

---

[10]On writing as a trace, see "Signature Event Context," in Jacques Derrida, *Limited Inc.*, ed. Samuel Weber (Evanston: Northwestern University Press, 1988), 1–24.

to demonstrate that the mixed category ("both/and") of many oppositions is, in fact, *not* the exception. It may rather, quite unexpectedly, prove to be the *rule*. Perhaps, for example, the ideas of absolute presence and absolute absence are, themselves, a *mirage*; maybe the radical divide between animate and inanimate is ultimately *permeable*; it could be that mathematics and poetry are *joined* by as much as they are *separated*. Maybe—just maybe—the commonsense organization of our lives into binary oppositions is a gross simplification, one that violates the truth and that distorts our perceptions.

How does this help us read "The Purloined Letter"? For one thing it helps us understand what is so *odd* about the letter, and why the Prefect has such a hard time locating it. Faithful to a simple logic of either/or, the Prefect picks apart the Minister's apartment, looking for something that is the *same* as the letter that was lost; anything that is *different* he sets aside. What he cannot fathom is that the letter might be *both* the same *and* different. Here is Dupin's description of the envelope he discovered on the card rack:

> In this rack, which had three or four compartments, were five or six visiting cards and a solitary letter. This last was much soiled and crumpled. It was torn nearly in two, across the middle—as if a design in the first instance, to tear it entirely up as worthless, had been altered, or stayed, in the second. It had a large black seal, bearing the D—— cipher *very* conspicuously, and was addressed, in a diminutive female hand, to D——, the minister himself. . . . To be sure, it was, to all appearance, radically different from the one of which the Prefect had read us so minute a description. Here the seal was large and black, with the D—— cipher; there it was small and red, with the ducal arms of the S—— family. Here the address, to the Minister, was diminutive and feminine; there the superscription, to a certain royal personage, was markedly bold and decided; the size alone formed a point of correspondence. But, then, the *radicalness* of these differences, which was excessive. . . . In scrutinizing the edges of the paper, I observed them to be more *chafed* than seemed necessary. They presented the *broken* appearance which is manifested when a stiff paper, having been folded, is refolded in a reversed direction. . . . It was clear to me that the letter had been turned, as a glove, inside out, re-directed, and re-sealed.

So, the letter is not concealed within a chair-leg or beneath paving stones, as the Prefect assumed; instead, the letter is disguised, oddly enough, *as a letter*, one that is the *same* (in size, in paper, etc.), yet *different* (inverted, redirected). Left casually on the card rack, where one ordinarily keeps visiting cards and correspondence, the letter is "hyperobtrusive," *both* hidden *and* concealed. Moreover, as if to complete the mathematical theme, the letter hesitates between oddness and evenness, between "one-ness" and "two-ness": it is a "solitary" letter (odd), but one that is torn *nearly* in two; it is caught between a "first instance," in which someone attempted to rip it in half, and a "second instance," when this attempt was stayed.

Once we begin pulling on the thread of both/and, the fabric of the story begins to run. How, one might wonder, can the Minister have been so clever, especially when the Prefect discounted him as little more than a foolish poet? The narrator himself questions the Prefect's assertion, asking Dupin, "But is this really the poet? . . . There are two brothers, I know; and both have attained reputation in letters. The Minister I believe has written learnedly on the Differential Calculus. He is a mathematician, and no poet." "You are mistaken," Dupin replies, "I know him well; he is both. As poet *and* mathematician, he would reason well." D—— incarnates the conjunction of these supposed opposites, combining the logic of mathematics (equations of quantity and form) and the *analogic* of poetic analogies and metaphors (equations of quality or characteristic).

Finally, Dupin's supremacy in the affair depends on his own ability to be "even" with the "oddness" of his adversary. His detailed commentary on mathematics demonstrates that he is skilled in that field, and yet when the Prefect rails against poets, Dupin mutters through a puff of his meerschaum that he has "been guilty of certain doggerel" himself. Both poet and mathematician, Dupin is on a par with D——, and to remain on equal footing, he dons green spectacles when he pays the Minister his visit, in order, he says, to be *even* with him. Finally, one begins to suspect that there is more than an intellectual affiliation between the Minister and Dupin. When the narrator refers vaguely to the Minister having a sibling, when Dupin professes to know D—— so well, and when the quote he leaves in the facsimile letter refers to a myth involving sibling rivalry (Atreus and Thyestes), the reader may well wonder whether some more fraternal bonds might not link the two.[11] This would seem perfectly consistent with the logic of the story, for what could be more the same, and yet different, than two brothers?

Even *and* odd, poetry *and* math, hidden *and* concealed, Dupin *and* D——: this sensitivity to simultaneous sameness *and* difference is one of the hallmarks of poststructuralist thought. Deconstruction condemns certain kinds of structuralism for being too mathematical, for being too much like the Prefect. To be sure, the various triangular structures outlined toward the beginning of this discussion are not necessarily "wrong" from a deconstructive point of view; however, insofar as they acknowledge only sameness (Scene 1 = Scene 2 = Scene 3, etc.), they prove terribly reductive. Nevertheless, although one can criticize reductive readings and champion the cause of difference, ultimately one cannot possibly avoid reduction, or at least distortion. As we see even in the Minister's clever inversion of the letter, there is always a kind of "surplus" involved in representation, an excess that is either the product of the representation itself or that eludes representation—it is that which representation, like Procrustes, always amputates. The summary of "The Purloined Letter" included at the beginning of this chapter is no exception: it is a "repetition" of "The Purloined Letter" that is in no sense "even" with the story itself. Even the deconstructive discussion of the richness of the text leaves plenty of loose ends—which is why one can even deconstruct a deconstructive

---

[11]On the fraternal ties, see Liahna Klenman Babener's essay, "The Shadow's Shadow: The Motif of the Double in Edgar Allan Poe's 'The Purloined Letter,'" in *The Purloined Poe*, 323–334.

reading of a text. (And, in fact, "The Purloined Letter" has been subjected to this kind of chain of deconstructions—to somewhat tiresome effect.) What this means in general is that *all* representations (be they interpretations, paintings, photographs, etc.) are caught in the web of simultaneous sameness and difference; in some sense they replicate the object they represent, and yet replicate it *differently*. Surprisingly, the logic of both/and, which is so often held to be inferior or monstrous, begins to look like the rule.

If you hadn't already guessed, deconstruction is a very *philosophical* approach to literature; it tends to appeal to readers who like puzzles in logic, who enjoy solving mysteries, who, in short, fancy themselves to be a little like Auguste Dupin. Those who don't go in for this angle often object to it on the grounds that it appears to be a bit infatuated with itself, that it takes playful liberties with the text, and that it draws conclusions that can be diametrically opposed to what the text seems to be about at first glance. The deconstructive analysis of "The Purloined Letter" avoids at least *some* of this criticism because the story contains a sort of "self-deconstructive" impulse; the reflections of Dupin seem entirely consistent with a questioning of simple binary logic. Most other texts are considerably more recalcitrant, and many work hard to create the kind of airtight constructions that poststructuralists like to deflate. Nevertheless, one needn't become a dyed-in-the-wool deconstructionist to make use of certain poststructuralist concepts. Although we can scrutinize a text to decipher its particular, individual logic, we can also benefit from some general principles that might broaden our perspective. For instance, we might try to keep an eye out for what is presented as scandalous or irrational in a text, and attempt to figure out how this scandal is defined. Or, even more generally, what would happen if we, as readers, challenged certain of our habits—say, our tendency to think that particular details in a text are insignificant, or our sense that certain elements that lie on the "edge" of a text (prefaces, epigraphs, quotes from other works, etc.) are of marginal importance? (Did anyone bother reading the epigraph to this chapter?) Is it possible that the "insignificant detail" may actually prove to be the most important, or that we should *center* our attention on what is most *peripheral?*[12] The presence of details that are simultaneously marginal and important is standard practice in murder mysteries, where it is often essential that clues be both present and yet unrecognized as clues. Why should this not apply in our other readings?

Moreover, is it possible that texts might be, in some sense, "hypocritical" or "self-contradictory," that there might exist a tension between what a book is "about" and the way the topic is presented? When Melville invokes science, for example, in the first, encyclopedic portion of *Moby Dick*, there is nothing "scientific" about it: the long, detailed descriptions of whales and whaling are there for *rhetorical* reasons (and rhetoric is often considered to be the antithesis of science), not the least of which is to lend a kind of

---

[12]Derrida investigates the implications of such a recentering in *The Truth in Painting*, trans. Geoff Bennington and Ian McLeod (Chicago: University of Chicago Press, 1987).

authority to the narrative. However, these crossed purposes do not necessarily *weaken* a narrative; in many cases the kind of hybrid that results can strike us as particularly compelling.

Finally, nearly all those features that so attract poststructuralists—binary oppositions, logical impasses, monsters, and scandals—are to be found in more exaggerated form in public discourse. The "hot" issues of the day, such as race, abortion, gun control, and so forth, all tend toward dramatic polarization as each group demonizes its opponent. Of course, nothing produces more spurious logic than inflamed passions. Deconstruction encourages us to reflect on the sanctity of oppositions that have traditionally gone unchallenged. Is there a clear-cut distinction between life and death? What is the interrelationship between victims and oppressors? What does it mean when groups that seem diametrically *opposed* (Jews and Arabs in the Middle East, say) use the *same* kinds of images to refer to one another?

Might it even be possible to call into question the most *fundamental* of distinctions, such as the venerable opposition between rational and irrational, between *sanity* and *madness*? And if so, what might this produce? That, as it happens, points us to the next chapter.

FURTHER READING

Deconstruction and Poststructuralism:

Culler, Jonathan. *On Deconstruction: Theory and Criticism after Structuralism.* Ithaca, N.Y.: Cornell University Press, 1982.

De Man, Paul. *Allegories of Reading: Figural Language in Rousseau, Nietzsche, Rilke, and Proust.* New Haven: Yale University Press, 1979.

Derrida, Jacques. "Differance." In *Speech and Phenomenon.* Evanston: Northwestern University Press, 1973.

Derrida, Jacques. "Structure, Sign, and Play in the Discourse of the Human Sciences." In *Writing and Difference,* translated by Alan Bass. Chicago: University of Chicago Press, 1978.

Hartmann, Geoffrey, et al. *Deconstruction and Criticism.* New York: Continuum, 1979.

Johnson, Barbara. "Melville's Fist: The Execution of Billy Budd." In *The Critical Difference.* Baltimore: The Johns Hopkins University Press, 1980.

Klages, Mary. "Structuralism/Poststructuralism." Available on the World Wide Web at: http://www.colorado.edu/English/ENGL2012Klages/1derrida.html

Miller, J. Hillis. "The Critic as Host." *Critical Inquiry* 3 (1977): 439–447.

Rorty, Richard. "From Ironist Theory to Private Allusions: Derrida." In *Contingency, Irony, and Solidarity.* Cambridge: Cambridge University Press, 1989.

Voice of the Shuttle Web links on deconstruction: http://humanitas.ucsb.edu/shuttle/theory.html#deconstruction

Postmodernism:

The Anti-aesthetic: Essays on Postmodern Culture. Edited by Hal Foster. Port Townsend, Wash.: Bay Press, 1983.

Voice of the Shuttle Web links on postmodernism: http://humanitas.ucsb.edu/shuttle/theory.html#postmodern

4

THE REMEMBRANCE
OF THINGS PAST
■■■
Psychoanalysis

The first concerns arose when, on the afternoon of September 22, 1969, eight-year-old Susan Nason, of Foster City, California, failed to come home. The tale followed an all-too-predictable and grisly plot. Calls went out, searches began, inquiries were made; all fruitless. It came to an end some two months later when the child's beaten and decomposing body—her skull had been smashed by a rock—was found near Crystal Springs Reservoir.

The investigation went nowhere for a long while. Then, twenty years later, when little Susan's friend, Eileen Franklin-Lipsker, looked into the eyes of her own six-year-old daughter (whose hair color, eye color, name, and age resembled those of her childhood playmate), the floodgates opened. Little Susie's startled glance as she looked up from her coloring replicated the last stare eight-year-old Susan had directed at Eileen before the rock came crashing down on her head—a large stone held by Eileen's own father.

No one was more surprised by the discovery than Eileen Franklin-Lipsker herself: for two decades she had shared the general ignorance regarding the fate of her chum. Then suddenly, in a series of memories triggered by that fateful glance, the events from the past surged forth. She had watched her father, she testified in court in 1990, as he raped little Susan and then murdered her at the bottom of a wooded hill; she remembered that he had threatened to kill *her*, too, if she breathed a word of the crime to anybody. So, apparently, she had swallowed hard and *forgotten* what she had seen, an act of forgetting that remained successful for a generation. Yet the memories were well preserved, and their vividness and precision proved compelling enough to land George Franklin in prison; in 1990 he became the first person ever convicted of murder on the basis of a repressed and recovered memory.[1]

The Susan Nason case was wrenching for all the reasons that ordinarily make us shrink from horrific stories of child molestation. However, it unleashed an energy in the popular press that far outstripped the gruesome particulars of the crime. On the one hand, recovered memory was suddenly mainstreamed: reports of long forgotten physical and sexual abuse—already on the upswing—multiplied wildly across the nation, and in the years since the Nason case, between twenty-five and fifty *thousand* adult victims have claimed to have "recovered" memories of childhood abuse. On the other hand, skeptics of all stripes have launched campaigns to challenge the validity of repressed memory. Some hope to demonstrate how the courts have failed to understand the complexities of repression; others are bent on showing that the notion is, for lack of a better term, a lot of hooey.

The problem appears to be that some of the repressed memories don't stack up: in spite of all their intensity they sometimes clash with known facts of the case, and frequently they elude any sort of corroborating evidence. In 1994 a young man named Steven Cook accused a cardinal in the Catholic Church, Joseph Bernardin, of molesting him some seventeen years earlier; but when it later occurred to him that the memory had actually been "planted" by his psychotherapist, he retracted his claims.[2] Later in that same year a policeman in Washington State, named Paul Ingram, under repeated and intense examination, confessed to sexually abusing his two daughters, then to allowing others to abuse them, then to participating in satanic rituals, and finally to killing forty prostitutes who had been found murdered between 1982 and 1984. When some of the confessions were recognized as patently absurd and materially impossible, and when an expert witness described Ingram as a "weak, easily influenced man," the validity of his memories was called into question, though the patient himself continued to believe many of them. (He was actually convicted on the child abuse charges, the ones that, although shaky, could not actually be disproved.[3]) In May of 1994 another landmark was set when a father accused of sexual abuse won a malpractice suit against two therapists he claimed had planted the idea in his daughter's mind.[4] Finally, in a dramatic reversal, the conviction against George Franklin—the man sentenced in the Susan Nason murder trial—was overturned in 1995 by a higher court.[5]

Are all these pasts being recovered, or fabricated? Skeptics—often those who felt they had been wrongly accused—established the False Memory

[1]Details from the trial and of the events concerning Susan Nason and Eileen Franklin-Lipsker are drawn primarily from the following sources: "Daddy's Little Girl," *Time*, June 4, 1990; "Forgetting to Remember," *Newsweek*, February 11, 1991; "Judge Upsets Murder Conviction Focused on 'Repressed Memory'," *The New York Times*, April 5, 1995.

[2]See "Was It Real or Memories?" *Newsweek*, March 4, 1994.

[3]"Oedipal Wrecks," *World Press Review*, 41, October 1994, 30–31.

[4]Reported in "Dubious Memories," *Time Magazine* 43, May 23, 1994.

[5]Reported in *The New York Times*, "Judge Upsets Murder Conviction Focused on 'Repressed Memory,'" April 5, 1995.

Syndrome Foundation in 1992, and in the following years "false memory" rivaled "recovered memory" for space in the popular press.

The virulence of the recovered memory controversy should not surprise anyone: since its founding a hundred years ago, psychoanalysis (and all its spin-offs) has sparked a level of contentiousness usually reserved for religious fanaticism. In the intellectual world nothing has been more repressed than Sigmund Freud (1856–1939); nor, in keeping with the resilience of the repressed, has anything been more recurrent. In the 1990s the field is as polarized as ever, with defenders of various psychoanalytic movements championing their cause. Detractors—especially those who were once enamored of psychoanalysis—viciously deride its founder, attacking Freud as if he were one of these fathers whose abuse they have suddenly recalled.[6]

The current mass hysteria over recovered versus false memories can actually trace only part of its heritage back to Freud. True, it does rely on some understanding of repression, albeit an extraordinarily simplified one, and it does focus primarily on sexual experience. However, in stark contrast to recovered memory therapists, who often suggest to patients what their likely problem is even before therapy begins, Freud made it clear in his theoretical statements (if not always in his clinical practice) that the analyst's job is to listen. He or she must take pains to avoid generating interpretations to which suggestible patients might cling. Moreover, psychoanalysis today no longer makes any of the curative claims often advertised by other forms of psychotherapy. It has become, instead, a voyage of self-discovery in which patients are accompanied by the analyst in an effort to make sense of their own thoughts, memories, dreams, and behaviors. This means, for one thing, that most modern psychoanalysts can set aside the notion that has proven so vexing for advocates and detractors of recovered memory: "veridicality"—that is, the assessment of the accuracy of recounted memories. The legal system is notoriously intolerant of ambiguity, and in the case of belated recollections, it demands (quite understandably, given what lies in the balance) that memories be classified as true or false. Yet in the nonjuridical setting of analysis, how *truthful* a memory is (in the sense of how faithfully it reproduces an external, lived reality) becomes less important than how *meaningful* it appears. Also of considerable interest (at least to the patient) is the idiosyncratic logic operating in the production of meaning, a logic that, as we shall see, is often quite poetic.

In other words, psychoanalysis is a lot like reading. It is, though, a particular kind of reading, and one that is often intensely personal. Skeptics of the psychoanalytic approach complain that the interpretations it produces—

---

[6]The main points of view in the debate are represented in the following: Louis Berger, "Cultural Psychopathology and the 'False Memory Syndrome' Debates: A View from Psychoanalysis," *American Journal of Psychotherapy* 50, no. 2 (Spring 1996):167–177; J. Ahrens, "Recovered Memories: True or False? A Look at False Memory Syndrome," *University of Louisville Journal of Family Law* 34, no. 2 (1996):379–401; Frederick Crews, "The Revenge of the Repressed," *The New York Review of Books*, Nov. 17 and Dec. 1, 1994; Lenore Terr, *Unchained Memories* (New York: Basic Books, 1994); Elizabeth Loftus and K. Ketcham, *The Myth of Repressed Memory* (New York: St. Martin's Press, 1994).

especially when removed from the constraints of external verification—are essentially "unfalsifiable." Falsifiability is one of the key standards for scientific proofs. It requires that one be able to imagine circumstances in which a given theory might be *disproved*. For example, a claim that the earth is flat yields to demonstrations to the contrary; or again, our understanding of gravity—namely, the idea that masses attract each other—could be shaken if, one day, we released a stone from our raised hand and it refused to fall. However, not everything submits to this kind of scrutiny. The idea of God, for instance, as a ubiquitous and omniscient presence, and yet one that utterly eludes detection or measure by scientific instruments, falls outside the scope of science. Likewise, psychoanalysis is difficult to confirm in any objective sense. Even in a caricature of psychoanalytic interpretation, in which every cigar figures as a phallic symbol, it is hard to fully dismantle or discredit such a reading, and the ultimate test of validity remains the intuition of the reader: does the analysis *feel* like it makes sense? Although the same might be said of most literary approaches (as we saw in the *Super Word Circles* of chapter 1, virtually *no* interpretation is entirely falsifiable), psychoanalysis probably represents an extreme.

CONFRONTING THE UNCONSCIOUS

What makes jokes funny? It is a truism that nothing is less humorous than trying to explain jokes, but that didn't stop Freud; he dedicated a book to the topic. Here is one of the wisecracks he cites:

> Mr. and Mrs. So-and-So live in fairly grand style. Some people think that the husband has earned a lot and so has been able to lay aside a bit; others think that the wife has lain back a bit and so has been able to earn a lot.[7]

A number of features go into the construction of a joke, and this one is tightly worked. Structurally it relies on two parallel statements, one regarding the husband and the other the wife. But the terms of the structure are *inverted* (earning . . . laying aside; lying back . . . earning), resulting in what classical rhetoric calls a *chiasmus* (from the Greek letter *chi*—X—which illustrates how the terms cross over). Moreover, the causal connection between the terms is reversed: in the first phrase it is earning that allows the laying aside; in the second lying back results in earning. Finally, the meaning of laying and lying changes from the first part to the second, sliding from an indication of wise banking to a hint of rather unorthodox promiscuity.

Jokes generally come at someone's expense, and jibes based on class, ethnicity, and sex (to name just a few of the relevant categories), regularly deride whole groups. Furthermore, they cross over limits, suggesting things that

---

[7]The joke, and its analysis, can be found in Sigmund Freud, *Interpretation of Dreams, Jokes and Their Relation to the Unconscious*, vol. XIII of *The Standard Edition of the Complete Psychological Works of Sigmund Freud*, trans. James Strachey and A. Freud (London: Hogarth Press, 1953).

we often feel "ought not to be said." Dirty jokes provide the best example because they, by definition, deal with taboo topics. One of the pleasures for connoisseurs of this kind of humor is the thrill of transgression. But what makes this transgression possible and permissible is that it is rarely overt. In the example above, "lying back" evokes a taboo topic without actually stating it. Such jokes present obscenity in disguise. Indeed, one of the pleasures of jokes in general is their surprising duality: frequently they mask the very ideas they seek to reveal.

Freud thought that jokes served as a good illustration of the operation of repression. He theorized that ideas which, for whatever reason, we consider inappropriate or undesirable cannot appear in their original form; to rise to the surface, to consciousness, they must be disguised as *something else*.

How does all this work? An old, eighteenth-century view of the mind regarded it as a well-organized (albeit complicated) piece of machinery operating according to certain principles of logic. "Mind" was generally linked to rationality; consciousness was the blinding beam of light that illuminated everything save the last remnants of the primitive and the irrational. Although the term hadn't been invented yet, and although he never formulated the idea this way, Freud was in a sense responsible for *deconstructing* this model of the Mind. First, he turned the model on its head by asserting that consciousness (rationality) was in fact *the exception* in mental processes, and that the irrational (what he came to call the unconscious) dominated our psyche. Instead of a blinding ray, consciousness ends up, for Freud, more like a feeble, underpowered penlight, whose beam can penetrate little and truly illuminate less.[8]

Second, Freud created a scandal by suggesting that even consciousness is not the rational force it believes itself to be. Actions, ambitions, and interests we may be inclined to think perfectly reasonable may, in fact, be motivated by causes we do not recognize: suddenly, the unconscious—which operates according to its own idiosyncratic logic—was in the driver's seat.[9]

If this doesn't remind you of poststructuralism, it should. What Freud created was a *monster*: a consciousness that was both rational *and* irrational, an unconscious that was both concealed *and* revealed, minds that were both adult *and* permanently infantile. What's worse, he presented this monster as being *the norm*.

Of course, over the past few decades Freudian psychoanalysis has been reworked, sometimes quite significantly, especially by the French analyst Jacques Lacan (1901–1981), but also by a host of others, including such big guns as Luce Irigaray, Sarah Kofman, and Julia Kristeva. Certain ideas (especially those dealing with gender) have come under fire and undergone significant revision, but the idea of *repression*, which Freud saw as the very

---

[8]It would be difficult to limit Freud's model of the mind to a single essay, because the ideas were polymorphous and in constant evolution. But a good place to begin is in his 1915 essay, "The Unconscious," in *The Standard Edition*, Vol. XIV, 159–216.

[9]Freud's most famous—and perhaps clearest—development of this idea of a secret logic of the unconscious comes in *The Interpretation of Dreams*, especially chapter 2, "The Method of Interpreting Dreams: An Analysis of a Specimen Dream," in *The Standard Edition*, Vol. IV, 96–121.

cornerstone of psychoanalysis, has remained amazingly intact and still occupies a privileged position in most forms of psychoanalytic interpretation.

Repression is the process by which we push out of mind thoughts we find unpleasant or even painful.[10] It is not the same as casual forgetting, the way, for example, I can't remember what color shirt I wore three days ago, or what day of the week my last birthday fell on; most memories, as psychologists tell us, simply atrophy over time. Repression, though, is a more deliberate, active kind of forgetting. Paradoxically, in spite of all the effort it entails, it is also less permanent than casual forgetting, for repressed memories have a nasty habit of coming back. Don't we all have a secret cache of embarrassing moments we wish we could commit to oblivion? If you are like me, you may go blithely about your everyday activities for weeks or months when abruptly, quite unexpectedly, one of these moments will spring to mind, making you wince until you can rid yourself of it once again. Repression of a memory requires eternal vigilance and a constant expenditure of energy, and the more we try to forget something (that is, the more painful or traumatic the memory), the greater the tendency of the memory to resurface.

THE RETURN OF THE REPRESSED

If we are working so hard to forget certain elements of our past, how can they *ever* make it into consciousness at all? According to Freud, they can never do so directly. Instead, repressed memories slip into the forefront of our minds by hook and by crook. In the case of the embarrassing flashbacks I mentioned above, they may be triggered by any number of unforeseen stimuli—an unexpected word, a surprising smell—which, by their link to the past, may call to mind one of these memories before our mind has time to steer clear of it. (Thus in Marcel Proust's famous novel, *The Remembrance of Things Past*, the narrator's entire childhood is conjured up by the flavors of tea and a madeleine pastry.) Other memories—especially the ones we repress most carefully—may only appear in disguised form. Consciousness, Freud says, is like a very small, select gathering in the mind, and unwanted guests will be stopped at the door by the mental equivalent of a bouncer. Unwelcome memories, then, will only work their way in by *pretending to be something else*, something considerably less painful than the memory itself.

This is where reading comes into play. Dreams, for example, apparently engage in such masquerades regularly, and most forms of psychotherapy, Freudian and otherwise, assume that the webs of fantasy we spin during our sleeping hours are anything but arbitrary. A dream's apparent (or "manifest") content may often be found to share a structural, thematic, or metaphorical relationship with a hidden (or "latent") meaning. Frequently, in traumatic dreams the latent meaning may even start to become manifest as the dream

---

[10]See Freud's 1915 essay, "Repression," in *The Standard Edition*, Vol. XIV, 141–158.

evolves (as when an apparently innocent dream begins to take on sinister undertones, turning nightmarish). Usually this is the point at which the bouncer springs into action to put a stop to it all; as a result, we wake up, and within moments a wrenchingly real illusion fades like a spirit at dawn.

The process of distortion is fundamentally literary. Present almost everywhere, it is perhaps most strikingly apparent in those timeless little fictions we call fairy tales. One need not be a card-carrying psychoanalyst to agree that certain stories tell of quite terrifying dangers in camouflaged ways: *Little Red Riding Hood* may send a shiver down the spine of a child, but that's nothing compared to what might happen to a real kid meeting a wolf in the woods. The "manifest" story has the job of reworking the latent message into something bearable, yet without sapping the text of its emotional energy.[11]

The problem, however, lies in the method for *reading* these stories and memories. How does one decipher what distortion has taken place? According to what logic can one disentangle the hidden message? When does one know when the final veil has been removed in order to reveal the truth? It's not surprising if clinical psychoanalysts have sought inspiration from the likes of Sophocles, Shakespeare, Hoffmann, Poe, and other writers whose mastery of metaphor offers excellent training in poetic logic. Still, it remains a tricky business, and one that is largely intuitive. In the recovered memory crisis discussed at the beginning of this chapter, a better understanding of repression may usefully enrich the discussion, but it does not necessarily lead to a better understanding of what *occurred*. When a daughter abruptly "recalls" a tale of abuse, is this memory a truth that had been veiled in unread symptoms for so many years? Or is this memory itself a distortion, rendering bearable a different and even more unendurable story? For example, imagine how inflammatory it would be to suggest that this memory actually represented, in disguised form, the *daughter's* desire for the *father*, a taboo desire that made the child feel so guilty that she shifted the responsibility, in the rearview mirror of memory, onto her father, thus inverting the dynamic. Outrageous? Perhaps. In fact, it is precisely the kind of suggestion that got Freud in hot water with certain feminists.[12] However, in the absence of external corroboration, the interpretation is just as unfalsifiable as its opposite.

Consequently, psychoanalysis is much less useful as a theoretical truth detector than as a way of understanding the relationship between metaphorical layers of stories. Its strength lies in its exploration of the individual logic of a given text, a logic that is often quite puzzling.

Psychoanalysis revels in such puzzles, the pieces of which often consist of language, visual imagery, or some rebuslike combination of the two. Rebuses actually provide a good model for understanding the language of the unconscious.

---

[11]It is the psychoanalyst Bruno Bettelheim, in *The Uses of Enchantment* (New York: Knopf, 1976), who suggested that fairy tales fulfilled this function, among others.

[12]The most famous of these episodes involves the "Dora" case history, in which Freud clearly crosses the line, forcing an outrageous interpretation on a patient. See Freud's "Dora" case history ("Fragments of an Analysis of a Case of Hysteria," in *The Standard Edition*, Vol. VII, 3–124).

A rebus is a picture-puzzle, of the sort you probably made in third or fourth grade. Or perhaps you watched them on television on the 1970s game show "Concentration." They are sometimes simple and fairly universally understood, such as the one in Figure 4.1, which was a popular bumper sticker some years ago.

Figure 4.1   I love New York.

However, rebuses can also engage in stranger, more personal logic, playing not just on familiar associations (heart = love, or NY as a common abbreviation for the city), but also on sounds and even spatial arrangement, such as the one in Figure 4.2.

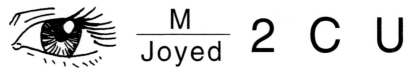

Figure 4.2   I am overjoyed to see you (eye m [over] joyed two c u)

In extreme cases, they become practically unreadable to everyone but their creator (see Figure 4.3).

Figure 4.3   Gold is the source of our discontent (Goal+d is thesaurus of hour disk [on] tent)

Rebuses communicate according to secret, idiosyncratic logics, although these logics interact with the laws of standard discourse. They often take liberties with syntax, and they show blatant disregard for the divisions between words and for the difference between words and images, and they may create links between disparate ideas based on little more than sounds or shapes.

Appreciating the importance of the rebus requires some understanding of the role of language in the psychoanalytic model. Freud tells an illuminating tale about a game a one and a half year old boy, who was extremely attached to his mother, devised for himself. When put to bed, he would take a toy of his, a small, wooden spool with a string attached to it, and toss it off his cot. As the spool disappeared over the edge, the boy would coo and utter the word "gone!"; as he pulled on the string, drawing the piece back onto his bed, he would smile and exclaim "here!" These actions he repeated tirelessly.

Freud surmised that the boy was compensating for his mother's absence by a symbolic game: the toy *represented* his mother, and by the magic words "here!" and "gone!" he could make his mother come and go as he pleased. Language served as a symbolic substitute for what was missing in the boy's life: the spool took the place of his mother, and language gave him control over the situation.[13]

These words mark that tot's entry into language and into what Jacques Lacan called the Symbolic Order.[14] The Symbolic Order is that collection of signifying, organizing systems—language, law, etiquette, religion, and so forth—that constitute the codes and structures of our public sphere. It is the realm of rules and limits, the conventions of which must be respected if we are to function successfully with others. Not surprisingly, psychoanalysis sees the entry into the Symbolic Order as occurring in very early childhood. It is preceded by the so-called mirror stage.[15] Many parents recall this stage from observing their own children's infancy. At between six and eighteen months of age, the human infant develops a fascination with its image in a mirror. (Day care centers always provide mirrors in infant and toddler rooms, but they are not strictly necessary: the same fascination will develop with any other moving human form, such as a playmate. Nor is the mirror stage always arrived at by visual cues; a blind child uses other senses.) The infatuation with this mirrored likeness signals the infant's development of a self-image: she is *not*, in fact, just a part of her mother; she is an autonomous being, one that looks like the image reflected back at her.

This realization of selfhood, and the identification with a group of others who look like her (a kind of "imprinting") gives rise to mixed emotions. On the one hand—as many parents will attest—the child's revelation coincides with a certain jubilation; the infant's new-found control over herself prompts giddiness. On the other hand, this psychic separation from the mother creates the awareness of a distressing *gap*. It is language that will flood in to fill that gap, language that—like the little boy's wooden spool—can only fill it symbolically. However, this symbolism will not necessarily be comprehensible to others: the first, perhaps most lasting symbolic creations are of an intensely personal nature, pieced together by the resources (spools, string, sounds . . .) at the child's disposal. Only later does the child learn public language and ritual, the true Symbolic Order, which she will always learn as a second, and somewhat foreign language. And because she enters into a system that is *pre-existing* (that is, we learn a grammar, an etiquette, and a code of conduct that exist before us and independently of us), her desires will necessarily be molded to fit previously constructed forms and laws. This is to say that the structure

---

[13]On the *fort/da* game, see Freud, *Beyond the Pleasure Principle*, in *The Standard Edition*, Vol. XVIII, 12–16. On language in general, see Jacques Lacan, "The Function and Field of Speech and Language in Psychoanalysis," in *Ecrits: A Selection*, trans. Alan Sheridan (New York: Norton, 1977), 30–113.

[14]See Jacques Lacan, "On a Question Preliminary to any Possible Treatment of Psychosis," in *Ecrits: A Selection*, 179–225.

[15]See "The Mirror Stage as Formative of the Function of the I," in *Ecrits: A Selection*, 1–7.

of our language and conventions largely predetermine what we can say and do. But taking on a ready-made system, like buying a suit off the rack, isn't always a good fit, and the Symbolic Order may leave no avenue for expression of some of our deepest feelings. The result is already a form of repression. Our most intense desires and our own personal symbolism can only bubble through the surface occasionally, and even then only in distorted form. When they do so, and if they are recognized as such, we call them symptoms.

Learning to read the language beneath the language becomes one of the jobs of psychoanalysis, which looks upon symptoms as a kind of metaphorical writing by the unconscious.

So let's see how it works. "The Fat Kid" (1952) is a tight, powerful little story by the German author Marie Luise Kaschnitz, and it offers a fascinating interplay of memory, desire, and fantasy.[16]

■

The Fat Kid

It was late January, soon after Christmas vacation, when the fat kid came to see me. That winter I had started to lend books to the neighborhood children: they were supposed to borrow and return them on a specified day of the week. Of course I knew most of the children, but once in a while there would be strangers who did not live on our street. And while most of them stayed just long enough to exchange books, there were a few who would sit down and begin to read right then and there. I would sit at my desk and work, and the children would sit at the small table near the book wall, and their presence was a pleasure and did not distract me.

The fat kid came on a Friday or a Saturday, at least not on the day designated for the book exchange. I was planning to go out later and was just carrying a snack I had fixed into my study. I had had company, and my guest must have forgotten to close the door to the apartment. This would explain why the fat kid suddenly stood before me, just as I had put the tray down on my desk and was turning around to get something else from the kitchen. She was a girl of about twelve, wearing an old-fashioned loden coat and knitted black knee socks and carrying a pair of skates by a strap, and she seemed familiar to me, but only in a vague sort of way, and I was startled because she had appeared so silently.

"Do I know you?" I asked in surprise.

The fat girl said nothing. She only stood there and folded her hands over her round belly and looked at me with eyes as light as water.

"Did you come for a book?" I asked.

---

[16]Marie Luise Kaschnitz, "The Fat Girl," in *Circe's Mountain: Stories by Marie Luise Kaschnitz*, trans. Lisel Mueller (Minneapolis: Milkweed Editions, 1990). I have modified the translation slightly, most noticeably in the title.

Again the girl didn't answer, but that didn't surprise me too much. I was used to shyness on the part of the children, and that you often had to help them along. So I pulled out several books and spread them out in front of the strange girl. Then I got ready to fill out one of the cards on which I recorded the borrowed books.

"What's your name?" I asked.

"They call me Fatty," the girl said.

"Do you want me to call you that?" I asked.

"I don't care," the girl said. She did not respond to my smile, and now I seem to remember that she winced at this point. But at the time I paid no attention.

"When is your birthday?" I continued

"In Aquarius," the girl said calmly.

Her answer amused me and I entered it on the card as a sort of joke, and then I turned back to the books.

"Are you interested in a specific book?" I asked.

But then I realized that the strange girl was not looking at the books at all, but at the tray with my tea and sandwiches.

"Perhaps you'd like to eat something," I said quickly.

The girl nodded, and her acceptance contained something like hurt surprise that I should think of this only now. She started to eat the small sandwiches, one after the other, in a peculiar manner I couldn't define until sometime later. Then she sat there again, letting her cold, listless eyes wander around the room, and there was something about her that filled me with anger and revulsion. No question about it, I hated this girl from the beginning. Everything about her repelled me, her sluggish body, her fat, pretty face, her way of talking, apathetic and arrogant at the same time. And though I had decided to give up my walk for her sake, I did not treat her with kindness, but coldly and cruelly.

Because it certainly couldn't be called kind, my sitting down at my desk with my work and saying over my shoulder, "Go on and read," when I knew perfectly well that the strange girl did not wish to read. And then I sat there intending to write, but I couldn't do it because of an odd sense of torment, similar to the torment experienced by someone who is asked to solve a riddle he can't figure out, and who knows that unless he succeeds nothing will ever be the same again. And for a while I stood it, but not for long, so I turned around and started a conversation, though only the usual silly questions occurred to me.

"Do you have brothers and sisters?" I asked.

"Yes," the girl said.

"Do you like to go to school?" I asked.

"Yes," the girl said.

"What's your favorite subject?"

"Pardon?" the girl said.

"German maybe?" I asked.

"I don't know," the girl said.

I twisted the pencil between my fingers and something arose in me, a feeling of dread that was quite disproportionate to the appearance of the girl.

"Do have friends?" I asked, trembling.

"Oh yes," the girl said.

"I imagine there's one you like best?" I asked.

"I don't know," the girl said, and the way she sat there in her hairy loden coat she resembled a fat caterpillar; and she was like a caterpillar in the way she had eaten and the way she was now checking out her surroundings again.

That's it, nothing more to eat for you, I thought, filled with an odd desire to get even. Nevertheless I went and got bread and cold cuts, and the girl stared at them with her impassive face, and then she began to eat the way a caterpillar eats, slowly and steadily, as if driven by instinct, and I looked at her silently and with hostility.

Because by now things had come to a point where everything about this girl began to upset and annoy me. What a silly white dress, what a ridiculous stand-up collar, I thought, when the girl unbuttoned her coat after eating. I went back to my desk to work, but then I heard the girl smack her lips behind me, and this sound was like the slow plop of a black pond in the woods somewhere, and it reminded me of everything murky, everything heavy and brackish in human nature, and it irked me a great deal. What do you want with me, I thought, go away, go away. And I would have liked to take my hands and push the girl out of the room, the way one gets rid of an unwanted animal. But then I did not push her out of the room; instead I started to address her in the same unfeeling manner as before.

"Are you going to go skating now?" I asked.

"Yes," the fat girl said.

"Are you a good skater?" I asked and pointed to the skates she was still carrying.

"My sister is good," the girl said, and again there was an expression of pain and sadness on her face, and again I paid no attention.

"What does your sister look like?" I asked. "Is she like you?"

"Oh no," the fat girl said. "My sister is thin, and she has curly black hair. In summer when we're in the country and a thunderstorm comes up in the night, she gets up and sits on the railing of the highest balcony and sings."

"And you?" I asked.

"I stay in bed," the girl said. "I'm scared."

"But your sister isn't, is she?" I asked.

"No," the girl said. "She's never scared. She dives from the highest diving board. She dives in and then she swims way out . . ."

"What does your sister sing?" I asked, curious.

"She sings what she feels like singing," the girl said sadly. "She makes up poems."

"And you?" I asked.

"I don't do anything," the girl said. And then she got up and said, "I have to go now." I held out my hand, and she took it, and I don't know exactly what I felt—something like an invitation to follow her, an inaudible, urgent call. "Come back sometime," I said, but I didn't mean it, and the girl said nothing and looked at me with her cool eyes. And then she was gone and I should have felt relieved. But as soon as I heard the entrance door close, I went out into the hall and put on my coat. I ran down the stairs and reached the street just as the girl disappeared around the corner.

I've got to see this caterpillar skate, I thought. I've got to see how this lump of fat moves across the ice. And I walked faster, so as not to lose track of the girl. It had been early afternoon when she arrived in my room, and now it was nearly dusk. I had spent some years in this town as a child, but was no longer thoroughly familiar with the layout, and though I managed to follow the girl I soon had no idea where we were going, and the streets and squares we passed were totally strange to me. Also, I was suddenly conscious of a change in the air. It had been cold, but now a thaw was setting in, and with such a vengeance that the snow was already dripping from the roofs and large clouds were moving across the sky. We came to the edge of town, where the houses are surrounded by large gardens, and then there were no more houses, and the girl suddenly disappeared down an embankment. And what I saw below me was nothing like the expected skating rink with booths and bright lights and a glittering surface full of noise and music. What I saw was the lake, which I had pictured as encircled by houses by now: there it was, solitary and ringed by dark woods, looking exactly as it had when I was a child. This unexpected view affected me so much that I almost lost sight of the girl. But then I saw her again; she was crouching at the edge of the lake, trying to cross one leg over the other and clamp the skate to her boot with one hand while turning the key with the other. The fat girl dropped the key a number of times, and then she dropped down on all fours and scooted around on the ice, searching, and she looked like an outlandish toad. In the meantime it had been getting dark, and the landing pier for the steamer, which jutted out into the lake a few yards from where the girl was, lay pitch-black on the broad surface, whose uneven silvery glint, a little darker here and there, was an indication of the thaw. "Hurry up," I called out impatiently, and the fat girl actually did, though not because of my urging, but because there was someone waving and shouting, "Come on, Fatty," at the end of the long pier, someone skating in circles, a bright, buoyant figure. It occurred to me that this must be the sister, the dancer, the stormy weather singer, a girl after my own heart, and I was now convinced that it was solely the wish to see this graceful creature that had brought me here. At the same time I realized that the children were in danger. What had started all of a sudden were the strange groans, the deep sighs the lake seems to emit before the ice breaks up. These sighs ran like a shuddering dirge through the deep lake, and I heard them, but the children did not.

Surely they could not have heard them. Otherwise the fat girl, this timid creature, would not have set out on the lake, forging ahead with scraping, awkward movements, and her sister out there would not have been laughing and waving and turning like a ballerina on the points of her skates, only to return to her beautiful figure eights, and the fat girl would have avoided the dark places, which now frightened her and which she nevertheless crossed, and her sister would not have suddenly straightened up tall and skated away, far off towards one of the small, secluded bays.

I was able to observe all of this quite well, having started to walk out on the pier, step by step. Though the planks were ice-covered, I was moving faster than the fat girl below, and when I turned around I would see the expression on her face, impassive and filled with desire at the same time. And I could see the cracks that were now beginning to appear everywhere, and the foaming water that seeped through them like the foam that seeps through the lips of a madman. And then of course I saw the ice breaking beneath the fat girl. It happened in the place where her sister had danced, only a few arm's lengths from the end of the pier. I should point out right here that the breakthrough did not threaten her life. The lake freezes in layers, and the second layer was only three feet below and still firm. All that happened was that the fat girl stood in three feet of water. True, it was ice-cold and filled with crumbling floes, but all she had to do was wade a few feet through the water to the pier, where I could help her pull herself up. But I suspected she would not make it, and for a while it looked that way, because she just stood there scared to death, trying a few awkward gestures while the water flooded around her and the ice broke under her hands. Aquarius, I thought, the water-bearer, now he will pull you down, and I felt nothing, not the slightest sense of pity, and did not move. But suddenly the fat girl raised her head, and because it was now quite dark and the moon had come from behind the clouds, I could see that something in her face had changed. Her features were the same and yet not the same; they were broken open by passion and determination, as if now, in the face of death, they were drinking in life, all the life that was burning in the world. I was convinced she was about to die and that this was final, so I bent over the railing and looked down at the white face, which looked back at me like a mirror image. But then the fat girl reached the post. She reached out and started to pull herself up, holding on rather skillfully to the nails and hooks that projected from the wood. Her body was too heavy, her fingers were bleeding, and she kept falling back, but only to try again. I was watching a long struggle, a terrible wrestling for liberation and transformation, like the breaking apart of a shell or cocoon, and now I wanted to help the girl, but I also knew that my help had become unnecessary, because now I knew who she was.

I don't remember walking home that night. I only remember that on the stairs I told a neighbor there was still a piece of lakeshore with green banks and black woods, but she replied that I was mistaken. And that the papers on my desk were all mixed up, and somewhere in that jumble I came across an old snapshot of myself in a white wool dress with a stand-up collar, with light, watery eyes, and very fat.

"The Fat Kid," obviously rapt with fantasy, offers compelling reading for the psychoanalytically inclined. But *what*, exactly, is one to analyze? That is, if psychoanalysis denotes an activity between therapist and patient, just who *is* the "patient" in a literary encounter? Some have suggested that you, the reader, are actually in the role of the patient, and the text plays the part of the analyst. Like the trained clinician, the text emits utterances with which readers may more or less freely associate; because the text offers no confirmation—or condemnation—of the reader's reactions, your own desires and obsessions will manifest themselves as you force yourself to respond to the story. This perspective is not as hallucinatory as it may at first appear, for individual readers do have different axes to grind, and they often bring as much to (literary) analysis as the text itself.

Nevertheless, most readers are more comfortable assuming the position of the analyst. Perhaps the most obvious, or the most seductive, model encourages us to undertake an analysis of the author, and we might thus expect "The Fat Kid" to shed light on the childhood of Marie Luise Kaschnitz in turn-of-the-century Karlsruhe. Such an approach is entirely possible (and, in fact, was a favorite among early psychoanalytic critics), and in this case it might even prove fruitful. The fat girl announces she is an Aquarius, and the story takes place "in late January"; Kaschnitz's birthday was January 31. However, much of the story is cast in exceptionally vague terms: we don't know what town the woman is in, when the story took place, or even if the account is autobiographical. Although the story is related by a first-person narrator, it would be unwise of us to assume that the narrator is identical with Kaschnitz, who may be telling a tale inspired by some other source. As we saw in chapter 1, anchoring texts in authors' lives is risky business, one that many readers have largely abandoned.

Another possibility consists of analyzing a given character in the story—such as the girl or the narrator. This type of interpretation, often quite rewarding, may seek to demonstrate how certain childhood experiences mark a character over the long haul, expressing themselves in some form of symp-tomatic behavior. Alluring in its own right, character analysis works best with certain kinds of texts, especially long narratives that give the reader a sense of a character's development over the long haul.

"The Fat Kid," of course, doesn't offer us this luxury: compressed into a few pages we have an account of limited scope. Analyzing such characters as the young visitor or her sister proves tricky for a variety of reasons, not the least of which is that the story calls into question their very existence as autonomous individuals. The most likely candidate for analysis—the narrator herself—poses other problems, notably our almost total ignorance of her past. Still, we needn't abandon the narrator altogether. Her tale smacks of reverie, of the dream world; Freud called dreams the "royal road to the unconscious," and he favored them for analysis. Although we may not be able to determine the source of the drama, we may well manage to identify some of its mecha-nisms. Focusing on the narrator's tale, we can examine it with an attention to various psychoanalytic processes or concepts. This approach, one that exploits a specific text in order to illustrate general concepts, has spanned the history of psychoanalysis: Freud drew on Sophocles' *Oedipus Rex* as a nearly inex-haustible resource for psychoanalytic study; decades later Jacques Lacan would read Ophelia's role in *Hamlet* as an illustration of the operation of desire. Many readers have found literary texts illuminating when read essentially as allegories of psychoanalysis itself.

I would propose we look at "The Fat Kid" in a rather two-faced way, using it to explain certain aspects of psychoanalysis at the same time that we harness the power of psychoanalysis to shed some light on it.

The simplest, barely psychoanalytic reading of the story might cast it as a literary version of the recovered memory cases this chapter opened with: like Eileen Franklin-Lipsker suddenly rediscovering that her father had brutally murdered her best friend, the narrator in "The Fat Kid" would seem, through a similar revelation, to have reconnected with the memory of a traumatic mo-ment in her own past: the day she fell through the ice and nearly drowned. The text does not disqualify such a reading. At the very least, this interpre-tation underscores the link between the narrator's past and present. First, the story takes place in a town where the narrator had "spent some years as a child"; then the final paragraph, in which she happens upon a photograph of herself as a young girl wearing "a white wool dress with a stand-up collar, with light, watery eyes, and very fat," drives home (were there still any doubt) the image of the fat kid as an early version of the narrator herself.

However, there are details that discourage our reading the event as the full and transparent recovery of a lost past. Peculiar details (the familiar streets gradually leading to a different time, the supernaturally rapid thaw of the ice, the face-to-face encounter between the narrator and her former self) all demonstrate that a certain amount of distortion has occurred: surely the events did not unfold quite as the narrator relates them.

One of the cues that this story constitutes more than a simple walk down memory lane comes from the overwhelming presence of what Freud referred to as the "uncanny." The uncanny, frequently present in tales of the supernatural, consists of those unsettling images that strike the reader as simultaneously strange and familiar. Images of ghosts, dismembered bodies, automata, for example, all exhibit qualities that typically send a shiver down our spine. If we find these ideas eerier than, say, smoke, meatloaf, and toasters, it is at least in part because they represent familiar, *nearly* human forms in strange ways. One needn't read "The Fat Kid" with a jeweler's glass to detect the uncanny within it: the odd little girl who comes to visit is referred to as "*familiar* to me, but only in a *vague* sort of way," and she is described as a "*strange* girl" several times, one who has a "*peculiar* way" of eating, who inspires in the narrator a "feeling of dread," and whose very humanity is unsettled by the repeated references to her first as a caterpillar, and then as a toad. In a similar vein, when the narrator follows the girl to the lake, she is struck by how the town she knew grows increasingly foreign to her, eventually becoming "totally *strange*." And yet the girl leads her to a scene that she recognizes as entirely *familiar*, the lake that looked "exactly as it had when I was a child." In the end the story culminates with the uncanniest moment of them all as the narrator realizes that she has encountered her double: "I wanted to help the girl, but I also knew that my help had become unnecessary, because now I knew who she was."

This tale is riddled with uncanny images, and for Freud the uncanny signals the presence of repression. Remember that repressed memories can only come back *in disguise*; and yet, to be effective, they must be able to elicit reactions similar to those memories they conceal. That is, they must be simultaneously strange and familiar: half understood. In "The Fat Kid," nothing fulfills this condition better than the girl herself, who so rattles the narrator. Like the repressed idea—that "unwelcome guest" within consciousness—the girl enters the scene surreptitiously, unannounced, and presumably because someone had "forgotten to close the door." "Go away, go away," the narrator thinks to herself with an urgency that she failed to understand, wishing that this harmless, dull little creature would leave as swiftly as she arrived. As the narrator's coldness develops into "cruelty" and even "hostility," she reveals her desire to make the girl disappear, aching to take her hands and "push the girl out of the room, the way one gets rid of an unwanted animal." Strangely, she acts on none of these impulses, and finds herself paradoxically attracted to the source of her revulsion. When the girl finally takes her leave, the narrator calls out to her to "come back sometime" in spite of herself; the narrator then undertakes to follow this creature she so desperately wished to banish.

Strange yet familiar? Repulsion yet attraction? Present yet past? The text is a puzzle, one filled with strange symbols requiring interpretation. This should come as no surprise, however, for the narrator makes the comparison herself: "I sat there trying to write, but I couldn't do it because of an odd sense of torment, similar to the torment experienced by someone who is asked to solve a *riddle* he can't figure out."

Riddles bring us back to rebuses, those picture puzzles that merge their peculiar logic with the language of everyday usage. They are, in a sense, like dreams—especially those dreams we find troubling, as if they *mean* something we can't quite put our finger on. And what does the narrator say in "The Fat Kid"? That she felt like "someone who is asked to solve a riddle he can't figure out." What if we read this story like a riddle, like a rebus, as if it were telling us a story very different from an adventure on the ice, as if *another* story were metaphorically bubbling to the surface here?

One of the quirks of the hidden logic of symptoms may remind you of structuralism (indeed, latter-day psychoanalysts rely heavily on structuralist concepts). I refer here to the importance of repetition, a feature of particular interest in psychoanalytic approaches, for it is the hallmark of the repressed: repressed thoughts recur *endlessly*, often changing their disguises. Some of these repetitions may take the form of descriptive details. Take, for instance, the image of water in "The Fat Kid," which appears everywhere in the story: the fat girl's eyes are "as light as water"; she is born in Aquarius, the sign of the water-bearer; she reminds the narrator of everything that is "watery and brackish" in human nature; the smacking of her lips makes a sound like that of a "black pond in the woods somewhere"; her appearance coincides with a sudden thaw, melting the snow; she leads the narrator to a lake, skates on the ice, and nearly drowns in the "foaming water that seeped through [the cracks] like the foam that seeps through the lips of a madman." Another motif in the story, which appears with similar insistence, though in different forms, is the promise and realization of great change, of metamorphosis. The time of year in the story sets this theme in motion: starting in January, after the Christmas holidays, the story opens in conjunction with a *new* year; next, the introductory scene will be marked by an *interruption*, by the sudden appearance of an unknown caller; the thaw marks a dramatic change in the weather; during the journey to the lake the familiar becomes unfamiliar; once there, the ice will crack, yielding to water; the girl's face changes ("her features were the same and yet not the same . . ."); she suddenly reaches for life, struggling "for liberation and transformation, like the breaking apart of a shell or cocoon"; finally, she appears to us as the narrator. This roly-poly girl, the "caterpillar," emerges from her chrysalis profoundly transformed.

As does the narrator. It is worth noting that the metamorphosis occurs precisely at the moment of recognition. When the narrator becomes convinced the girl is on the brink of death, she bends over the rail on the pier and "looked down at the white face, which looked back at me *like my mirror image*." In the next sentence the girl is reaching for the post, pulling herself up, becoming suddenly self-sufficient, even skillful.

From a psychoanalytic view, it is hard to read this scene without thinking of the mirror stage, that crucial and ambivalent moment of self-recognition that separates us from the mother, endows us with an idea of our own autonomy, and prepares us for entry into the Symbolic. Certainly such a reading is encouraged by the emphasis on transitions, for the mirror stage is a phase, one resulting in the traumatic and yet exhilarating birth of the self. The girl's emergence from the water, her sudden discovery of her ability to save herself, and her shedding of the cocoon, all suggest this kind of rebirth, triggered by her "mirror image."

Along the same lines, "The Fat Kid" tells the tale of the girl's entry into the Symbolic. The narrator, of course, has already made this transition. Indeed, as a writer (this is the work she performs in her study), she specializes in the Symbolic, and her association with the realm of symbols and language is further reinforced by her operating a small lending library—notably one for children, those who need initiation into the world of words and codes. The little girl who arrives seems to be on the far side of the threshold of language: she appears "silently," and to the first questions the narrator asks her she replies nothing, remaining utterly mute. When she does finally speak, the words come in dribs and drabs, many of her responses appearing in the form of monosyllables, or even vague gestures, sometimes indicating incomprehension. Thus when the narrator asks her about school, focusing particularly on the study of language and literature, the girl is confused:

> "What's your favorite subject?"
> "What?" the girl said.
> "German, maybe?" I asked.
> "I don't know," the girl answered.

This refusal on the part of the girl to engage in conversation, and in particular to show any interest in or knowledge of a subject matter dealing with reading and writing—with *language*, that is to say—disturbs the narrator profoundly, as she fidgets with the tool of her own symbolic trade: "I twisted the pencil between my fingers and something arose in me, a feeling of dread that was quite disproportionate to the appearance of the girl." That the narrator's reaction is out of proportion, excessive, signals that things are not as they appear; the girl touches a deeper nerve than the narrator has recognized.

The young visitor's disconnection from language is acute, going beyond mere mutism and indifference. Psychoanalysis frequently insists on the importance of the *name* as anchoring a person in the Symbolic, but this girl doesn't even have that: "They call me Fatty," she says. In addition, her vaguely stated birthday ("In Aquarius") shows her to be awash, unmoored by the constraints of such symbolic undertakings as record keeping. More interested in eating and loafing, the girl strikes the narrator as animal-like, indifferent to books and language. Yet she reveals a sense of jealousy when speaking of her sister, the thin, beautiful skater who exudes independence, who is fearless, and who sings during storms. A poet ("She makes up poems," the fat girl says of her), the sister is thus similar to the narrator herself; perhaps it is for this that the narrator refers to the older sibling as "a girl after my own heart."

The real trick of "The Fat Kid" is the way the story camouflages the idea of language, and specifically the notion of writing, as *another* activity. The fat girl shows up in the study/library, but with no manifest desire to read or write:

she has come to *skate*: "She was a girl of about twelve, wearing an old-fashioned loden coat and knitted black knee socks and carrying *a pair of skates by a strap*." The skates are not included in the photograph the narrator discovers at the end of the story, so they have been grafted onto this memory. Significantly, this story of books, of poems, of writing changes direction midstream and is suddenly transformed into an excursion to the ice. Here, as the narrator watches from a distance, the fat girl who is too afraid to do anything takes her first hesitant steps on the lake. Handling her old-fashioned skates with the clumsiness of a child wielding a pencil, she can barely clamp them to her feet, dropping the key (which, metaphorically, is also the key to the riddle the narrator wishes to solve) several times, and finally forges ahead with "scraping, awkward movements." The ice bears the marks of these movements like so many inscriptions; it is like paper. The analogy is made all the more apparent by the arrival of the sister; her skill in singing and writing takes the form here of skating, as she "draws beautiful figure eights" on the surface of the frozen lake.

Significantly, it is when the girl reaches the spot where her sister had danced her figures, inscribing them on the ice, that the creaking surface finally gives way. The fat girl goes down, mired in freezing water, paralyzed. The narrator describes the water rushing through the cracks as resembling "the foam that seeps through the lips of a madman": in the water lies madness, the state of those locked in the terms of a personal, uncanny logic, those who are unable to function in the conventional terms of the Symbolic. The fat girl is immobilized, half submerged, caught between two worlds. Associated with water throughout the story, figuratively *of* the water if we are to believe her birthday, she seems about to submit to it: " 'Aquarius, the water-bearer,' I thought, 'now he will pull you down.' " But when the narrator looks down at the girl, as their eyes meet, their faces reflecting each other, the girl is transformed, and she begins to claw her way to safety. Suddenly different, she acts with skill and determination, becoming in essence both her sister and the narrator.

"The Fat Kid" is a fascinating example of memory at work. Operating like a puzzle, like a rebus, it presents the convergence of conscious and unconscious logics. Like the ice it describes, "The Fat Kid" presents a surface that is "cracked," where the seething foam of madness oozes into the supposedly rational world. Yet, if the unconscious is present everywhere, it is visible nowhere: it tells its tale in disguise. The distortions we have had to interpret are numerous and peculiar:

1. The story divides a single individual into three characters (the narrator, the girl, her sister);
2. These three characters of different ages (the adolescent girl, her older sister, an adult narrator) are used to tell the tale of a fourth, earlier age: the memory of an infantile experience; the mirror stage and the entry into the Symbolic;
3. Water becomes associated with madness;

4. Skating becomes associated with writing;

5. Writing becomes metaphorical for the entrance into the Symbolic;

6. Entrance into the Symbolic is represented as a transformation.

What unsettles some readers in this kind of interpretation is that *none* of these distortions is much more than the result of speculation on the part of the interpreter. The "substantiation" for such an analysis lies primarily on the parallels it holds with psychoanalytic theory, which is itself a highly speculative enterprise. Moreover, there is the potential for a dangerous double bind: this interpretation of the story can be used to clarify and confirm psychoanalytic theory at the same time that psychoanalytic theory is used to clarify and confirm *it*. Nevertheless, as discussed earlier, science can brandish falsifiability as the sine qua non of its world without all other worlds having to fall into locked step. After all, one of the most intriguing things about a story like "The Fat Kid" is the way it remains resolutely ambiguous. Like the narrator, we may find ourselves oddly tormented by the story, "similar to the torment experienced by someone who is asked to solve a riddle he can't figure out."

FREUD THE IRREPRESSIBLE

Psychoanalysis often deals with nasty, gritty topics: trauma, taboo, sex, violence, obsession, rape, and incest, just to name a few. A lot of people might be happy to leave the psychoanalytic method to the sterile corridors of mental hospitals, or at least to the halls of college literature departments—which for some may not seem much different. Lock Freud up with his own id, and let the rest of us go about our business. Yet this is one point on which psychoanalysts of all stripes have formed common ground: topics such as repression, compulsion, desire, and fetish are, they say, *everyone's* business. Some individuals are obviously in need of serious psychiatric help, but we are none of us clear-thinking, unified agents acting on the basis of reason. Desire and its repression, memory and its distortion, the experiencing of symptoms, these are, according to psychoanalysis, *universal* phenomena, even if their manifestations are local and idiosyncratic, and often culturally based. We all engage in subliminal strategies and unconscious motives; this is what Freud called the "psychopathology of everyday life." For the psychoanalytic reader, the fact, for example, that I "forgot" my mother's last birthday surely means *something*. As does the fact that this example concerns my *mother* and not my *father*. Or that I felt compelled to make up for leaving my father out of the first example by adding him to the second. Or that I feel I need to provide any personal examples at all. We are all scattered, fragmented souls, animated by competing, conflictual forces. The "I" we so dearly cling to as the mark of some inner core, some unified and absolutely irreducible "me-ness" is, from this viewpoint, a mirage.

It is important to understand the universality of psychic mechanisms not just so we can obey the advice of the Delphic Oracle—"Know Thyself"—but also because these forces operate at a variety of levels. Historians and cultural critics have used psychoanalytic theory to shed light on movements, events, and beliefs in whole populations. One of the lessons of repression is that unacceptable or unpleasant ideas will veil themselves in order to find expression, to come into the open, where they can circulate like wolves in sheep's clothing. Because these wolves are so hard to spot, so hard to recognize *as wolves*, we tend to focus our energies on easier targets. These targets, unfortunately, are at best decoys; at worst they become scapegoats—unwilling proxies for real problems. The displacement of our attention from the unbearable to the merely unpleasant would suggest that we are often treating little more than symptoms. And like a lump in the carpet, symptoms pushed down in one place will only resurface elsewhere. So, rather than determine what the real nature of our problems might be, we opt most frequently for quick fixes, for surface changes—for prescribing political and social Prozac.

So why, if Freud and his followers are telling important truths, does there continue to be such tremendous *resistance* to psychoanalysis? Well, of course, as we have seen, some of these truths are decidedly unpleasant; they take us out of control and show us to be the playthings of our own desires. But ignoring these ideas is a bit like closing your eyes to escape from monsters. Not seeing them doesn't make them any less present, and, in fact, it probably makes them all the more dangerous, all the more monstrous. Indeed, disavowing Freud allows us to maintain and even create monsters in the society around us. Admitting, for example, that incestuous or murderous desires are universal (even if acting on them is not) would force us actually to *identify* with some of the unhappy individuals the tabloids put before us. How much easier, how much more reassuring, to brand these people as inhuman, as fundamentally different, *other*. As we saw in poststructuralism (chapter 3), we prefer to ignore, or even to obliterate the "monstrous," those crossover figures like the Minister D—— in Poe's story. So, we keep the lid on our own desires, blissfully unaware of how symptoms—the safety valve of repression—manifest themselves; and the more tightly we keep this lid clamped, the greater the danger it may blow.

Nevertheless, if psychoanalysis has found the "royal road to the unconscious," the route is often rocky. Freud has been roundly criticized, and probably rightfully so, for skewing some of his data in an attempt to render this new field of knowledge more credible in the eyes of science. What is even more important and more controversial is the way his work has been received, debated, and revised by theorists of a feminist bent.[17] Freud's misogyny is by

---

[17]On feminist reworkings or interrogations of Freud, see Juliet Mitchell, *Women, the Longest Revolution* (New York: Vintage, 1974); Julia Kristeva, *Revolution in Poetic Language*, trans. Margaret Waller (New York: Columbia University Press, 1984); Luce Irigaray, *This Sex Which Is Not One*, trans. Catherine Porter and Carolyn Burke (Ithaca: Cornell University Press, 1985); Sarah Kofman, *The Enigma of Woman: Woman in Freud's Writings*, trans. Catherine Porter (Ithaca: Cornell University Press, 1985), Shoshana Felman, *What Does a Woman Want?* (Baltimore: The Johns Hopkins University Press, 1993).

now legendary, and although one might excuse it as the product of late nineteenth-century, bourgeois Viennese culture, the mark it left on psychoanalysis is, perhaps, permanent. Revisions of Freud continue to be problematic on the question of sexual difference, which many theorists consider the single most formative discovery of a child's life. Much of the problem lies in the assumption that the Symbolic Order—that realm of public institutions and organizations ranging from the judicial system to language—is fundamentally *patriarchal*, masculinist. This means that when a little *girl* enters into the Symbolic, her experience is different from that of the little *boy*. While *he* learns the rites and practices of system that will privilege him, *she* submits herself to a structure that will, by design, subjugate her. The little girl learns early on that she is different from the standard. An obvious example of this difference can be seen in the way many languages mark gender: in French, for example, the feminine is usually marked by the addition of an "e" to the supposedly standard male form of nouns and adjectives. (What is worse, we perpetuate this notion of the masculine as the standard in the way we teach language. Check any French grammar manual or dictionary: *none* will show masculine forms as derived from a feminine standard, even though such an approach is entirely possible and no less logical than the prevailing approach.) And because we learn language and social codes so intimately, we come to think of them as transparent and neutral. We thus remain largely unaware of how gender, among other factors, forces us into predetermined positions.

Does this strain of psychoanalysis tell us a fatalistic truth about gender that we don't want to hear? Or is it just wrong? Some have found the gender bias to be sufficient grounds to reject psychoanalysis altogether; others have worked to revise psychoanalytic thinking about gender, casting it in less rigid—or even reversed—terms. In any case, the debate has become heated and complicated in recent years. As we will see in the next chapter, new conceptions of gender have a lot to do with it.

FURTHER READING

General Psychoanalysis:

Freud, Sigmund. "The Unconscious." In *The Standard Edition of the Complete Psychological Works of Sigmund Freud*, translated by James Strachey and A. Freud. Vol. XIV, 159–216. London: Hogarth Press.

Freud, Sigmund. "Repression." In *The Standard Edition*. Vol. XIV, 141–158.

Klages, Mary. "Jacques Lacan." Available on the World Wide Web at: http://www.colorado.edu/English/ENGL2012Klages/lacan.html

Klages, Mary. "Sigmund Freud." Available on the World Wide Web at: http://www.colorado.edu/English/ENGL2012Klages/freud.html

Lacan, Jacques. "The Mirror Stage as Formative of the Function of the I." In *Ecrits: A Selection*, translated by Alan Sheridan. New York: Norton, 1977.

Lacan, Jacques. "The Agency of the Letter in the Unconscious, Or Reason since Freud." In *Ecrits: A Selection*, translated by Alan Sheridan. New York: Norton, 1977.

Mitchell, Stephen, and Margaret Black. *Freud and Beyond*. New York: Basic Books, 1995.

Voice of the Shuttle. Web links on psychology and psychoanalysis: http://humanitas.ucsb.edu/shuttle/theory.html#psycho

Psychoanalysis and Literature:

Freud, Sigmund. "The Uncanny." In *The Standard Edition.* Vol. XVII, 217–256.

Lacan, Jacques. "Desire and the Interpretation of Desire in Hamlet." In *Literature and Psychoanalysis: The Question of Reading Otherwise,* edited by Shoshana Felman et al. Baltimore: The Johns Hopkins University Press, 1980.

Lacan, Jacques. "Seminar on 'The Purloined Letter'." In *The Purloined Poe: Lacan, Derrida, and Psychoanalytic Reading,* edited by John Muller and W. Richardson. Baltimore: The Johns Hopkins University Press, 1988.

Muller, John, and W. Richardson, eds. *The Purloined Poe: Lacan, Derrida, and Psychoanalytic Reading.* Baltimore: The Johns Hopkins University Press, 1988.

Wright, Elizabeth. *Psychoanalytic Criticism: Theory in Practice.* London and New York: Methuen, 1984.

Psychoanalysis, Gender and Language:

Mitchell, Juliet. "Femininity, Narrative, and Psychoanalysis." In *Women: The Longest Revolution. Essays on Feminism, Literature and Psychoanalysis.* New York: Vintage, 1974.

5

GENDER GAPS

■ ■ ■

Feminism and Gender Studies

It used to happen in the delivery room amidst the bustle of nurses and the moans of those who had just become parents. Now it comes even earlier, in the placid surroundings of the OB/GYN office. As the technician glides the magic wand of the sonogram over a swelling abdomen, scanning the blurry screen to detect the presence or absence of a tiny finger of flesh, it is not uncommon to hear some civilized, modern version of the old cry "It's a boy!" or "It's a girl!"

Thus are we defined. Gender has served as the primary human sorting feature since time immemorial. Long before christening, before length and weight have been established, even before the doctor announces an APGAR health score, the infant is identified as male or female. And this inaugural identification influences many of the identifiers to come: the color of the bonnet the hospital places on the child's head, the name, the toys, the games, the clothes, the haircuts, the sports, the companions, the roles, the education, the jobs, the privileges, the rewards, the very *style* of living.

Our lives are steeped in distinctions based on gender, and these distinctions have a real, demonstrable impact on the way people live and interact. There is no shortage of data available on the effects of gender in the schools, for example: girls tend to be encouraged by teachers, parents, and other students to study different subjects than boys, and to work in different ways; boys, it is often presumed, come by technical aptitude quite naturally, and many parents seem inclined to view a love of contact sports as a sex-linked trait. The social and psychological force of such assumptions can be witnessed in the lengths young people, especially adolescents, will go to fit the role that we have prescribed for them. The surge of anorexia and other eating disorders among adolescent girls is one of the most dramatic manifestations of this susceptibility, making individuals strive to refashion themselves in ways utterly incompatible with their bone structure, metabolism, and general health.[1] When boys "beef up" on steroids, modeling themselves on the Incredible Hulk, a similar violence is accomplished. Furthermore, in addition to social encouragements to conform to certain standards, we have established significant *disincentives* for straying across gender boundaries: nothing is more stigmatizing for a young boy than to be called a *girl* (or one of the slew of similar slights: "fem," "wimp," etc.); some little girls may enjoy being called a tomboy, but if their unladylike behavior continues too long (notably, through puberty), they become "butch," which is pregnant with more sinister overtones.

No, in terms of sexual identity we are commonly taught that there exist two and only two possibilities. It's the public restroom phenomenon: our society is comprised of Ladies and Gents. Transgressions are not tolerated—except by small, accompanied children, who, presumably, are not yet fully sexed.

In many senses, this state of affairs is not particularly surprising: in chapter 2 we saw how the human mind tends to structure things by binary oppositions. And even if you don't generally go in for sweeping generalizations, you would be hard pressed to deny that the male/female opposition has been one of the most enduring and formative in the history of human societies, often providing the basis for how communities will function in areas as diverse as government, religion, and the distribution of labor and wealth. (It has been estimated that women perform three-fifths of the world's work, and that they do it for one-tenth of the world's wages.[2]) Certainly the tension between women and men has provided the raw material (at least on the level of plot) for a significant literary and cultural tradition peopled with memorable pairs: Ulysses and Penelope, Romeo and Juliette, Cathy and Heathcliffe, Scarlet and Rhet, Rick and Ilsa. In addition to being one of the most widespread of oppositions, the male/female pair is also among the most rigorously maintained—or even policed. First, gender is traditionally an all-or-nothing proposition, more so than most other oppositional pairs. Compare it, for example, to the political realm: some people may think you puzzlingly inconsistent if you admit to having voted Democratic for one office and Republican for another, but few (well, perhaps more than one might think) will accuse you of being a *monster*. However, what would it mean to say that, sexually, you belong to the Independent Party? There is but limited tolerance for sexual cross-identification: when done "all for fun" (as in the recurrent "drag" theme in the popular cinema—witness *Tootsie* [1982] and *Mrs. Doubtfire* [1993]), as we will see later, it generates laughter; when taken seriously (as in the 1992 film, *The Crying Game*, or as in certain kinds of cross-dressing or in sex-change operations), it can prove profoundly troubling.

This discussion may seem to have little application to anything as remote as the practice of reading. However, literature has historically maintained an interesting and complicated relationship with notions of gender. First, books

---

[1]Mary Pipher, *Reviving Ophelia: Saving the Selves of Adolescent Girls* (New York: Putnam, 1994).
[2]See Ruth Sidel, *Keeping Women and Children Last* (New York: Penguin, 1996).

have long served as one of the primary vehicles for the communication of gender roles. The most flagrant examples can be found in the kinds of early readers many of us were raised on in grade school, in which stories abound about mothers baking blueberry pies with aproned daughters at their side and fathers spending weekends training their sons with tools. And these role models were not limited to the printed page, but even found their way into our

Figure 5.1 In this early reader, *I Want to be a Carpenter*, published in 1959 and reprinted in 1969, Don learns how to hammer a nail in straight. His sister, Ellen, lends moral support, while Dad and Buster look on. The copy I looked at has been pulled from the library and is stamped "Not suitable for school use"; most of the books in this series seem to have been removed from circulation because of dated views of gender or class identities. *Photo courtesy of Julia Steinmetz.*

living rooms: most of us have also been subjected to a couple of decades of gender-indoctrinating sitcoms—and those who escaped the first incarnations of *I Dream of Genie* or *Leave it to Beaver* have ample opportunity to make up for lost time, thanks to Nick-At-Nite.[3]

A genre of special interest, and one that spans the breach between the printed page and the silver screen, is fairy tales. Often among the first formal narratives we encounter in our childhood, these tales can be revelatory when put to critical scrutiny. They also yield to some forms of this scrutiny without much resistance: one discovers in short order that certain kinds of roles are regularly doled out on the basis of the sex of the characters. Women and girls generally display passive, domestic behaviors (one need only think of Snow White, Cinderella, or Little Red Riding Hood), whereas the men (as in "Tom Thumb" or "Jack and the Beanstalk") are busy questing, risking, and otherwise testing themselves.[4] Women who *do* show some initiative—Bluebeard's wife comes to mind—usually end up paying dearly. Even certain morals are "gendered": more than one critic has pointed out that in "Beauty and the Beast," it is Beauty—the woman—who has to learn to look beyond ugliness to find the inner beauty of her hideous companion. But the lesson doesn't apply to males, and the Beast gets to have his cake and eat it, too.[5] This is not to suggest that anything is necessarily *wrong* with the books we read as kids; in fact, a convincing argument could be made that these books reflected the social realities of the time, and that attempts to use children's literature to promote uncommon and untraditional gender roles (a practice fairly widespread in the current market) transmit manipulative and potentially deceptive messages about today's society. Nevertheless, these early readers did not *merely* reflect social realities; they also clearly *reinforced* them, which is arguably just as manipulative (although, perhaps, unintentionally so) as anything on the shelves today.

Children are not the only readers with a stake in the "engendering" of literature and literary debates. In the nineteenth century, for instance, it was widely argued that novels presented dangerously licentious views of women and that female readers, judged to be susceptible and generally shy on common sense, should avoid them at all costs.[6] Today publishers clearly target certain audiences, whole series being geared to groups defined not just by economic strata, cultural background, or race, but also—and often most fundamentally—by gender.

---

[3]See Susan Douglas's clever and entertaining study, *Where the Girls Are: Growing Up Female with the Mass Media* (New York: Times Books, 1994).

[4]On gender roles in fairy tales, see Maria Tatar, *Off with Their Heads: Fairy Tales and the Culture of Childhood* (Princeton, N.J.: Princeton University Press, 1992); Jack Zipes, *Don't Bet on the Prince: Contemporary Feminist Fairy Tales in North America and England* (New York: Routledge, 1989).

[5]See Maria Tatar, "Beauties and Beasts," in *Off with their Heads*.

[6]This becomes clear, for example, in the 1857 censorship trial against Gustave Flaubert's *Madame Bovary*. In this novel, a young woman is drawn to financial ruin and moral debauchery—and, ultimately, suicide—because she wants her life to measure up to the tripe of sentimental literature. Although the novel is actually, in part, a mordantly ironic undercutting of such literature, the censors feared that impressionable female readers might not survive their reading of the volume unscathed.

The process of identification that occurs between readers and characters is but one of the ways in which notions of gender insinuate themselves into literature and reading. A more fundamental and yet less obvious point pertains to the engendering of that basic building block of literature that is language itself. Although English is not commonly considered a language particularly laden with gendered aspects (compare, for example, French, Spanish, or German, which flag gender regularly in their nouns, articles, and adjectives), samples of such markings are not hard to come by. Sometimes the distinction is made quite obviously, as in the vocabulary we use to describe certain occupations: men who play theatrical roles are "actors," whereas women are "actresses." Sometimes the engendering of our language manifests itself in the mere resonance or connotation of certain words. Thus the actor from the previous sentence may be "handsome," a word that functions as a masculine adjective (even when one speaks of a "handsome woman" the phrase hints at a certain virile quality); an actress, on the other hand, will almost certainly be judged (partly or wholly) in terms of "beauty," a word with a decidedly feminine ring to it.[7] More surreptitious than the connotation of given words, though, certain *ways* of using language can bear gender tags. Gossip may be deemed a female enterprise, whereas orders may have a certain masculine smack. Research shows that women tend to give more feedback than men when in the role of the listener, providing all those "yes . . . yes . . . mmmm . . . uh-huh" words that reassure the speaker that someone is paying attention.[8] In many cases silence itself—especially when found in mixed company—may be gendered female: men tend to be more active, or aggressive, or even domineering in discussions.[9] So, the way we use and perceive language every day helps to construct and reinforce our divided, gendered, binocular vision of humankind.

Finally, even such intangible, supposedly literary aspects of language as "point of view" do not escape potential gender identification. Point of view is one of those items that often go entirely unquestioned in reading—as it does, too, in such visual arts as painting, photography, and film (the fields from which the term is borrowed). If point of view passes unnoticed, it may well be because it exists in the work only by implication. We are so accustomed, for example, to think of photographs as transparent chronicles of reality that we rarely stop to think about *whose eye* the lens of the camera imitates. Certainly, though, when vacationers shoot snapshots of the changing of the guard at Buckingham Palace, of the Taj Mahal, or of bear snouts at Yellowstone

[7]On the gendering of language, see Luce Irigaray, *This Sex Which Is Not One*, trans. Catherine Porter and Carolyn Burke (Ithaca: Cornell University Press, 1985).

[8]Roman Jakobson, in his study of communication, points out that this "phatic" function of language (the use of utterances to verify that an interlocuter is, indeed, present) is *crucial* to a felicitous instance of communication. See Jakobson, "Linguistics and Poetic," in *Style in Language*, ed. Thomas Sebeok (Cambridge: Technology Press of the Massachusetts Institute of Technology, 1960).

[9]See Deborah Tannen, *That's Not What I Meant!: How Conversation Style Makes or Breaks Your Relations with Others* (New York: Morrow, 1986); and *Women and Men in Conversation* (New York: Morrow, 1990).

Park, the point of view is not "objective," or "universal" in any sense: the pictures, which focus on things the locals care little or nothing about, clearly reproduce the perspective of the transient outsider.

Not surprisingly, point of view can also be gendered. To take an extreme, pictures presented in magazines like *Playboy* or *Penthouse* presuppose a point of view that is calculated to correspond to a certain idea of male desire. In some shots, the camera pretends to look at certain scenes voyeuristically; in others it is on the receiving end of the model's sultry gaze, making the (supposedly male) reader feel that it is he himself who is the target of sexual advances. More problematically, pictures in women's magazines often do the same kind of thing. The cover shot of *Cosmopolitan* is always a good example: it almost invariably presents an alluring young woman who sports an impressive

Figure 5.2   Never come across *Glitz* before? Well, this is just a mock-up (somewhat tamer than the real thing, actually) designed to give you the idea. *Cosmopolitan, Glamour, Elle, Allure, Shape, Vogue,* and *Mirabella* all declined our request to reproduce a cover *Photo courtesy of Julia Steinmetz.*

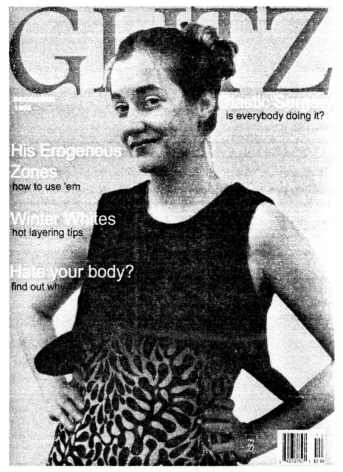

décolleté and gives the camera a look that ranges from teasing to frankly seductive. In a so-called men's magazine, such a pose is readily understandable, but why these covergirls should be attempting to seduce the reader of *Cosmopolitan* defies common sense—except insofar as it suggests that women readers have learned to look at other women (and probably themselves) from a *male* point of view.[10] Sound far-fetched? Take a close look at women's fashion magazines and ask yourself whom these pictures are meant to attract. Other women? Although the men's magazines appear calculated to satisfy male desire, certain women's magazines seem geared to helping women desire to become the objects of desire for the male gaze. In short, one might argue that the function of *Cosmopolitan* is to turn readers into women who could appear in *Playboy*, if they wanted to.

Examples from the visual domain are often the easiest for us to understand, but it is important to note that the same kinds of ploys occur in written texts; and indeed, they may be all the more effective *because* we are less aware of their presence in linguistic form. But what happens, for example, when a female reader happens upon a long, titillating description of feminine beauty? Is she not required to look, like the reader of *Cosmopolitan*, through the eyes of a male narrator? What are the effects of this kind of shaping of the reader's perceptions? What are the implications of gender in literary studies?

FEMINISM

These kinds of questions have been the subject of significant literary debate reaching back at least three decades. Early feminist criticism, beginning in the mid-1960s, represented the first serious investigations into the role of gender in literature and literary history, and these studies often met with enormous resistance. Of course, feminist critics were working against the grain of a colossal tradition. As we saw in chapter 2, binary oppositions are rarely evenhanded, one term of the pair almost always enjoying privileged status over the other. So, overturning the dominance of the male in literary studies proved to be as challenging as reversing magnetic poles. Moreover, binary oppositions tend to travel in crowds, so that oppositions of the ilk good/bad, rational/emotional, strong/weak, successful/unsuccessful, memorable/forgettable have all piggybacked throughout the ages on male/female. You can probably surmise which of the terms in each opposition has been aligned with female; there is something of a pattern.

It should not surprise you to find that the literary hall of fame houses a preponderance of male writers (most of whom are embalmed). Feminist

---

[10]See Laura Mulvey, "Visual Pleasure and Narrative Cinema," in *Visual and Other Pleasures* (Bloomington: Indiana University Press, 1989). In this influential essay, Mulvey demonstrates how the traditional Hollywood film layers ways of looking: the gaze of the male actor (often focused on the beautiful heroine) will be imitated by the camera (which often lingers, voyeuristically, on the female body), and subsequently by the audience—both men *and* women, who find themselves forced to partake of the male gaze of the hero.

criticism sought to correct the imbalance, striving to compensate for the privileging of gents in the literary canon by focusing on the category that had been largely overlooked. This impulse took a variety of forms. Some readers simply began to pay greater heed to female characters in novels and plays, characters who had not received their due in earlier scholarship.[11] Perhaps, for example, enough had been written about Hamlet to allow one to think a little about Ophelia (who, by the way, did herself in because of gender roles). Others embarked on projects of broader scope, attempting to demonstrate the kinds of subservient roles female characters occupy in general in Western literature, where their literary function may often amount to highlighting male characters—the way blockbuster movies today use actresses to ornament the Arnold Schwarzeneggers and Harrison Fords—especially in books by male authors. Surely the most involved project, though, and one that continues to our day, has concentrated on women *as writers*. The number of women authors to have been ensconced in the literary pantheon has been ridiculously small (Sappho, Eliot, Austen, Woolf . . . how many more can you think of?), and over the past thirty years remarkable advances have been made in the rediscovery, rereading, and reenjoyment of writings that had slipped into the silt of time. This is no small feat. Because many of these authors had been forgotten, one often didn't even know whom one was looking for in library catalogs or institutional archives; unearthing neglected works has often been a bit like searching for a particular volume in Borges's Library of Babel. The find of an important text has often entailed all the serendipity of the discovery of the Dead Sea Scrolls, as well as problems of interpretation worthy of the Rosetta stone. Yet the foregrounding of women writers has broadened the literary field enormously and has even helped to expand the commonplace notion of what falls into the definition of the "literary text": letters, memoirs, and diaries have recently become recognized and rewarding areas of study. Provocative questions have given rise to considerable debate: Do women write differently from men? If so, how? How is the female experience translated into predominantly male literary conventions, or how are these conventions adapted or subverted? And what about women as *readers*? Do women experience literature differently?

However, just as readers were discovering these exciting new possibilities, a tension began to develop between feminism and certain other critical approaches. Structuralism and poststructuralism (see chapters 2 and 3) encourage readers to dethrone the author, to divest him—or her—of authority, to ignore the writer's biography, as well as authorial intentions. These directives were very large pills to swallow—and poisonous ones at that—for a feminist movement that had just succeeded in *resuscitating* a large number of authors. Just as these female ghosts of the past had begun to speak, poststructuralism arrived on the scene to exorcise them. To make matters worse, the principles of post-

---

[11]For an excellent summary of the complementary enterprises of feminist critics during the sixties and seventies, see Elaine Showalter's "Feminist Criticism in the Wilderness," in *Critical Inquiry* 8, no. 2 (Winter 1981):179–205; see also the readings collected in Showalter's edited volume, *The New Feminist Criticism: Essays on Women, Literature, and Theory* (New York: Pantheon, 1985).

structuralism called into question some of the basic assumptions of feminism. While the feminist movement had sought to *invert* a certain binary opposition, privileging at least for a time female over male, poststructuralists were building careers by *deconstructing* such oppositions. While feminist readers implicitly relied on the notion that an abyss—the so-called gender gap—separated male and female, deconstruction seemed to suggest that genders are not separated by an abyss at all. Rather, it suggests, gender is actually *in* the gap; it is, in some sense, *missing* as a positive term. The division between male and female, poststructuralism hints, may not be so rigorous after all. By what right, then, could one distinguish between male and female authors?[12]

The crossing of feminism and poststructuralism resulted in heated debate. But it also produced an interesting hybrid that combines some of the strengths of both sides. This new creature is omnivorous, feeding indiscriminately on art, literature, current events, medicine, law, and whatever else is at hand. The movement has come to be known as *gender studies*. It poses some radical questions, or, as often as not, shows how certain of these questions are already implied in its objects of study.

ENGENDERING LITERATURE: A CASE STUDY

From the story of this movement's genesis, let's move to another tale. This one is a short story called "The Hidden Woman" written in France in 1924. We'll talk about the author a bit later; for now, let's skip to the story.

The Hidden Woman

He had been looking at the swirl of masks in front of him for a long time, suffering vaguely from the intermingling of their colors and the synchronized sound of two orchestras too close together. His cowl pressed his temples; a nervous headache was building between his eyes. But he savored, without impatience, a mixture of malaise and pleasure which allowed the hours to fly by unnoticed. He had wandered down all the corridors of the Opéra, had drunk in the silvery dust of the dance floor, recognized bored friends, and wrapped around his neck the indifferent arms of a very fat girl humorously disguised as a sylph. Though embarrassed by his long domino, tripping over it like a man in skirts, the cowled doctor did not dare take off either the domino or the hood, because of his schoolboy lie.

---

[12]Judith Butler, in the opening chapter of *Gender Trouble: Feminism and the Subversion of Identity* (New York: Routledge, 1990), lays out the complexities of the gender question quite thoroughly. Her illustration of the "constructed-ness" even of our notion of biological sex represents a serious incursion of poststructuralist thought into gender inquiry.

"I'll be spending tomorrow night in Nogent," he had told his wife the evening before. "They just telephoned and I'm afraid that my patient, you know, that poor old lady . . . Can you imagine? And I was looking forward to this ball like a kid. It's ridiculous, isn't it, a man my age who's never been to the Opéra Ball?"

"Very, darling, very ridiculous! If I had known I might never have married you . . ."

She laughed, and he admired her narrow face, pink, matte, and long, like a thin sugared almond.

"But . . . don't you want to go to the Green and Purple Ball? You know you can go without me if you want, darling."

She trembled with one of those long shivers of disgust which made her hair, her delicate hands, and her bosom in her white dress shudder at the sight of a slug or some filthy passer-by.

"Oh, no! Can you see me in a crowd, all those hands . . . What can I do? It's not that I'm a prude, it's . . . it makes my skin crawl. There's nothing I can do about it."

Leaning against the balustrade of the loggia, above the main staircase, he thought about this trembling hind, as he contemplated, directly in front of him, on the bare back of a sultana, the grasp of two enormous square hands with black nails. Bursting out of the braid-trimmed sleeves of a Venetian lord, they sank into the white female flesh as if it were dough. Because he was thinking about her, it gave him quite a start to hear, next to him, a little "ahem," a little cough typical of his wife. He turned around and saw someone in a long and impenetrable disguise, sitting sidesaddle on the balustrade, a Pierrot by the looks of the huge-sleeved tunic, the loose-fitting pantaloons, the skullcap, the plaster-like whiteness coating the little bit of skin visible above the half-mask bearded with lace. The fabric of the costume and skullcap, woven of dark violet and silver, glistened like the conger eel fished for by night with iron hooks, in boats with resin lanterns. Overcome with surprise, he waited to hear the little "ahem," which did not come again. The Pierrot-Eel, seated, casual, tapped the marble balusters with a dangling heel, revealing only its two satin slippers and a black-gloved hand bent back against one hip. The two oblique slits in the mask, carefully covered over with a tulle mesh, allowed only a smothered fire of indeterminate color to pass through.

He almost called out, "Irene!" but held back, remembering his own lie. Not good at playacting, he also decided against disguising his voice. The Pierrot scratched its thigh, with a free and uninhibited gesture, and the anxious husband sighed in relief.

"Ah! It's not her."

But out of a pocket the Pierrot pulled a flat gold box, opened it to take out a lipstick, and the anxious husband recognized an antique snuff-box, fitted with a mirror inside, the last birthday present . . . He put his left hand on the pain in his chest with so brusque and so involuntarily theatrical a motion that the Pierrot-Eel noticed him.

"Is that a declaration, Purple Domino?"

He did not answer, half choked with surprise, anticipating, as in a bad dream, and listened for a long moment to the thinly disguised voice—the voice of his wife. The Eel, sitting there cavalierly, its head tilted like a bird's, looked at him; she shrugged her shoulders, hopped down, and walked away. Her movement freed the distraught husband, who, restored to an active and normal jealousy, started to think clearly again, and calmly rose to follow his wife.

"She's here for someone, with someone. In less than an hour I'll know everything."

A hundred other purple or green cowls guaranteed that he would be neither noticed nor recognized. Irene walked ahead of him nonchalantly. He was amazed to see her roll her hips softly and drag her feet a little as if she were wearing Turkish slippers. A Byzantine, in embroidered emerald green and gold, grabbed her as she passed, and she bent back, grown thinner in his arms, as if his grasp were going to cut her in half. Her husband ran a few steps forward and reached the couple as Irene cried out flatteringly, "You big brute, you!"

She walked away, with the same relaxed and calm step, stopping often, musing at the open doors of the boxes, almost never turning around. She hesitated at the bottom of a staircase, turned aside, came back toward the entrance to the orchestra stalls, slid into a noisy, dense group with slippery skillfulness, the exact movement of a knife blade sliding into its sheath. Ten arms imprisoned her, an almost naked wrestler roughly pinned her up against the edge of the boxes on the main floor and held her there. She yielded under the weight of the naked man, threw back her head with a laugh that was drowned out by other laughter, and the man in the purple cowl saw her teeth flash beneath the mask's lacy beard. Then she slipped away again with ease and sat down on the steps which led to the dance floor. Her husband, standing two steps behind, watched her. She readjusted her mask, and her crumpled tunic, and tightened the roll of her headband. She seemed calm, as though alone, and walked away again after a few minutes' rest. She went down the steps, put her arms on the shoulders of a warrior who invited her, without speaking, to dance, and she danced, clinging to him.

"That's him," the husband said to himself.

But she did not say a word to the dancer, clad in iron and moist skin, and left him quietly, when the dance ended. She went off to have a glass of champagne at the buffet, and then a second glass, paid, and then watched, motionless and curious, as two men began scuffling, surrounded by screaming women. Then she amused herself by placing her little satanic hands, all black, on the white bosom of a Dutch girl with golden hair, who cried out nervously. At last the anxious man who was following her saw her stop as she bumped up against a young man collapsed on a banquette, out of breath, fanning himself with his mask. She leaned over, disdainfully took his handsome face, rugged and fresh, by the chin, and kissed the panting, half-open mouth . . .

But her husband, instead of rushing forward and tearing the two joined mouths away from each other, disappeared into the crowd. Dismayed, he no longer feared, he no longer hoped for betrayal. He was sure now that Irene did not know the adolescent, drunk with dancing, whom she was kissing, or the Hercules. He was sure that she was not waiting or looking for anyone, that the lips she held beneath her own like a crushed grape, she would abandon, leave again the next minute, then wander about again, gather up some other passer-by, forget him, until she felt tired and it was time to go back home, tasting only the monstrous pleasure of being alone, free, honest, in her native brutality, of being the one who is unknown, forever solitary and without shame, whom a little mask and a hermetic costume had restored to her irremediable solitude and her immodest innocence.[13]

Curious, isn't it? "The Hidden Woman" is a troubling, unsettling tale, one full of surprising turns. It offers some interesting twists on the standard story of adultery. On the one hand, it reads like a small morality tale reinforcing proverbial wisdom: the deceiver is himself deceived: the husband who lied to his wife finds himself the victim of her deceit. On the other, as we shall see, it challenges proverbial wisdom in a variety of ways.

Just who *is* the "hidden woman" of the story's title? We might at first assume that the term refers to the dutiful wife hidden behind the mask, concealed beneath the "Pierrot" costume. The "hide-and-go-seek" resonance of the story's title plays into this theme of apparel and disguise, suggesting that the fabricated costume screens the real, authentic woman underneath. The costume, however, serves as only the most obvious indication of concealment. More shocking—to the husband, at any rate—is that in this story one woman hides another. We recognize the forward, almost promiscuous Pierrot of the Opéra masked ball to be the same person as that delicate soul the husband had left earlier the same day. Simple enough. But *which* woman is the *hidden* one? That is to say, is this proper, upper-middle-class wife simply cutting loose and playacting for an evening, taking on the persona of a vixen the way one becomes Miss Scarlet or Professor Plum in a board game? Or is it the reverse? Does the Pierrot of the ball show this physician's wife

[13]"The Hidden Woman" (originally translated as "The Other Woman") by Sidonie Gabrielle Colette, in *The Collected Stories of Colette*, trans. Matthew Ward (New York: Farrar Strauss Giroux, 1984). I have modified the translation in a few passages.

dropping her mask of propriety and subservience, letting her "true colors" come to the surface?

These questions are already problematic, for they cast the issue in the kind of binary logic poststructuralism has urged us to scrutinize closely. Must the "hidden" woman be *either* the wife *or* the Pierrot? Must one be the real, authentic individual, while the other remains merely a passing disguise? What if both were authentic? What if neither was?

We may be tempted to identify with the thoughts of the husband, through whose eyes we witness the events. He, of course, feels that he is living a lie, that his costume serves only to conceal the person he "really is" underneath. "Not good at playacting," he tries to remain as invisible as possible. His wife, however, displays a disturbing naturalness in both her roles. In the role of wife, when she contemplates the idea of attending the ball in her husband's absence, the very depth of her shudder would seem to qualify her reaction as genuine: "She trembled with one of those long shivers of disgust which made her hair, her delicate hands, and her bosom in her white dress shudder at the sight of a slug or some filthy passer-by." And yet, it is actions as involuntary and as unpremeditated as this shudder that, when the husband observes them on the part of the Pierrot, first reassure him that the costumed figure is really somebody else: "The Pierrot scratched its thigh, with a free and uninhibited gesture, and the anxious husband sighed in relief. 'Ah! It's not her.'" Only when he becomes convinced that it is, indeed, his wife, do such actions become cause for even greater concern. He is amazed to see her roll her hips as she walks, altering her gait, even expressing active sexual desire. If this woman can adopt poses, attitudes, and emotions that strike even her husband as compellingly genuine, what are we to make of the notion of disguise? Is the slightly priggish doctor's wife the real McCoy? The ending of the story shows that the foundation of the husband's life has been shaken, as he imagines that that night, by a dizzying interplay of masks, he has glimpsed a view of the naked truth. He pictures Irene returning home in the evening, "free," and "honest," having enjoyed her "native brutality"; these qualities he sees neither as created nor borrowed, but rather *restored* to her by that "little mask" and "hermetic costume"—a costume no more impenetrable, we suspect, than the one she wears in everyday life.

All this talk about costume and disguise, about parts being played, places us directly in the context of the theater. Why not? The story takes place at the Opéra, the site of theatrical performances, and it presents us with a cast of costumed characters ranging from the Pierrot of the commedia del arte to naked wrestlers, from Byzantine lovers to little Dutch girls. As a masked ball, it partakes of the spirit of the carnival, a topsy-turvy celebration in which paupers dress as princes and the normal taboos of polite society are briefly suspended. At such gatherings we may take on roles the way one plays a dramatic part.

"The Hidden Woman," however, carnivalizes the carnival, turning it upside down so that the "real" performance seems to be taking place *outside* the Opéra, during ordinary life. Or rather, it blurs the line between costumed balls and the masquerade of the everyday. Playacting, that rather exceptional activity (at least for adults), reveals itself to be the norm. The story suggests that our identities, those precious little definitions we have of ourselves, are not very different from dramatic roles.

PLAYING ROLES

We commonly use the word *roles* to describe the various identities we "take on" in life, like so many dramatic parts into which we have been cast. Most of us are at least dimly aware of the vast number of roles we play simultaneously: husbands, wives, lovers, brothers, sisters, parents, children, providers, team members, leaders, followers . . . women, men. The simultaneous advantage and disadvantage of identifying our various interactions as particular kinds of roles is that roles are, in some measure, previously *scripted*. This means that we come to them with preconceptions, with some idea of how we think brothers, lovers, employers, and so forth, should "act." So, when we come to a new role, we often already know something about how we think we are expected to behave. This somewhat comforting feature, though, can turn constraining when we feel the urge to do something "out of character," when we wish to act or speak in ways that are incompatible with traditional definitions of the parts we play. Strong social injunctions exist against breaking character, as much today as ever. For instance, certain groups lobby hard to enforce what they consider to be traditional family values, which would require that roles be played a certain way. On a more personal level, we may find that the parts we play vary ever so slightly when we interact with different friends, or we "act" somewhat differently with professional associates than we do with long-standing companions. Our roles vary with the scene we are playing, and there is considerable pressure to remain faithful to the part. But do our chameleon characters mean we are by turns true and unfaithful to some "core" identity? Do we have, in fact, any identity that *precedes* our role-playing, our taking-on of masks? Or are our identities more or less *constructed*, formed by the parts we play?

"The Hidden Woman" argues in the direction of the latter. However, it goes beyond demonstrating the fundamental artifice of the roles we play; it also shows how these roles are profoundly marked by *gender*. The story is told from the husband's point of view, and this is already a gendered element of the tale. As we saw earlier, when considering such publications as *Playboy* and *Cosmopolitan*, point of view is regularly gendered male, regardless of the sex of the main character. That is, women and men are both trained to view the world through the filter of male desire. In this case the husband has maneuvered to put himself in a situation that is not much different from poring over a girlie magazine: attending the ball alone, thoroughly disguised, he plays the peeping Tom, gazing voyeuristically at the bodies on display, seeing without being seen. This dynamic, which grants him the power *to look*, while limiting the role of women in the story as the lot of *being looked at*, reinforces the stereotypical gender dynamic.[14] And because this point of view is rigidly adhered to in the story, the reader, regardless of his or her own predispositions, has no choice but to share it.

What happens, though, in this story is that the privileged point of view is undermined—indeed, booby-trapped. When the husband discovers his own wife at the ball, the scene becomes considerably more complicated, especially with its implications concerning gender. First comes the double standard: although his ruse for attending the ball without Irene is but a "schoolboy lie," *her* deception is cause for absolute shock, a veritable scandal. Boys will be boys, of course, so he is not overly ashamed of having misled his wife; but *girls* are supposed to be *ladies*. The fact that the husband seems unaware of the bias of his judgment is typical of double standards; self-critical blindness is conveniently built into them.

More disconcerting, though, for the husband is the fact that the male point of view loses ground throughout the story. The husband-wife relationship is rather neatly described in the opening paragraph when the husband fibs about not being available to attend the ball:

> "Can you imagine? And I was looking forward to this ball like a kid. It's ridiculous, isn't it, a man my age who's never been to the Opéra Ball?"
>
> "Very, darling, very ridiculous! If I had known I might never have married you . . ."

Agreeing with him, mimicking his emotions and feeding his own words back to him, she serves as a mirror for the male ego. At the beginning, then, Irene plays the perfect housewife. Things go haywire, though, when she begins to voice her own desires. His narcissistic assumption that his wife desires him alone is shattered when, at the ball, she levels her voyeuristic gaze on her disguised husband, thinking he is somebody (anybody) else. The husband experiences, for the first time perhaps, what it is like to be cast as an object of desire:

> "Ah! It's not her."
>
> But out of a pocket the Pierrot pulled a flat gold box, opened it to take out a lipstick, and the anxious husband recognized an antique snuffbox, fitted with a mirror inside, the last birthday present . . . He put his left hand on the pain in his chest with so brusque and so involuntarily theatrical a motion that the Pierrot-Eel noticed him.
>
> "Is that a declaration, Purple Domino?"
>
> He did not answer, half choked with surprise, anticipation, nightmare, and he listened for a long moment to the thinly disguised voice—the voice of his wife.

---

[14]Laura Mulvey, in "Visual Pleasure and Narrative Cinema" (cited above), described the essential quality of the traditional heroine as "*to-be-looked-at-ness*": her role is to attract the gaze.

To make matters worse, the husband isn't even the *sole* object of desire. This he learns as his wife leers at others and slinks about the room. What he discovers, in effect, is a gaze that parallels and even overpowers his own. In fact, the husband's impotence grows as he follows Irene through the crowd; already feminized by *her* gaze, he ends up powerless, silent, crushed. Not surprisingly, Irene's own transformation contributes to this emasculation, for she takes on a number of male attributes. Dressed in the costume of a male character, wielding a masculine, desiring gaze, she out-leers her husband, whose long domino made him "like a man in skirts" anyway. Perhaps it is for her assertiveness that she is described as "an Amazon," one of those manly women of Greek mythology. Her mask includes a beard, thus accentuating her masculinity. She maneuvers through the crowd aggressively, skillfully, with "the exact movement of a knife blade sliding into its sheath." Finally, after downing her drinks at the bar, she "amused herself by placing her little satanic hands, all black, on the white bosom of a Dutch girl with golden hair, who cried out nervously." Just what is becoming of the passive, modest Irene we encountered at the beginning of the story? She seems to be gravitating toward another pronoun, swapping "she" for "he."

It is precisely this gender confusion, this blending of supposed opposites, that casts Irene in the role of monster. The image of the conger eel ("The fabric of the costume and skullcap . . . glistened like the conger eel fished for by night with iron hooks") is bad enough by itself, but when joined with the image of the woman—in those passages in which Irene is not just compared to the serpentine creature but actually referred to as "the Eel," or even "the Pierrot-Eel"—the monstrous combination of human and animal doubles the intertwining of male and female, turning Irene into a Melusina, a mythical creature, half woman, half serpent, usually associated with oversexed, masculinized women.

If "The Hidden Woman" presents Irene as alternately male and female, or as some strange composite of the two, it is perhaps because the blending of gender she incarnates somehow *eludes* representation.

One could possibly dismiss the story's waffling on the gender issue as dishonest, or at least as disingenuous: clearly Irene is a woman in drag, one might reasonably assert, and any attempt by the text to cloud the issue is disingenuous. According to this logic, Irene's masculinity is feigned; it is part of her costume, an act she is playing. Underneath it all lurks the "real" woman she fundamentally "is." However, this assertion is neither inevitable nor incontrovertible, and her husband himself seems unsure about which woman is the authentic Irene. One might suggest, though, that *neither* representation (that is, neither that of a male nor that of a female) is authentic—or that *both* are. How could this be? Well, the story seems calculated to help us to see beyond binary oppositions, to see that identities—including gender identities—are not always unambiguous. This is a difficult ambiguity even to talk about, for it falls between the cracks of our language, which provides us only with a binary option—"he" or "she"—when we speak of people. Demonstrating gender ambiguity, one that eludes

*Un peuple est sans honneur, et mérite ses chaines
Quand il baisse le front sons le Sceptre des Reines.*

Figure 5.3   A Melusina from the late seventeen hundreds; in this case it's a representation of Marie-Antoinette getting too big (and serpentine) for her britches: she is sapping power from the king.

the standard categories of our language, would have to be done against the grain of the language. The narrator needs to stretch language, distort it, so that, by some sleight of hand, it might represent something not ordinarily "representable."

There is nothing too unusual about this, for representations are often full of distortions. Take a simple example: remember those little moving pictures you used to make at school in the margins of textbooks you were supposed to be reading? A water balloon in the upper-right-hand corner of page one would appear slightly lower in the margin of page three, lower again on page five, and so on, descending the margin of odd-numbered pages until somewhere around page fifty you depicted it bursting spectacularly over the head of your teacher? Then, when you fanned the pages before your eyes the balloon appeared to drop in one continuous motion. You could adjust the speed of the attack as you desired, and you could replay the scene for yourself or your friends as often as you wished. Of course, in this elementary movie, nothing actually moves: the *illusion* of movement is created from a series of static images. Thus can representation approximate something that technically falls beyond its power, something that, at least in the limits of a given medium, is properly *unrepresentable*. You could make another of these paperback movies, this time simply placing a colored dot in the upper right-hand-corner of the pages. (This book will serve nicely.) But if you *alternate* the color of these dots, using, for example, blue and pink, when you make these dots flicker rapidly before your eyes, you will see neither color distinctly: a pleasant lavender emerges. Again, what is evoked by the representation surpasses the raw materials of the medium.

Similarly, if the language used in "The Hidden Woman" oscillates between the "maleness" and "femaleness" of Irene, perhaps the effect of this oscillation is to blur the distinction between these two opposites. The question is, is this *just* an illusion? Is it an attempt to create the image of something that does not exist, or does the oscillation help us to glimpse an "in-between-ness" that otherwise eludes representation? Perhaps the categories we use in describing gender are not airtight—at least insofar as they pertain to this particular story. The possibility of other categories is at least hinted at in "The Hidden Woman." "He was sure she was not waiting or looking for anyone," the text reports as the husband watches Irene cruising through the ball. He knew that she would "gather up some other passer-by, forget him, until she felt tired and it was time to go home, tasting only the *monstrous* pleasure of being alone, free, honest. . . ."

Monstrous? The word is of special interest in the light of poststructuralism. You may recall from chapter 3 that "monstrous" is the label often applied to that which eludes simple binarities, which occupies the space of neither/nor or both/and. The notion is vexing in "The Hidden Woman," for just what *is* a person who is neither male nor female, or both at once? Could this refer to anything other than castrati or hermaphrodites? Clearly, "The Hidden Woman" seems to suggest, we have something eccentric on our hands.

DEFINING GENDER

However, we need to clean up what we mean by "male" and "female," by masculine and feminine. Has Irene lost her femininity because she acts like a man? Is maleness defined by behavior, or by anatomy, or by desire? Identity, we saw above, can be likened to roles that we play, without there being much in the way of essential, "inner" qualities. Gender is a part of our identity; is it also as artificial or as "constructed" as identity in general? Although social roles are largely "scripted," they should not be impervious to rewriting, nor should individuals be unable to recast themselves. If such rewritings are possible in career and family roles, why would the same not hold true in gender roles as well?

Gender studies have given this last question a great deal of thought, and the very name of the movement begins to imply the complexity of the problem. What do we mean when we speak of "gender"? Certainly the term cannot be reduced to biological sex. Nor does it refer solely to behaviors, nor again to sexual orientation. Instead, current uses of the term *gender* generally imply a *mix* of these fields, and more.[15]

Society, we know, likes to keep things simple; gender studies, however, entails a certain amount of complication. First, let's divide "gender" into four components, keeping in mind that even this division is probably too simple-minded. Our initial categories will include biological sex, physical appearance, sexual orientation, and behavior. All of these have traditionally been conceived of in terms of oppositional pairs: that is, an individual is either genetically male (XY chromosomes) or female (XX); bears physical traits that are either masculine (male genitalia, angular features, etc.) or feminine (female genitalia, smoother features, etc.); is oriented toward either a male or a female sexual partner; and speaks, acts, and dresses like either a woman or a man. This kind of distillation can seem forced or artificial. We don't often think of gender in all these layers because we have generally learned to expect an unproblematic coincidence of the categories of sex, appearance, orientation, and behavior: we may be inclined to assume, for example, that biological males will look, speak, and act like "men," and that they will desire the opposite sex. Analogous expectations, of course, are made of biological females.

These assumptions can be, well, *assumed*, and they can even, to some extent, be enforced. But they are not unassailable. Homosexuality, for one thing, throws a monkey wrench into this understanding of sexual desire. Transsexuals—those who have had their sexual apparatus surgically transformed, thus placing their physical appearance "at odds" with their biological genotype—also trouble the gender grid as we conventionally conceive of it. Exceptions, these? "Monsters," like Irene? *Maybe*, but let us not be hasty. For, if nothing else, these apparently exceptional cases bring to light those complications of simple binarities that society would happily overlook. A fuller rendering of the gender possibilities would invite us to look at the logical complications of the male/female opposition—as well as the complication of

---

[15]Eve Kosofsky Sedgwick, in *Epistemology of the Closet* (Berkeley: University of California Press, 1990), demonstrates quite amply the fluidity of sexual and gender identities. The nearly insurmountable problems associated with establishing a stable vocabulary form, in part, the subject of her often cited chapter, "Axiomatic" (*Epistemology of the Closet*), 1–66.

Biology

either XY (chromosomal male)	or XX (chromosomal female)
neither XY nor XX (asexual)	both XY and XX (bisexual; hermaphrodite)

Anatomy

male physical traits	female physical traits
neither male nor female (children? castrati?)	both male and female (chromosomal hermaphrodite; castrati?)

Behavior, speech, mannerisms

masculine (stereotypical male)	feminine (stereotypical female)
neither masculine nor feminine (certain religious orders?)	both masculine and feminine ("effeminate" males; "masculine" females)

Sexual orientation

toward the female (heterosexual male)	toward the male (heterosexual female)
toward neither the male nor the female (absence of sexual desire)	toward both the male and the female (bisexual)

Figure 5.4

each of the attendant oppositions characterizing gender. As we saw in chapter 3, simple either/or propositions can be expanded to include other possibilities: the *exclusion* of both elements, or their *combination*. Thus the categories of "male" and "female" allow for the logical *possibility* (even if we can think of no concrete examples of these possibilities) of elements being neither male nor female, or of being somehow both at once. If we apply this logic to the various levels of gender, the number of permutations quickly turns vertiginous. Each layer could be drawn schematically as follows (with the terms in parentheses indicating samples of entities we might assign to each category). Again, as we saw in poststructuralism (chapter 3), the shading of the lower quadrants reflects the general reluctance of our society to recognize these complications. Sometimes there are compelling reasons for this blindness: the statistical occurrence of biological hermaphrodites, for example, is vanishingly small, and it would surely be impractical of us *not* to ignore such anomalies in our everyday interactions. However, that should not encourage us to overgeneralize the pattern, applying the same assumptions to every situation. Narrow thinking might well presume that the "both/and" categories of anatomy, behavior, and orientation, although *theoretically* possible, are in reality as anomalous as hermaphrodites. This, combined with our feeling that the different layers of gender should be aligned with one another, might lead us to think, for example, that only truly chromosomal hermaphrodites should exhibit ambiguity in their behavior, appearance, and desires. Of course, this is just "thinking of convenience," and there is no necessary coincidence of these categories. Thus there have been cases of dizzying complexity, such as a recent instance in which a woman underwent a sex-change operation because she felt not only that she wanted to be a man, but a *homosexual* one at that. This made her a woman desiring to be a man who desires other men.[16] A "traditional" understanding might have suggested that this orientation toward the male identified her precisely as the anatomical woman she already was. Moreover, the slipperiness of these concepts leaves in question what, exactly, it is that this woman desired. To the extent that, for her at least, her own gender was not anchored in biology, by what criteria could she identify the "men" to whom she was "homosexually" attracted? Our own phrase "orientation toward the male" takes on an unanticipated ambiguity.

This is an extreme case, one filled with anguish for all the participants. But it is meant to illustrate the multilayeredness of current understandings of gender. Each layer reveals another, and another, and yet another—until we get to the center of this philosophical onion, only to find that, *just maybe*, there is no *core*. Or, at the very least, this core may be less of a precise identity than a kind of biological *tether*, allowing a much broader range of possibilities than we might have thought ourselves open to. In this model, gender becomes less an expression of some immutable inner truth than a ragtag, variable combination of physical predispositions, social influences, family dynamics, and more.

Although the scenarios we have looked at above seem *extreme*, gender studies would suggest that they are not exceptional, and certainly not monstrous. Though many of us choose or accept to play conventional gender roles, many people now believe that behaviors and sexual orientation bear much looser links to biological, chromosomal sex than was previously thought. The idea is not altogether new: already Freud, early in the century, theorized that bisexual impulses were actually the standard, but that same-sex desires were regularly repressed.

Of course, pointing out that heterosexuality is not a universal inclination, and that its inevitability or naturalness is open to challenge, does not amount to saying that gender has *no* grounding in biology, that *nothing* is hardwired. (That remains one of the hot topics in gender studies: how

---

[16]See Amy Bloom, "The Body Lies," *The New Yorker*, July 18, 1994, 38–49.

much of us is swayed by genetics, and how much by social forces?) But new models help us understand gender more broadly, allow us to see how gender roles can be multiplied beyond the traditional two, and how these non-traditional roles have nothing monstrous or unnatural about them. Indeed, when we look closely, it is perhaps the traditional roles themselves that seem encrusted in artificiality, because they are being endlessly reinforced and reconstructed by social institutions as divergent as religion, law, and the media.

Of course, Irene is not a transsexual, and nothing suggests that she is a hermaphrodite. How much more comforting, though, it might be for some to relegate her to one of these extreme categories. What is, perhaps, more troubling is that "The Hidden Woman," by its manipulation of notions of gender and identity, demonstrates the flexibility of roles, as well as the malaise that this elasticity can elicit. The author seems to want to suggest that Irene remains simultaneously revealed to and hidden from her husband.

Ah yes . . . the author. Do you look at authors with the same voyeuristic gaze that the husband in the story uses to study Irene? Do you read with a mind to unmasking the writer, to unveiling, like Dorothy in Oz, the "man behind the curtain"? If so, what is your conclusion? Do you peg "The Hidden Woman" as the handywork of a man or a woman? What aspects of the work, what themes, devices, or stylistic tics sway your guess? Clearly the story is told from a male point of view, but as we saw in the discussion of *Cosmopolitan*, that doesn't guarantee anything.

In the light of the discussion above, the very value of this question can itself be called into question. What, exactly, do we mean by a "male" or "female" author, and how artificial is the distinction? At any rate, many would argue that it is probably not *altogether* artificial: because society has policed gender pretty effectively over the years, forcing most of us into one category or the other, we have certainly been molded by the roles we have been forced to play. Thus it would hardly be surprising to find that the two halves of the population, raised, educated, and indoctrinated in different ways, might very well write differently. As it happens, "The Hidden Woman" was written by the French writer Colette (1873–1954), a woman—though one who was not without gender issues of her own. So the author repeats Irene's ruse, taking on a male mask (in this case, the point of view), only to unsettle notions of gender identity altogether.

REMAKING DESIRE

One of the problems confronted by authors dealing with notions of gender is that many readers—like Irene's husband—don't *want* gender problematized. After all, life is complicated enough without somebody messing around with what used to be a pretty simple idea. The claim has been made that popular art, ranging from Hollywood classics to pulp fiction to Disney animations, has reinforced traditional gender roles so efficiently that books and films that challenge orthodox views fail to connect with our established patterns of desire. They turn us off. As a result, the films flop at the box office; the books, their front covers ripped off, collect dust in half-price stores. So, the next time around, publishers and producers take a long, hard look at anything that doesn't pander to public demand. And once this vicious circle has been engaged, it perpetuates itself marvelously, gathering nearly unstoppable momentum.

As we saw in chapter 4, one way to bring the unorthodox to the surface is by humor: jokes regularly perform this service, evoking taboo topics and triggering that slightly nervous laughter that accompanies them. The arts have never left the attraction of humor unheeded, even when gender is the issue. Films like *Tootsie* (1982) or, more recently, *Mrs. Doubtfire* (1993) were both tremendous box office hits: watching Dustin Hoffman or Robin Williams prance about in nylons and high heels pushed the funny button. What allows audiences to enjoy films like these, however, is precisely the fact that they never have to take cross-dressing or other gender-related topics *seriously*: jokes work because they allow us to consider unbearable or threatening topics in an outlandish, manifestly impossible form. As a result, *Mrs. Doubtfire*, in spite of its subject matter, participates in the perpetuation of conventional gender roles.[17]

This is not to suggest that any work that rocks the gender boat is doomed to failure. In "The Hidden Woman" a different strategy is used, and one of the story's chief accomplishments lies in its ability to seduce the reader in spite of its subject matter. It does this by a ruse working a bit like the Trojan horse. This story, which *begins* as a voyeuristic tale conforming to conventional desires, suddenly turns into something else. First the reader is hooked by the appeal to masculine desire, by the male point of view; then the narrator begins to reel in. The truth that so disturbs Irene's husband simultaneously disturbs those who initially identified with him.

Nevertheless, "The Hidden Woman" presents gender trouble rather subtly, and there is enough going on in the story that readers can choose to dodge that particular issue if they are so inclined. A better example of the Trojan horse approach can be found in the film *The Crying Game* (1992), a Neil Jordan movie that turned comedies like *Mrs. Doubtfire* on their ear.[18] In this

---

[17]The reversal of gender roles is closely related to what the Russian critic M. Bakhtin referred to as the logic of the "carnival": such reversals are tolerated, or even encouraged, because they provide a release of tension. However, it is a *temporary* release, and the upside-down world of the carnival is righted in short order. The carnival, then, ultimately serves to *reinforce* the very world it superficially *subverts*. See Mikhail Bakhtin's introduction to his book *Rabelais and His World*, trans. Helene Iswolsky (Cambridge: Technology Press of Massachusetts Institute of Technology, 1968), 1–58.

[18]The notion of a work of art operating like a Trojan horse comes from an essay by Monique Wittig: "The Trojan Horse," in *The Straight Mind* (Boston: Beacon Press, 1992), 68–77.

film the audience again shares the point of view of a male protagonist, a strikingly handsome hunk (Fergus, played by Stephen Rea) who flees from the Irish Republican Army. Hiding in central London he meets a girl of extraordinary beauty (Dil, played by Jaye Davidson), and whose shapely figure the camera never tires of caressing. The surprise comes midway through the picture when Fergus and Dil hit the sack. When Fergus initiates a little foreplay, and Dil eventually disrobes, Fergus leaps back in surprise: Dil is, at least anatomically, *male.*

At this point in the scene, Fergus doubles over and vomits. And the reaction of some viewers, in fact, was not so different: when the film opened in 1992, some audience members actually walked out of the movie theater at this point. But only *some* of them. The others, sufficiently engrossed by the first half of the movie, swallowed hard and decided to ride it out. As the film continued they began, like Fergus, to understand and even appreciate Dil.

What happens in *The Crying Game* is extremely interesting. Many viewers, had they known about Dil from the outset, might never have entered the theater. But the movie's opening scenes lull us into a sense of normalcy: it's a man's movie, filled with guns, violence, and tough-talking terrorists. Then it catches us off guard, hitting below the belt, as it were. Part of Fergus's horror when he discovers Dil's secret arises from his realization

Figure 5.5   Jaye Davidson as Dil, about to engage in her first kiss with Stephen Rea. No doubt about it; she's a looker.

that he had been sexually aroused by someone he later considered devoid of femininity, thereby troubling his understanding of his own desires. Viewers who had identified with Fergus, and who had enjoyed leering at Dil's curves and seductive gaze, may well share in Fergus's discovery, wondering about their own desires. Some will simply be repulsed and leave the theater; others may be shaken but intrigued, provided with an inkling of the unsuspected complexity of gender. The film will have tricked them into thinking the unthinkable.

The Crying Game, "The Hidden Woman," Mrs. *Doubtfire*—these are all inviting texts for gender studies; questions of desire, sexual identity, and gender all crop up quite explicitly. And yet, these stories are exceptional only for the degree of their questioning; relatively few texts make gender their central theme. But gender is everywhere, and it is difficult to see how any text could be entirely untouched by such concerns. As we have seen, such mundane vehicles as children's stories and popular magazines provide ample material. Indeed, the mere presence of gendered characters justifies a certain line of questioning. How are gender roles defined in this text? How, if at all, are they challenged? Are there conflicting definitions? How do these definitions operate within this text? How do they operate beyond the text, in the world in which we live?

Beyond the text . . . Gender studies has almost certainly been the critical school most closely allied with movements outside of literature and beyond the walls of the academy itself. In fact, gender has become one of the hottest political and social issues of the late twentieth century in America. The topic is not limited to such obvious causes as the gay/lesbian movement or the Equal Rights Amendment. Issues such as abortion, welfare, education, and, of course, the ubiquitous, if nebulous calls for "family values" are all riddled with assumptions about gender, assumptions that need at least to be recognized and understood. Gender studies undertake to provide us with the tools for asking some of the necessary questions.

FURTHER READING

Feminism:

De Lauretis, Teresa. "Upping the Anti [sic] in Feminist Theory." In *The Cultural Studies Reader*, edited by Simon During. New York: Routledge, 1993.

Showalter, Elaine, ed. *The New Feminist Criticism: Essays on Women, Literature, and Theory.* New York: Pantheon, 1985.

Showalter, Elaine. "Feminism and Literature." In *Literary Theory Today*, edited by Peter Collier and Helga Geyer-Ryan. Ithaca: Cornell University Press, 1990.

Voice of the Shuttle Web links on feminism: http://humanitas.ucsb.edu/shuttle/gender.html#women

Gender Studies:

Butler, Judith. *Gender Trouble: Feminism and the Subversion of Identity.* New York: Routledge, 1990.

Foucault, Michel. *The History of Sexuality. Vol. I, An Introduction.* Translated by Robert Hurley. New York: Vintage, 1980.

Voice of the Shuttle Web links on gender studies: http://humanitas.ucsb.edu/shuttle/gender.html

Gay/Lesbian Studies:

Abalone, Henry, et al., eds. *The Lesbian and Gay Studies Reader.* New York: Routledge, 1993.

Halperin, David. "Is There a History of Sexuality?" In *The Lesbian and Gay Studies Reader,* edited by Henry Abelove, M. Barale, and D. Halperin. New York: Routledge, 1993.

Sedgwick, Eve Kosofsky. *Epistemology of the Closet.* Berkeley: University of California Press, 1990.

Voice of the Shuttle Web links on gay/lesbian and queer studies: http://humanitas.ucsb.edu/shuttle/gender.html#queer

The Gendering of Point of View:

Mulvey, Laura. "Visual Pleasure and Narrative Cinema." In *Visual and Other Pleasures.* Bloomington: Indiana University Press, 1989.

6

THE IMPORTANCE OF CONTEXT

■■■

New Historicism and Cultural Studies

What does a grimace mean?

Let's say you are a beginning psychology student at a large state university, and you have volunteered to participate in an experiment. Heading for your first appointment, you wander into a large building on campus and begin to wend your way through the labyrinth of halls and offices. Following the directions you received, you find yourself in a deserted corridor leading to a glass panel that, in turn, looks upon a bright, sparsely furnished room. Seated in the center of the chamber, staring up toward you, is a young man with a tortured expression on his face. As you watch, his expression relaxes into one of mere anxious anticipation. Then, after a few moments, his hands suddenly clench the arms of his chair, his back arches, and his face wrenches into a grotesque contortion. As you press your face up to the glass, you realize that broad Velcro bands clamp his arms and legs in place, and that he is belted to the chair. Tendril-like wires climb above the collar of his shirt and become entwined as they loop above the floor, trailing off toward the wall.

What's going on?

The convulsion lasts only an instant before the body in front of you again collapses into relative, if anxious calm. As you watch, realizing that the subject on the other side of the glass cannot see you, the process repeats itself several times, the attacks coming at unpredictable intervals, but apparently increasing in intensity, for now the subject's screams—barely audible outside the room—accompany his contortions. Scanning the room you notice another glass panel on the wall to the left; apparently you are not the only witness to the event.

Working your way down a side corridor, you turn the corner and come to a heavy metal door. Through the panel of safety glass you see a young woman, dressed in a white lab coat, standing at a counter, jotting notes on a clipboard. From where you stand you see her from behind, and beyond her, through the observation panel, the young man in the room is clearly displayed. Finishing her notes, the woman reaches to the controls before her, giving a dial a small turn and pressing a red button; the subject is suddenly racked with pain. When he settles, she again records notes on her sheet. Checking her watch, she reaches for the dial again.

What's going on?

If this is some kind of experiment, it is surely inhuman. The torture before you has crossed a line, has exceeded what we can tolerate in the name of science. You enter the room to stop this clinical victimizer, to restrain her, or at least to grill her about what she is up to, but when you push open the door, you discover that she is not alone: an older man, also in a lab coat, is seated at a desk to the side. He is in the midst of giving her instructions, but upon your intrusion, he leaps to his feet, asking what you want, barking at you to get out, hollering that you are interrupting an experiment. You babble something about a person in pain, but are cowed by the violent gesticulations of the man, by the sharp gaze of his assistant.

Your mind reeling, you back out of the room, just fast enough to keep from having the door slammed in your face. After a moment's hesitation you realize that you can't just retreat, that you need to talk to someone, alert someone, and you start down the hall, where light shines from the next office door. Without stopping to knock, you turn the knob and burst in, only to surprise a small group of people seated before a glass panel looking into the office you just left. They look around at you and smile.

What's going on?

What's going on is that you have already participated in the experiment you volunteered for. Only the subject of the experiment wasn't the poor soul in the chair; it was *you*. The entire operation has been staged to measure "Good Samaritanism," to see how far a person will go to intervene on behalf of a fellow human. And your lack of resolve, your willingness to withdraw, didn't do much to honor the species.

The scenario may seem like a bit of a stretch, but in fact, mind-bending experiments like this are conducted with some frequency. The most famous of this sort are probably the Milgram experiments done at Yale in 1960, in which unwitting students were ordered to deliver what turned out to be fake electrical shocks to trained "victims" who feigned reactions to the jolts.[1] These experiments can reveal a great deal about human psychology (as it turned out, many students happily administered potentially "fatal" shocks when they were doing so at the orders of superiors), but for our purposes they demonstrate the importance of *context*.

For the grimace that caught our attention in the first place means little or nothing by itself. We may take it either as a sign of surprise or of pain, but

---

[1]Stanley Milgram, "Behavioral Study of Obedience," *Journal of Abnormal and Social Psychology* 67 (1963):371–378.

it is not until we study the circumstances, noting the straps and the electrical wiring, that we begin to suspect that something is seriously awry. As we expand our frame of reference, showing first the lab assistant, then the supposed director, our assessment of the situation undergoes constant revision. Then, when we discover that the "experimenters" themselves are under observation, and that this observation focused not on the ostensible victim, but on *us*, our initial interpretations are turned on their ear.[2]

What the scene means—and how we interpret it—depends largely (some might say entirely) on context. Thus, our understanding of a grimace requires, in part, that we be aware of the forces producing it: from a superficial recognition of the constriction of certain facial muscles, we deepen our view, coming to interpret the grimace first as an expression of pain, then as an imitation of this expression, and finally as nothing more than a *decoy*. Moreover, the anecdote I have fabricated and related above can mean different things when transplanted into different contexts, when appropriated into other discussions. Although the experiment itself is supposedly designed to tell us something about Good Samaritanism, in the context of the present discussion, I have recruited it to demonstrate the importance of contexts. Yet it could be pressed into service by others to show, for example, my poor understanding of contemporary psychology, or the way in which the Milgram experiments have been used to bolster arguments foreign to their original intent.

From a certain point of view, context is everything, and our reading of any action or utterance (or of anything else we have decided to look at as a text) requires that we understand the circumstance surrounding the object of study. It sounds commonsensical, doesn't it? And yet, the attention to context bucked a long trend in literary study, reaching back to early structuralism and American New Criticism, both of which narrowed their sights to focus on the text itself, as if it existed without ties to the world around it. Strangely enough, it was the poststructuralists who helped prepare the way for a reassessment of the role of context. When Jacques Derrida, one of the founders of deconstruction, argued that, "Nothing lies outside the text," he was breaking open the floodgates.[3] The poststructuralists began to deconstruct the opposition between "inside" and "outside," demonstrating that our knowledge of what seems to lie "outside" the text is often already implied in our understanding of the text itself.[4]

Here deconstruction does not undermine structuralism so much as supplement it. To take a simple example, the word *black* derives much of its

---

[2]A famous variation on this "grimace" is to be found in Clifford Geertz's essay, "Thick Description," in *The Interpretation of Cultures: Selected Essays* (New York: Basic Books, 1973). Therein Geertz plays with an idea introduced by Gilbert Ryle regarding the inscrutability of a *wink* (pp. 5–10). The lesson is that interpretation always depends on knowledge of a context; however, context is ever-expanding.

[3]"Il n'y a pas de hors-texte." Jacques Derrida, *Of Grammatology*, trans. G. C. Spivak (Baltimore: The Johns Hopkins University Press, 1976), 158.

[4]Jacques Derrida's most developed critique of the inside/outside opposition is to be found in *Truth in Painting* (trans. Geoff Bennington and Ian McLeod [Chicago: University of Chicago Press, 1987]), where, in part, he investigates the relationship between frames and their content.

meaning from its opposition to *white*, and from its association with such words as *dire* or *dark*. This much conforms to structuralist principles. Deconstruction, however, suggests that meanings are not limited to the associations and oppositions within a given text; instead, words and images carry tremendous baggage, bearing traces of all past usages and associations. So, the fact that *black*, depending on the context, may invoke notions of race (African American), or ethics (as in a "black" lie), or an interest in the macabre ("black" humor), or even personal associations based on homonymy or metonymy ("slack," "block," "cat," "coat and tie," etc.) means that *all* of these meanings (and more) can be present, in some measure, in any given usage. Thus, the word always harks back to its ancestral *blek* (Old Icelandic for "ink") *and* all its current resonances (official and unofficial), at the same time that its meaning is always provisional, subject to change by *future* usages.[5] Like Scrooge in Dickens's *Christmas Carol*, words are "haunted" by the spirits of all usages past and present, as well as those yet to come.

Most readers are not interested in taking things to such extremes. But the point remains that when we read something and profess to understand it, we have always already made a myriad of assumptions about context, most of which we make unconsciously.

Emphasis on context has become the bailiwick of a relative newcomer to the literary scene known as *cultural studies*. The label covers a broad array of activities—so broad, in fact, that it would seem to encompass almost everything: what, after all, is not cultural? Accordingly, cultural studies may focus on topics ranging from literary texts to historical events, from film to shopping malls.[6] In some cases, people seek to "read" events or objects using techniques borrowed from literary study. For those who fix their gaze on more traditional texts, the object often consists of disentangling the troubled relationship between books or films and the cultures that produce and consume them.

CIRCUMSTANTIAL EVIDENCE

If one is to glean meaning from context, *how much* context is enough? In the rather perverse psychological experiment presented at the beginning of this chapter, the unwitting visitor makes a series of discoveries: that of the scream-

---

[5]The indeterminate, ever-changing, and always provisional nature of meaning is the key to the Derridean notion of *differance* ("difference" spelled differently—with an "a"). The neologism is a play on words, indicating that meaning is (a) always established by a word's *difference* from other words (this idea goes back to Saussure's linguistics), (b) always indeterminate (different from any "fixed" meaning we may have in mind), and (c) always *provisional* (that is, always "deferred"), because the context is constantly evolving.

[6]Stephen Greenblatt's new historical works on Shakespeare (*Learning to Curse: Essays in Early Modern Culture* [New York: Routledge, 1990]); on Columbus (*Marvelous Possessions: The Wonder of the New World* [Chicago: University of Chicago Press, 1991]), and others, thus fits neatly into the cultural studies enterprise. On the "reading" of shopping malls, see Meaghan Morris, "Things To Do with Shopping Centres," in *The Cultural Studies Reader*, ed. S. During (New York: Routlege, 1993).

ing victim, that of the straps restraining him, that of the lab testing him, and that of the crowd observing it all. Each link in the chain provides crucial information for understanding the situation, and by the final step, the "victim" of the experiment has radically reoriented his thinking. Yet, had the process of discovery been interrupted or diverted at any point, he would likely have interpreted the scene differently. Likewise, nothing guarantees that his last discovery will be sufficient: as unlikely as it may appear, it is just possible that further investigation would reveal, for example, that the group of observers is itself under observation . . . and so on. Crucial evidence may always remain undiscovered.

The unsettling implication is that one can *never* be sure of adequately understanding contexts. Contextual interpretations are always provisional, always subject to modification should new information come to light. How, though, does one draw the line? Most readers implicitly measure context according to a kind of "ripple model." A stone dropped into a pool of water creates a field of concentric ripples, expanding asymptotically—that is, always diminishing in magnitude, but never (at least in theory) quite leveling out. The tacit assumption made in cultural readings is that contexts, too, diminish in importance as they become further removed (geographically, temporally, politically, economically, etc.) from the text under study. In the end, just how far into the field of cultural ripples one needs to travel in order to make sense of a reading is a judgment call, often based on little more than an intuition that further contextualization is more likely to reinforce than to undercut our reading.

The ripple model is a useful metaphor for visualizing the dynamic range of contextual influences; however, it is a poor image for modeling other aspects of the problem. When we drop a stone in a pond, the ripples are the direct *result* of impact, and cultural studies frowns on simplified notions of cause and effect. It is true that a literary work can make something of a splash (winning over the public, creating a scandal, or even generating a wave of hysteria, as in Orson Welles's original radio broadcast of *The War of the Worlds*)—but the text is also *already* an effect, bearing the imprint of its time. The entanglement of the text with its context, in which there exists an interaction between the two, has been referred to as a *negotiation*, an ongoing exchange of sorts between the work and the circumstances of its production and consumption.

This negotiation can be difficult, and yet fascinating, to fathom. Traditional literary study often supposed that a work provided a window onto another time or culture: *Great Expectations* gave us a sense of life in Victorian England; Sappho's (fl. c. 600 B.C.) poetry revealed something about the sentiments and experiences of women in Ancient Greece. Windows on the past? In part, yes; however, the problem remains that language is not as transparent as glass, and even if it were, the *position* of the window (that is, the point of view) would suffice to undermine the idea that any representation could be *entirely* neutral.

Nevertheless, texts can, and often do, chronicle elements of the culture of which they are a part: whenever a film or a book makes reference to actual places or events, it conforms to the model of the mirror, according to which texts reflect reality. However, because no reflection is objective, the representation of the world will always be more or less *distorted*; if texts are mirrors, then they are often carnival mirrors, stretching, shrinking, inverting the worlds they reflect. Investigating the nature, degree, and effects of this distortion lies at the heart of cultural studies.

Although the kinds of distortion that can occur are undoubtedly without number, we can point out a few of the major types:

Selection.   Even in a documentary film or a historical chronicle, representation cannot be exhaustive; the eye of the camera or that of the narrator can only capture a tiny sample of what actually occurs in a given scene, event, or context. This process of sampling—sanctioned in the sciences and social sciences as a relatively faithful and reliable method of representation—suggests that the part is representative of the whole.

Exaggeration.   Certain elements of a representation may be emphasized or de-emphasized (by a variety of techniques), thereby shaping our sense of their relative importance. When a camera takes an extraordinarily low-angle shot of a man, it exaggerates his height; when a passage from a murder mystery lingers over a detailed description of the corpse, it may well underscore a feeling of violence.

Fabrication.   A certain amount of exaggeration may pass unnoticed by many readers; however, when it goes too far, it smacks of the unreal. In science fiction or in tales of the supernatural (and in other genres involving fantasy), we may find things that do not exist, that no longer exist, or that cannot be known.

Allegory.   Distortions may be so complete that they no longer seem merely exaggerated or fantastic; they may look like something else altogether. George Orwell's *Animal Farm* may strike the uninitiated reader as a curious barnyard story, whereas others read it as telling a political tale of somewhat broader implications.

There are no pure instances of these forms of distortion. Texts of all sorts combine them, exaggerating here, selecting there; now fabricating, now allegorizing. Thus, such a fanciful form as fairy tales can show elements of realism (say, the existence of woods and grandmothers) while simultaneously exaggerating parts of that realism (say, the number and ferocity of wolves), and even allegorizing (as evidenced by the explicit and implicit morals). Nevertheless, although the various elements of distortion may exist in most texts, the mix will always be different, and this difference adds to the delightful particularity of everything we read. Texts written in the vein of realism tend to emphasize the mode of selection and downplay allegory; satires, on the other hand, often work in the mode of allegory, using a healthy dose of exaggeration. Other genres, such as propaganda, may weigh in with exaggeration and fabrication while trying to disguise them as "realistic" selections. The variety of permutations is limitless.

INVASIVE PROCEDURES

Have you seen the movie *Invasion of the Body Snatchers?* Real film buffs will respond by asking which one I mean, the 1956 version with Kevin McCarthy, or the 1978 remake with Donald Sutherland; film addicts—the kind who really need some help—will add to the list the most recent remake, which flopped resoundingly in 1993. We'll get to these remakes later; for now I want to concentrate on the "original" version of 1956. (I place quotes around original because the screenplay comes from an earlier serial, itself not without echoes of Robert Louis Stevenson's short story "The Body Snatcher" [1884],[7] made as a film of the same name in 1945, starring Boris Karloff and Bela Lugosi).

The 1956 version is a sci-fi thriller in the classic tradition of B movies. It takes place in California, and opens with a crazed man telling a wild story in a city hospital. "Well, it started . . . for me, it started last Thursday," he begins, as the scene dissolves into a flashback. We see our narrator, the suave Miles Bennell, M.D., as he returns to the town of Santa Mira after a business trip. As Sally, his secretary, drives him back to the office from the train station, he learns that things have been busy during his absence; a crowd of his regular patients have scheduled appointments, complaining of vague, bizarre symptoms. Yet when he returns to his office, the only person to show up is Becky Driscoll (Dana Wynter)—not a patient at all, but a former flame, returned home after the end of a bad marriage. Miles, ever gallant, picks up his courtship where it had left off years earlier, but he will soon be distracted by more pressing concerns: it appears that Becky is not the only newcomer to town. All around people are making outlandish accusations, asserting that their friends and relatives have been "changed," replaced by creatures that look and act like people, but aren't the real McCoy. Miles at first dismisses the allegations as the result of some strange mass hysteria; however, when things turn from eerie (inexplicable changes in personality occurring literally overnight in some of the minor characters) to downright weird (as when a half-formed adult body turns up in a friend's house), Miles and Becky, along with their friends Jack (King Donovan) and Teddy (Caroline Jones), take matters into their own hands. Yet the realization that strange beings are taking over the minds and bodies of the townspeople comes too late: the police, the town leaders, and even the phone operators succumbed early, and all contact to the outside world has been eliminated. When they are captured by the invaders, the foursome sweats it out, trying desperately to stay awake: they have learned that the enormous pods hidden everywhere grow into thinking, but unfeeling humanoids, cloning and killing their victims *while they are asleep.* One by one they surrender to the overpowering forces before them; Jack and Teddy make a break for it, but are caught. When Miles and Becky escape and head for the hills, hoping to reach the interstate highway, Becky falls asleep while hiding in a mine shaft; she wakes up feeling like a different person

---

[7]In *Robert Louis Stevenson: The Complete Shorter Fiction*, ed. Peter Stoneley (New York: Carroll and Graf, 1991), 325–340.

Figure 6.1   The foursome stares in horror as pods take shape in the greenhouse. Photo from *Invasion of the Body Snatchers. Courtesy of Republic Entertainment, Inc.*

and leads the charge on her horrified suitor. Only Miles, who makes it to the highway in the nick of time, escapes to the city, where he is placed under psychological evaluation, and we find ourselves in the city hospital of the beginning. They are about to lock him up for his own good when news comes in of a traffic accident involving a truck transporting the weirdest things: these strange, giant seed pods ... "Operator, get me the Federal Bureau of Investigation," an alarmed physician barks into the phone, "Yes, it's an emergency."

If you haven't seen *Invasion* before, check it out. The special effects have lost a little of their pizazz in the Spielberg age, but it is still a fine, hokey thriller.

What one is supposed to make of this movie, however, can be a tough question. Of course, the film may have a number of personal meanings—meanings we attach to it because of individual recollections or circumstantial connections. When I first saw the movie as a kid, for example, it was broadcast on New Year's Eve, one of the only nights I was allowed to stay up late. At the time I didn't appreciate the irony of the network schedulers: this film proclaiming the dangers of falling asleep showed on the one night I needed to stay awake. Of course, after watching *Invasion* at age ten or eleven, staying awake was no problem; pod people (and I had had doubts about my parents for some time) were everywhere.

Nothing is more common in reading than personal associations of this sort. When we devour a novel, view a film, or even follow a television series, our enjoyment of the text always involves our own individual makeup and experiences: a film set in our own hometown will resonate for us differently than for the general public; a novel dealing with sexual abuse will affect readers differently if they have suffered similar experiences themselves; a story we read as a kid may remain a favorite not because of any intrinsic qualities it has, but because of the happy (or troubled) past we associate with it. However, we can also expand this kind of reasoning. If individuals have reasons for the way in which they engage with material, then the same can be said of groups of individuals: these "communities"—be they small clusters of readers, entire segments of larger populations, or audiences on an international scale—share their cultural makeup to various degrees. This is to say that if *Star Trek*, for example, has succeeded in maintaining a tremendous following spanning more than two decades, the series plugs into the needs or desires of a large public. To the extent that the series does not enjoy *universal* appeal—Trekkies are a rare breed outside of North America (North Africa currently hosts no Trekkie conventions)—we can infer that the allure is *culturally* based: *Star Trek* is meaningful to Americans of a certain generation and a certain background in a way that it cannot be for others. This is why our reading of Shakespeare is today different from readings of the past, or, for that matter, why we might appreciate haiku poetry or Noh dance differently than, say, a Japanese audience, or even a Russian audience: the cultural background we bring to the text—our frame of reference—is different.

Looking at the cultural materials that appeal or flop at various historical moments in assorted places can teach us a good deal about the communities that produce and consume them; inversely, understanding aspects of a culture helps us get some purchase on how a text becomes meaningful in a given context. Why, one might wonder, was a film like *Invasion of the Body Snatchers* made in the United States at this particular moment? Why did it become so popular?

First, it helps to recognize that *Invasion* was not an entirely unanticipated movie; it participated in a kind of invasion itself, riding on a tide of science fiction and horror movies popular in the late forties and throughout the fifties. So the appeal of scenes of body snatching is part of a larger issue—namely, just why this whole genre of science fiction commanded such attention. Except in the eyes of the most paranoid of viewers, these films don't have much documentary value. Although it is true that *Invasion* provides some relatively transparent information about late-model cars from the fifties, and some entertaining background about contemporary notions of fashion, the bulk of the film revolves around a problem that *did not exist*, at least not in the form presented. Film critics with a cultural bent have pointed out how many sci-fi films played off the social and political anxieties experienced by Americans in the fifties.[8] Although this was a time of relative prosperity,

---

[8] See the delightful article by Peter Biskind, "Pods, Blobs, and Ideology in American Films of the Fifties," collected in *Invasion of the Body Snatchers*, ed. Al LaValley (New Brunswick and London: Rutgers University Press, 1989), 185–197.

moviegoers in the fifties were, after all, living in the aftermath of Hiroshima and Nagasaki; the Korean War had dragged on; the rhetoric of the Cold War maintained the illusion of an ever-present threat; and social and political pressures to conform to a particular model of citizenship were running high. The malaise underlying the *Leave it to Beaver* fifties provided fertile ground, from which sprang pods, giant ants, and a host of other Things. Films patched into different forms of paranoia differently, some showing how technology and scientists were leading America to destruction, some requiring civilian vigilantes to combat the creatures that the government could only dither about. All these films—as well as most thrillers today—capitalize on polarization, divvying up the world between Us (the good guys in the film and, by extension, the viewer), and Them (those robots, Martians, test-tube creatures, and mutants who seem hell-bent on picking Us off one by one).

Invasion of the Body Snatchers had its own particular allure, though. The fundamentally reassuring thing about the Creature from the Black Lagoon was that, even if he was about to devour you, you could hardly confuse him with somebody else. Giant lizards (*The Beast from 20,000 Fathoms*, 1953), oversized ants (*Them*, 1954), and gnats with human bodies (*The Fly*, 1958) were all easy to pick out in a crowd. Much of the eeriness of *Invasion* comes from the fact that, while They are diametrically opposed to Us, their difference is *invisible*. In fact, although the technical details are left a little sketchy in the film, it seems that We actually *become* Them: the pod people reproduce their victims in every measurable way—right down to fingerprints, voice, and even memories and habits, apparently draining it all from their victims. Only a slight change of attitude is detectable by the most sensitive of kin: Wilma complains to Miles that her Uncle Ira has lost that "special look"; little Jimmy screams that his mother is not his mother; entrepreneur Joe Grimaldi has let his vegetable stand slide because it was "too much work." Besides, who has time for vegetables when the fields are needed to grow more pods? When this new plant life takes over, it replicates its victims while filtering out all the "human" qualities; people will spend the rest of their lives "vegging out" in a big way. "Love. Desire. Ambition. Faith," one of the pod people drones on to Becky and Miles when they are captured, "Without them, life's so simple, believe me." Of human passion, only the pretense remains, the better to delude those not yet ensnared. "I don't want a world without love or grief or beauty," Becky says as she chokes back her tears, "I'd rather die." Too bad she falls asleep first.

Many readers may know that the situation in *Invasion*, in which wholesome Americans have been taken over by impassive look-alikes, has frequently been associated by film buffs with the Red Scare.[9] This allegorical interpretation has a lot going for it: these Godless pod people, devoid of emotion, not even entrepreneurial enough to run a miserable vegetable stand, infiltrate bit

---

[9]Peter Biskind, in the article cited above, links this film—and many others—to the Red Scare. See also Michael Paul Rogin's "Kiss Me Deadly: Communism, Motherhood, and the Cold War Movies," also in *Invasion of the Body Snatchers*, 201–205.

Figure 6.2 and Figure 6.3 The Beast from 20,000 fathoms compared to a pod person ("Danny Kauffman," center): which one looks more like *your* neighbor? *Invasion* plays on the notion of the indistinguishable "Other." *Courtesy of Republic Entertainment, Inc.*

by bit, often where we least expect them. Wasn't this the claim made by Joseph McCarthy (no relation to Kevin McCarthy in the film) in February of 1950, when he claimed that 205 Communists had infiltrated the State Department? Over the next few years McCarthy succeeded in persuading multitudes that the Commies were everywhere and that their numbers were growing. Red-blooded Americans were being transformed into poor, pink substitutes. Of course, as with Communists, so with mutant pods from interstellar space: they are all alike. What Becky fears in Santa Mira echoed the concerns of Americans more generally—namely that the expansionist Commies wanted everyone to be like them. And as Elmer Davis wrote so memorably in 1954, our "freedom can be retained only by the eternal vigilance which has always been its price." The call for vigilance—that eternal wakefulness—points out the dangers of letting down one's guard, of drifting off to sleep. *Invasion* takes the threat of this metaphorical slumber and makes it literal.

In this model, Miles Bennell plays the role of Joe McCarthy. The physician discovers the illness (at one point Miles muses that the problem may be mass hysteria, brought on by "worries about the world today") and sets out to cure it—or rather, to amputate the affected tissue. A lone crusader by the end of it all, Bennell escapes from Santa Mira with the truth; with the fervor characteristic of McCarthyism, he convinces the authorities that the attack he has described does not just exist within his mind. As they say, it's not paranoia if They really *are* out to get you.

Reading *Invasion* as an allegory of the Red Scare makes for a compelling case, one strong enough to withstand a couple of twists. First, the filmmaker, Don Siegel, flatly denied that the movie had any political motivations whatsoever. His concern was to design a good horror picture, and he apparently felt that his major innovation in the genre consisted of dedicating the bulk of his meager budget to securing acting talent; unlike others of that period, he refused to throw the whole sum at special effects. (It shows.)

What is the importance of Siegel's denial? In chapter 2 we saw how authorial intent *can* be immaterial to the way we read. That idea may apply here, at least in part. We want to be careful, though, not to invoke this structuralist principle simply to dodge the issue, or to silence the author altogether. After all, cultural studies generally place a premium on the material and social circumstances surrounding the text, so an author might reasonably be considered *part* of the context that informs our reading. On the other hand, if, as the poststructuralists suggest, "nothing lies outside the text," then we cannot look to the author for some kind of objective confirmation or invalidation of our reading. Rather, the author simply becomes part of the text itself, and we will need to "interpret" her or him accordingly. Suffice it to say that few directors in the mainstream B-movie line were thinking of their pictures as cultural commentaries; nevertheless, these pictures could hardly avoid being marked by the stresses of their time. Moreover, the popularity of *Invasion*, or that of any work of art, depends less on the conscious or unconscious intentions of the author than on the reception by the public. If nothing else, it would seem that *Invasion* piggybacked on paranoid dynamics that were still very fresh when the movie appeared. Assuming causality between McCarthyism and *Invasion* is not necessary. One does not necessarily depict the other; rather, one can view the Red Scare and the film as two related manifestations of a deeper malaise in 1950s America. In this light McCarthyism is not the "source" of the movie, but runs parallel to it: a cultural production in its own right, the Red Scare became a media event in 1954 (when 36 days of hearings were nationally televised), and one not devoid of theatricality. Neither *Invasion* nor the Scare limit themselves to reflecting the paranoia of their time; both undoubtedly exploit it and reinforce it.

The idea that *Invasion of the Body Snatchers* allegorizes a general susceptibility to paranoia rather than just a specific episode of political maneuvering is evidenced by the fact that the *Invasion*/Red Scare analogy is, in some respects, problematic. Yes, Miles Bennell *does* seem a bit like Joe McCarthy rescuing us from these all-cast-in-the-same-die Commies. However, the political stance of this reading (apparently pro-McCarthy) is also *entirely reversible*. Are the pod people—those unthinking, unfeeling beings who lack all but the semblance of individuality—really the emblem of Communism? Or, do they instead represent the growing number of witch-hunters, the ranks of McCarthy supporters who would require all Americans to conform to a particular model of citizenship? Is Miles the stand-in for McCarthy? Or is the honorable senator from Wisconsin really one of Them? Which of these two readings is the "right" one, and which is the interpretation that, like the pod people themselves, simply goes through the motions? In some sense, the question lies elsewhere. The fact that *both* readings, although entirely incompatible, are entirely convincing, lends the movie a wonderful ambiguity. It also underscores the idea that the allegorical reading reaches deeper, beyond the specifics of the Red Scare. The dynamics of the paranoid scenario are the same, regardless of which factions we plug into the model.

The plasticity of *Invasion*, which allows it to take on a number of meanings, helps to explain why it retains some of its punch even after the McCarthy years—even for ten-year-olds who have never heard of the Red Scare. Certain elements of the movie transcend the particular historical moment and will have special resonance in other situations, especially when paranoid feelings are running high. This means that the movie may attract individuals at any time, given their particular susceptibilities; it may appeal more broadly across the community when a sensitivity to the theme is generalized. This may account, in some measure, for the way in which some films or books enjoy recurring success, the tide of their popularity ebbing and flowing on a regular basis. It may also account for why some books and movies are rewritten, remade, as the years pass: elements of a story that once captivated an audience in the past can be "recycled," reworked, or "customized" for current circumstances.

Hollywood refers to these successive versions of films as remakes. Occasionally they focus on mediocre films that one remakes in hopes of finally "getting it right" (witness the long list of *Dr. Jekyll and Mister Hydes* gathering dust in film storage facilities); more often a remake capitalizes on a film with a proven track record. Asking Americans of the 1990s to connect with a picture shot forty years earlier goes against Hollywood principles, because mainstream cinema generally attempts to make the spectator's identification with a film as effortless as possible. Bridging the cultural gap between the nineties and the fifties—a gap made most visible by fashion, hairdos, gender roles, and the quality of special effects—requires "updating" a movie before it can be re-released as a new product. More important, though, these movies need to do more than dust off the superficial aspects of their presentation; they need to recast the way they connect with audiences emotionally if they are to be successful.[10]

Invasion enjoyed two such updates, the first in 1978, the second in 1993. The 1978 version (directed by Philip Kaufman), starring Donald Sutherland and Brooke Adams, remains faithful to the general plot structure of the original—although it eliminates the brief segments framing the flashback (where, in the 1956 version, we see Miles in the hospital). In 1978 Matthew Bennell is a government employee, a public health official, who whiles away his hours inspecting restaurants and food-service operations. Elizabeth Driscoll is his assistant. Together they watch as their friends and loved ones go over to the dark side. And, of course, they figure it all out too late. When Bennell tries to warn his superiors, they reply that they are aware of the problem, but ask him to maintain "extreme discretion" in order to avert a panic. As it turns out, the plea for discretion comes from a government already infiltrated. The Bennell/Driscoll love affair ends up repeating the scenario from 1956, and at the last minute Elizabeth turns into someone Matthew wouldn't exactly want to go to bed with. Unlike the Don Siegel movie, the 1978 Invasion ends with the pods winning out. In a drastic reversal of events, once the pod people have taken control by masquerading as humans, humans can only survive by acting like *them*. Thus, one of the good guys survives quite nicely in society, simply by pretending she is a pod when in public. When she spots Matthew on the street at the end of the film and assumes he is doing the same, how is she to tell? She can't—at least, not until he rolls his eyes and emits a monstrous screech, pointing her out for attack. In this conclusion, the film plays a trick on those who know the 1956 version and expect Matthew to remain the voice of humanity; instead, he has become one of Them. By relying on the viewer's knowledge of the earlier film, the 1978 Invasion uses the 1956 version as context.

The 1993 remake, entitled Body Snatchers: The Invasion Continues, twists things even more. Miles is still present, though now he is named Steve Mallone (played by Terry Kinney) and is an E.P.A. inspector, sent out to an army base to look into its handling of chemical waste. Moreover, he's a flake—so much so that when he is taken over by the pods we feel it is an improvement

---

[10]On the phenomena of remakes, see Thomas Leitch, "The Rhetoric of the Remake," *Literature Film Quarterly* 18, no. 3 (1990):138–148.

Figure 6.4   Matthew Bennell (Donald Sutherland) discovers some unsanitary conditions. *Courtesy of MGM-United Artists.*

in his quality of life. The real story focuses on his daughter, Marti (Gabrielle Anwar); as she comes to realize that this military base has been taken over and is propagating pods at an alarming rate, she attempts to escape it all with her boyfriend. Mom and Dad went to the other side long ago, and Marti doesn't seem to regret it much. Still, she and her boyfriend try to save her kid brother in the deal, but when even he turns out to be one of Them, they have to hurl the little creep from the helicopter. The film closes with the couple escaping and coming in for a landing at a military airport in Atlanta. It would seem reassuring, except that the personnel waving the chopper in for landing seem a little more deadpan than one might expect, even for the army. . . .

What is interesting in the remakes is the way in which the dynamics of paranoia are refashioned. In 1956 it is only the local government that has fallen to the pods, and when Dr. Hill barks "Get me the Federal Bureau of Investigation" into the phone, we know that order is to be restored. In 1978, the federal government is not only *not* the solution, it's the problem. In 1993 it is the military that has turned out to be the villain. What has happened is that the object of paranoid suspicion has gone full circle—moving from the Communist forces from which the American government and military must protect us, to the federal administration (which has always had certain pod-like qualities to it), to the very military that had insured our safety forty years earlier. The other major shift has to do with what we might call the social status of pods. Whereas the 1956 invasion is a grassroots movement, in 1978 the em-podding of people comes from the top down, socially speaking. Bennell comes across, early in the film, as a holdover from the sixties, an idealistic guy driving around town in a beater, performing a necessary if inglorious task. But what happens in the mid-seventies—not in the film, but in American society at large—is that the activists of the sixties settle down. As idealism yields to career decisions and family planning, the radicals become part of the establishment they had earlier attacked. Geoffrey, Elizabeth Driscoll's husband, who seemed to have difficulty expressing his feelings even before becoming a pod, is, of all things, a dentist—that cultural archetype for the drab. At the end of the film, when Bennell is walking podlike through the crowd, one is struck by what a civil, staid, three-piece-suit kind of society the pods have fostered.

In 1993, the elements become even trickier. Although the Bennell figure is an employee of the E.P.A.—an agency that probably *did* feel somewhat paranoid during the eighties—the role of government is far less impressive in the film than the role of *race*. From the lily white Santa Mira of the 1956 version, we find ourselves transported into the Deep South, where local demographics are further influenced by the racial effects of an all-volunteer army. From the opening scene, when a black man attacks Bennell's daughter, the film is already playing with our notions of otherness. The fact that this fellow turns out to be one who escaped from the pods, and who warns her of the danger, does little to change the initial force of racial difference, which will be picked up later in the film.

The fact is that the possible remakes of *Invasion* are innumerable, and one can imagine all sorts of ways for capitalizing on and fostering paranoia—especially paranoia of the invisible or indistinguishable other. Such is the fear generated, for example, by AIDS: the HIV-infected person looks and acts like

Figure 6.5 In 1993 the pod people are into army surplus; the infiltration also has racial implications. *Courtesy of Warner Brothers Studios.*

anybody else, yet is slowly being "taken over" by so many viral pods awaiting their opportunity for new territories, new hosts. Is it any wonder that the media in the nineties overflowed with stories about exotic epidemics, ranging from books like *The Hot Zone* (1994) to films along the lines of *Outbreak* (1995)? The calming words of the Center for Disease Control, apparently designed to help us keep threats in perspective and avoid mass hysteria, echo the government's plea, in the 1978 *Invasion*, for "extreme discretion." There are times when hysteria is ripe for the plucking.

CONTEXTUALIZING

Invasion of the Body Snatchers demonstrates less a dangerous onslaught of Communist thought than, for our purposes, another kind of incursion: that of textual analysis into cultural contexts. This way of reading (or of viewing or thinking) does not always come easily. We Americans have long held a preference for ahistorical perspectives, for looking at art objects—or, for that matter, rituals, politics, and even our daily activities—as if they exist in isolation. This somewhat cavalier attitude toward contexts is evident nearly everywhere: we can see it in the contexts we create, for it marks even the landscapes in which we live. When we drive through different parts of the country, the increasingly standardized architecture (be it the pole barns of rural America or the cost-efficient, cloned constructions of new housing developments) demonstrates a one-size-fits-all mentality. In commercial construction, the predominance of nationwide chains means that we will find nearly uniform building styles everywhere. The recent spread of gated communities bears witness to a desire to ignore some contexts—especially undesirable ones. At one extreme, this disregard for context leads to the "accidental tourist" syndrome; in Anne Tyler's novel of this name (*The Accidental Tourist*, 1985), the main character writes guide books for American business people who need to travel, but who seek accommodations abroad that reproduce home as closely as possible. That way, one can travel without changing frames of reference, without realizing that one has actually gone much of anywhere at all. At the other extreme, there are those who are infatuated with contexts, but with *simulated* ones. So, instead of bothering to figure out the contexts in which we live, we often create new ones—microcontexts that, although fabricated, give us what we think we want. For instance, in certain shopping malls we can, in the space of a few hours, shop in a Latin American *mercado*, practice scaling a mountain side, choose from among several cinematic experiences of other times and places, and dine in merry olde England, Nepal, or the O.K. Corral, depending on what we have a yen for. Nothing from these borrowed contexts need be authentic: they must only correspond to our preconceptions, reinforcing what we suspect these cultural differences ought to be. In the Nepalese restaurant, who is really going to know whether it's a Sherpa serving us or a high-school kid dressed in a costume of his own design? Choosing a restaurant when you are out shopping feels like taking the "It's a Small World" ride at Disneyland. Computer scientists champion their new wares in vain; virtual reality has been with us for some time.

One explanation for the resistance to contexts is, quite simply, that it takes a great deal of *time* to understand the cultural entanglements of any text or event, and time is the one commodity Americans have in short supply. Nevertheless, many students and professors are finding cultural studies, defined broadly, to be among the most exciting of approaches in the humanities. For one thing, it offers a kind of *grounding* to their study, demonstrating the "inter-connected-ness" of various disciplines and activities.

The implications of cultural studies for "casual" readers may initially seem less impressive, for who has the time to undertake an exhaustive study of an entire context? Who, for instance, when reading *Emma* (1816), can pull together a thorough understanding of Jane Austen's biography and couple it with an encyclopedic knowledge of the social, political, economic, and historical aspects of the early nineteenth century in England? Who can tease out the implications of the expanding British colonial Empire in this novel firmly entrenched in the placid countryside south of London? No casual reader can accomplish all this. In fact, no one at all can—not even Austen specialists in literature programs. However, this inability to master the context *exhaustively* derives not from any weakness or limitation on the part of the reader. The problem is not that exhausting the context requires too much time or too much energy; rather, the problem is that the context is, by its very nature, *inexhaustible*. There will always remain contextual rocks we have not turned over, leads we have not been able to follow. We might regard this situation with despair as a demonstration of the impossibility of ever grasping anything. Alternatively, we can find it liberating: with no imperative to know *everything*, we simply take things as far as we can. The working assumption in cultural studies is that knowing more about a context is generally more useful than knowing less. Still, we never, in any real sense, know *enough*. That means that cultural studies interpretations tend to be open-ended—always susceptible to revision as new information comes along.

The open-mindedness implied by such an approach is a lesson in itself. If we realize that all interpretations contain contextual elements—whether those elements allude to the culture from which a work has issued or to the culture of those interpreting it—we may well end up with a greater tolerance for conflicting interpretations in many walks of life. Indeed, a greater attention to context would help us deal with a whole host of issues, ranging from international politics and economics to gang activity in American cities. The same could be said for more local problems, where broadly disparate backgrounds foster misunderstanding between social classes and ethnic groups, or for that matter, in interpersonal relationships. Arguably, the more we expand the breadth of our understanding, the less we will be subject to the kind of paranoid undercurrents we detect in, say, *Invasion of the Body Snatchers*. This is *not* to suggest that, gee whiz, when you listen to them, the pod people really have a point; granting greater weight to contextual understanding does not mean that we end up *agreeing* with all points of view, along the lines of a value-neutral, "I'm okay, you're okay" style of reading. It simply broadens our understanding and informs the judgments we make.

FURTHER READING

New Historicism:

Greenblatt, Stephen. "Towards a Poetics of Culture." In *The Aims of Representation: Subject/Text/History*, edited by Murray Krieger. New York: Columbia University Press, 1987.

Greenblatt, Stephen. "Marvelous Possessions." In *Marvelous Possessions: The Wonder of the New World*. Chicago: University of Chicago Press, 1991.

Veeser, H. Aram, ed. *The New Historicism Reader*. New York: Routledge, 1994.

Cultural Studies:

Bakhtin, Mikhail. "Introduction." In *Rabelais and His World*, translated by Helene Iswolsky. Cambridge: Technology Press of the Massachusetts Institute of Technology, 1968.

Barthes, Roland. *Mythologies*, translated by Annette Lavers. New York: Hill and Wang. 1972.

During, Simon. *The Cultural Studies Reader*. New York: Routledge, 1993.

Morris, Meaghan. "Things to Do with Shopping Centers." In *The Cultural Studies Reader*, edited by Simon During. New York: Routledge, 1993.

Voice of the Shuttle Web links on cultural studies: http://humanitas.ucsb.edu/shuttle/cultural.html

Williams, Raymond. "Advertising: The Magic System." In *The Cultural Studies Reader*, edited by Simon During. New York: Routledge, 1993.

Postcolonial Studies:

Bhabha, Homi K. "The Other Question: Difference, Discrimination and the Discourse of Colonialism." In *Out There: Marginalization and Contemporary Culture*, edited by Russell Ferguson, M. Sever, T. Minh-La, and C. West. New York: New Museum of Contemporary Art, 1990.

Spivak, Gayatri Chakravorty. "Post-Structuralism, Marginality, Postcoloniality and Value." In *Literary Theory Today*, edited by Peter Collier. Ithaca: Cornell University Press, 1990.

Voice of the Shuttle Web links on postcolonial studies: http://humanitas.ucsb.edu/shuttle/cultural.html#postcolonial

7

CLICK HERE

■ ■ ■

Hypertext and Reader Response

The word *here* doesn't mean what it used to. Think about how words operate: they generally point to the things they represent. You might think of them as slightly more complicated versions of the printer's dingbat, called the "index," that adorned, throughout the nineteenth century, newspaper advertising. It looked like this.

Figure 7.1

In fact, that symbol pretty accurately depicts what is the first word for many a child, for whom pointing at desired objects while emitting inarticulate grunts suffices to send a parent scurrying. Similar to the index finger, a cluster of letters, such as b-o-o-k, doesn't actually *contain* any particular meaning; it simply refers us elsewhere, pointing to the idea of a book, or even (in a given sentence) to a particular bound object. The word *erase* does not actually exemplify what it means (thus effacing itself before our eyes); rather, it indicates some idea of an action that cannot be present within the word itself. The word *here* has served merely to point to the vicinity of the speaker. "Look over here," we might call to someone, beckoning them to turn in our direction. The phrase, "Set it down here" instructs one's interlocutor to place an object beside us.

These days, however, *here* has taken on a more literal meaning. When we read "click here," for example, on a page on the World Wide Web, *here* doesn't mean "hereabouts," "near to here," "close to the person uttering the word *here*"; it means *right* here, on the word *here* itself. The printer's dingbat is pointing, in some contortionist pose, at itself. This is just one of the ways in which the World Wide Web is making us rethink some of our assumptions about reading.

The Web is based on a single fundamental invention: hyperlinks. Anyone who has surfed or browsed a bit is familiar with them. The idea is extraordinarily simple: by clicking on a "hot" component (either text or graphic) of a Web page, the reader is suddenly transported from *here* (wherever that is) to *elsewhere*. The "elsewhere" that becomes one's destination may be a passage above or below the one left behind, or it may be an entirely new document. You may find yourself parachuted into a page on the same site or server, or the document conjured up could actually reside halfway around the world. Often you won't know the difference.

In spite of what you might think, the Web is not a new idea. It was first imagined in 1945 by a scientist named Vannevar Bush. In a fascinating article published in the *Atlantic Monthly*, Bush described a new system of information retrieval that, in spite of the fact that it was entirely mechanical (predating, as it did, the advent of personal computing by some three decades), already outlined the architecture for the Web. The invention he described, the "memex," was based on existing technologies, such as microfilm and punch-card selection, and worked with lights, cameras, and levers. The memex consisted of a workstation allowing for the photographing, storage, selection, and viewing of printed records. Its true innovation, however, lay in the way readers could *personalize* the indexing of records by associative links. Here is Bush's example:

> The owner of the memex, let us say, is interested in the origin and properties of the bow and arrow. Specifically he is studying why the short Turkish bow was apparently superior to the English long bow in the skirmishes of the Crusades. He has dozens of possibly pertinent books and articles in his memex. First he runs through an encyclopedia, finds an interesting but sketchy article, leaves it projected. Next, in a history, he finds another pertinent item, and ties the two together. Thus he goes, building a trail of many items. Occasionally he inserts a comment of his own, either linking it into the main trail or joining it by a side trail to a particular item. When it becomes evident that the elastic properties of available materials had a great deal to do with the bow, he branches off on a side trail which takes him through textbooks on elasticity and tables of physical constants. He inserts a page of longhand analysis of his own. Thus he builds a trail of his interest through the maze of materials available to him.
>
> And his trails do not fade.[1]

The linking of texts Bush describes is a radical innovation for a variety of reasons. First, it recognizes that ordinary ways of indexing and reading are the result of conventions that are at best inconsistent, and at worst incompatible, with the operation of the human mind. Standard indexing practices—including such time-tested systems as alphabetical order and the (somewhat more

---

[1] *Atlantic Monthly* 176 (July 1945), 107. George Landow discusses Bush and the memex in detail in *Hypertext* (Baltimore and London: The Johns Hopkins University Press, 1992), 14–18.

recent) Library of Congress cataloging numbers—exist because they partake of
an easily learnable system. The methods of human memory are too individual
and too transient for the management of immense amounts of data. For example, if I attempt to dredge up some memory of my year in the third grade,
knowing how to *spell* "third grade" is of very little use: my memories have not
been filed in alphabetical order. Instead, my route will be more circuitous and
idiosyncratic, moving, perhaps, from a visual memory of my classroom, to an
aural memory of the recitation of the Pledge of Allegiance, to an olfactory
memory of that kid who sat next to me. Moreover, the less often I think of
the third grade, the harder it will be for me to conjure up these memories:
trails linking memories to one another require thorough, frequent clearing
(what, in neuropsychology, is called *facilitation*[2]), without which trails become
overgrown, as it were, and sometimes lost forever: use 'em or lose 'em. Bush's
memex, then, is very different. Its trails "do not fade," and its links are both
idiosyncratic *and* communicable to others.

Associative thought is thus very different from the straitjacketed ways
we have of classifying knowledge. And it would appear incompatible even
with our conventions for reading, according to which we proceed inexorably
from the *beginning* of a text to its *end*, our path between these points consisting of a unidirectional line of printed characters that we follow, from left to
right, from top to bottom, in a prescribed fashion. Should we happen to personalize a text at all, we do so by the occasional insertion of marginal notes,
the placement of bookmarks, or by the nearly transgressive act of *not* reading
as prescribed, but rather by *browsing*.

The very vocabulary I have used here—browsing and bookmarks—should
set off some bells. The terms have become part and parcel of our reading of that
massive text we have come to know as the Web. Although the Web consists
only of electrons and we consult it by way of a screen, everything possible has
been done to package it in the reassuring metaphor of the physical book. Therefore we call the software used to surf the Web "browsers"; what we see are
"pages" (often with backgrounds imitating ruled paper or watermarks); forward
and back buttons allow us to turn the page (and in some programs the buttons
emit a slightly digital scrape, mimicking the crackle of newsprint); pages often
consulted we flag with "bookmarks"; some browsers even provide an index.

Comforting though the metaphor may be, it is all wrong: books are very
different from webs. As one thinker has categorized it, books adhere to the
model of the tree, whereas the Web is a *rhizome*.[3] The book is centered: from

---

[2]"Facilitation" is a term derived from Freud, who called it *Bahnung*, which refers to the blazing
of trails. It describes the way memory links become quicker, surer, with repetition. Although a hundred years old, the idea is still used in cognition studies.

[3]A rhizome, according to *Webster's* is "a somewhat elongated, usually horizontal subterranean
plant stem that . . . produces shoots above and roots below, and is distinguished from a true root in
possessing buds, nodes, and usually scalelike leaves." On hypertext as a rhizome, see Gilles Deleuze,
"Rhizome Versus Trees," in *The Deleuze Reader*, ed. Constantin Boundas (New York: Columbia University Press, 1993), 27–36. See also, Stuart Moulthrop, "Rhizome and Resistance: Hypertext and the
Dreams of a New Culture," in *Hyper/Text/Theory*, ed. George Landow (Baltimore: The Johns Hopkins
University Press, 1994), 299–319.

Figure 7.2 The tree of knowledge. This diagram, from the famous *Encyclopédie* of Diderot and D'Alembert (1772) shows the branching off of knowledge. The metaphor of the tree has dominated for hundreds of years. Even our vocabulary for books intimates the connection: in French and German the word for a sheet of paper (*feuille, Blatt*) also means "leaf"--much as when we speak of loose-*leaf* paper. *Photo courtesy of Julia Steinmetz.*

a single table of contents we can branch off in various directions, always knowing that the branches relate back to a single trunk. This image is ancient, and at least since the era when our ancestors used bark as primitive paper, the tree has served as the foundational metaphor for the dissemination of a centered, organic knowledge.

Rhizomes, however, are quite different: for one thing, they have no center. Take the example of crabgrass (it's not a very poetic image, but at least it's one most of us are familiar with). Crabgrass is difficult to eradicate because it grows *rhizomatically*, each new shoot potentially sending out its own roots and becoming a new organism, connected to others. The problem with crabgrass is not that neurotic groundskeepers have a hard time locating its central stem; it is rather that no such absolute center exists. In a tree, one can trace ramifications backwards—leaves leading to stems, stems to twigs, twigs to branches, and so on, all the way back to the trunk. In a patch of crabgrass, though, a shoot may lead to another shoot, or it may peter out, or it may join a labyrinth of other, related organisms. If the analogy holds, reading on the World Wide Web is rather different from most book reading: it tends to leap from text to text to text, no point of which is necessarily privileged as more central (key, important, meaningful) than any other. The act of reading becomes somewhat associative, and readings go in multiple directions, with readers forging paths, backing up, redirecting themselves, and, occasionally, arriving at dead ends.

The hopscotch style of reading we associate with the Web is not entirely new. Some readers will have dabbled in multidirectional reading with the *Create Your Own Adventure* series of books, or some similarly fashioned adolescent literature. In these adventures, at the bottom of each page, the reader is prompted to make choices about how the story should proceed. Want to go down the roller coaster that was just described? Go to page 44. Otherwise, go to page 102. Adolescents, however, don't have a corner on the market, for more high-minded literature has entertained similar ventures. In 1961 Raymond Queneau, the French novelist and poet, published a slender volume entitled *One Hundred Thousand Billion Poems*.[4] Fitting so many poems into such a small book might have required the extensive use of microfilm, but Queneau took a different route. The volume consists of ten principal pages, and although each page contains only ten lines of poetry (in French, ten lines can make a sonnet), the pages have been sliced up in such a way that each *line* of each sonnet is on a separate strip of paper, joined only at the binding. Because each line of poetry is a syntactic whole, the reader can lift the strips—joining, for example, line one from page one, line two from page ten, line three from page six, etc.—in order to make new, unanticipated (and metrically, syntactically, and grammatically correct) sonnets. The number of possible permutations—one hundred billion—comes close to justifying the book's title.

So, this kind of experimentation was already *possible* in print; digital text simply extends the capacities and begins to normalize what was originally an outlandish way of reading. More and more often now, fiction is appearing in digital form, and the use of hyperlinks is key to their operation. It would be awkward, in the context of this book, to "quote" a hypertext in its entirety: I can't very well include a hundred trillion poems, and "clicking" on a piece of paper doesn't generally get you very far. However, if you have worked with the Web at all, you should get the gist of what's going on here.

---

[4]*Cent Mille Milliards de Poèmes* (Paris: Gallimard, 1961). (Not available in English.)

Let's take a look at a famous example of hypertext literature. Michael Joyce's 1987 short story, "Afternoon" has been hailed as the "granddaddy of hyperfiction."[5] It comes on a floppy disk (unless you have downloaded it, or someone has sent it to you—illegally—as an e-mail attachment), and once you launch it on your computer, the adventure begins. At the opening screen, both similar and dissimilar to the cover of a book, you are invited to read the directions, most of which teach you how to operate a small navigational palette. By simple commands you can move forward and backward along whatever textual trail you blaze, answer yes or no questions, view available hyperlinks, add your own typed text, and print. Pressing the return key takes you to page one, the springboard for the rest of the story. From this single point of departure readers can create their own labyrinth, wending through 539 different blocks of text (some shorter, some longer), networked by some 950 textual links. Unlike links on a Web page, the links in Joyce's novel are invisible: certain words on each page are "hot"; most are not. However, double-clicking on any word will move the reading forward—either to the next default block of text, or to a specially linked one. The result is dizzying. Because Joyce could not know in what order various passages would be discovered by the reader— just as Queneau could not predict which strips of poetry a given reader might line up—the blocks of text must have a certain self-sufficiency about them: each one makes sense on its own. However, because the blocks can be linked only in certain ways, one's discovery is not altogether random (unlike the reading of Queneau's poems). What happens is that one's reading meanders,

Figure 7.3   The first screen from *Afternoon, A Story*, published by Eastgate Systems Inc. © 1987 Michael Joyce.

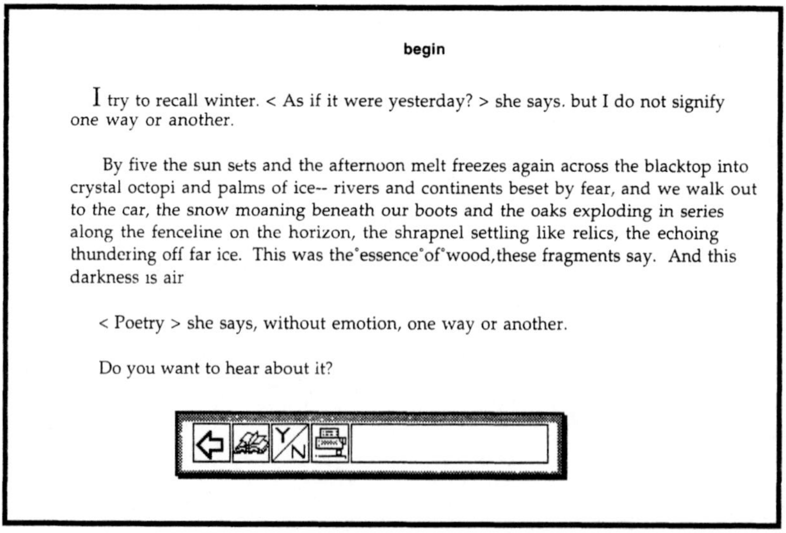

> **begin**
>
> I try to recall winter. < As if it were yesterday? > she says. but I do not signify one way or another.
>
> By five the sun sets and the afternoon melt freezes again across the blacktop into crystal octopi and palms of ice-- rivers and continents beset by fear, and we walk out to the car, the snow moaning beneath our boots and the oaks exploding in series along the fenceline on the horizon, the shrapnel settling like relics, the echoing thundering off far ice. This was the°essence°of°wood,these fragments say. And this darkness is air
>
> < Poetry > she says, without emotion, one way or another.
>
> Do you want to hear about it?

---

[5]Michael Joyce, *Afternoon, A Story* [Diskette] (Cambridge: Eastgate Press, 1987, 1992). "Grandaddy" status has been conferred on the work by Robert Coover, quoted on the "cover" (initial screen) of *Afternoon*.

and the textual trail often loops around and crosses over itself; you pass through text already read, only to emerge from it headed in a different direction. The *plot* of the story, which has to do with the narrator trying to determine whether his wife and son were killed in a car accident he spotted from afar earlier in the day, lurches forward and backward and frequently stalls. But the *thematic motifs*—ruminations on love, memory, sex—drift in and out quite musically, creating a sense of unpredictable inevitability.

"Afternoon" represents a slightly primitive version of what is currently occurring in the field of hyperfiction. In Joyce's later piece, "Twilight, A Symphony" (1994), a number of technical innovations have been introduced that have a sizeable impact on the reader's experience. First, the "text" has become a multimedia object, including color pictures, a variety of fonts, a movie, and sound. Second, as an attempt to alleviate the sense of disorientation experienced by readers in "Afternoon," "Twilight" provides a *map* of the textual sites visited during a reading session, although it is not certain that the map always provides a clearer sense of direction. Finally, a random feature has been added to the links, which means that after the first screen of the story, you are plunged into the text at a point different from many other readers. Although various readings of "Afternoon" drift slowly apart after the opening, in "Twilight" the trajectories arc in drastically different directions.

This kind of reading is *not* without its problems, and Michael Joyce is not even the most radical practitioner of hyperfiction. Other writers—or the programs they use—allow readers to add to the text, deleting or modifying what the author has created, sometimes even adding their own links. In this

Figure 7.4 A screen shot of the map from "Twilight"; the map can turn into a veritable jungle when one visits more "spaces" and activates more links. The ¶ labels indicate the titles of given spaces, the arrows indicate the direction of your reading, and the words floating between the spaces record the links used to move among the spaces. From *Twilight, A Symphony*, published by Eastgate Systems Inc. © 1995 Michael Joyce.

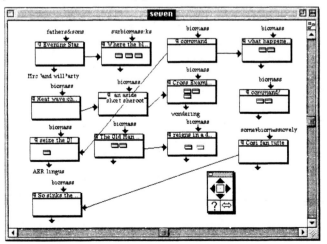

model, hyperfiction begins to resemble a miniature version of the World Wide Web, where anyone can post nearly anything, and where the "text" (and we could legitimately consider the Web nothing more than one monstrous, evolving text) is never complete, never centered. One of the largest problems, however, is that *no two people have ever read the same book.* Navigating through different passages in different order, readers have very little in the way of shared experiences, and this makes discussing a book difficult at best. Even if they started from the same paragraph, they will almost certainly *not* reach the same ending—largely because in most hyperfictions it is impossible to determine where the ending is, or if one even exists, or if there is more than one. You read a text like "Afternoon" for, well, an afternoon, and when you feel that the story has looped around sufficiently, when you have depleted its stock of surprises, you stop.

READERS

What does all this have to do with critical theory? After all, hyperfiction hardly represents a new *approach* to reading. Rather, it presents a new kind of textual object; it changes the *thing* being read. And even this idea is not altogether radical, for cultural studies has suggested that any cultural artifact can be "read" like a text, and film analysis has long shown the transferability of literary theory from one kind of text to another.

However, there are some important differences here, and they go so far as to challenge many fundamental assumptions we have about reading. Some of this is evident in the jargon tossed about in discussions regarding hyperfiction, where such odd words as *wreaders* and *riters* tug at our traditional distinction between those who *produce* texts and those who *consume* them. Playful though these terms are, their challenge is real. When we speak of "reading" a movie or a cultural event, we have not actually rethought, from the ground up, the role of the reader: in film analysis or cultural studies we continue to assume that the reader receives a preestablished object of study. In fact, a major area of critical study has precisely to do with the way *different* readers develop *different* interpretations of the *same* material. Hyperfiction, however, propels readers into more active roles, ones according to which they participate in the construction of the text, and the complexity of interpretation is increased by this added layer of involvement. The trend toward reader-constructed texts is significant for a couple of reasons. First, this trend will grow as hyperfiction becomes a more common medium. More important, just as the traditional conventions of readers guide their practice in this new medium (often making uninitiated readers extremely uncomfortable), the new habits and expectations readers develop with hyperfiction are likely to spill over into other, "older" kinds of reading as well. Thus the new media we confront today may well influence our interactions with the old.

The general study, however, of the reader's role in texts is far from new and has long been the domain of reader-response criticism. Reader response cannot properly be called a critical "school"; even more than most movements we have seen, it has evolved as a skein of loosely entwined strands of thought. Still, certain principles apply fairly broadly. As the name implies, reader-response criticism focuses less on the text as an autonomous object and more on the position and function of the reader. Interpretation, according to this model, results from the combination of these two entities—reader and text—and the multiplicity of possible interpretations springs largely from the diverse perspectives and backgrounds various readers bring to the text. Reading thus consists less of drawing meaning out of a text than it does of creating that meaning *intersubjectively*, by an interaction between reader and text.

But we have skipped rather too hastily over the definition of a key term—the deceptively simple idea of the reader. Where's the problem? A reader is a reader is a reader; you, if you are in the midst of this sentence, would appear to qualify as a reader. We might be tempted to describe a reader quite simply as "one who reads." But this isn't always true: not all readers read; nor do they necessarily exist. One can distinguish between *actual* readers and *implied* readers, for example.[6] You, holding this book in your hands, are an *actual* reader (at least, I hope you are); however, you are not necessarily the *implied* reader, the one I have in mind as I write these words. When we engage in an act of communication, we always have a recipient in mind[7]—we are always saying something to someone, even if we're talking only to ourselves. Novels, poems, films are no different in this respect, and they display a variety of deliberate or unconscious assumptions about the reader or viewer whom they address. Look at these three passages, and see how they cast their readers differently:

I. In the middle of the room there was a round table of Saint-Anne marble, bearing one of those white porcelaine tea sets, with half-visible streaks of gold, that you find everywhere today. The room, rather poorly floored, was paneled up to elbow height, the remainder of the walls being covered with wallpaper depicting the main scenes from *Telemachus*, the classical characters of which were colored.

II. On Friday, June 12th, I woke up at six o'clock and no wonder; it was my birthday. But of course I was not allowed to get up at that hour, so I had to control my curiosity until a quarter to seven. Then I could bear it no longer, and went to the dining room, where I received a warm welcome from Moortje.

Soon after seven I went to Mummy and Daddy and then to the sitting room to undo my presents. The first to greet me was *you*, possibly the nicest of all.

III. My dearest life,

If you do not impute to love, and to terror raised by love, the poor figure I made before you last night, you will not do me justice. I thought

---

[6]This is, in fact, the point of Wolfgang Iser's book, *The Implied Reader: Patterns of Communication in Prose Fiction from Bunyan to Beckett* (Baltimore: The Johns Hopkins University Press, 1974).

[7]See the discussion of Jakobson's model of communication in chapter 1.

I would try to the very last moment if, by complying with you in *every-thing*, I could prevail upon you to promise to be mine on Thursday next, since you refused me an earlier day. Could I have been so happy, you had not been hindered going to Hampstead, or wherever else you pleased. But when I could not prevail upon you to give me this assurance, what room had I (my demerit so great) to suppose that your going thither would not be to lose you for ever?

If nothing else is apparent, it should at least be clear that *none* of these voices is really directed at you or me personally. In each case, even though the pronoun *you* would appear to involve us, the text addresses a reader whom it assumes or postulates, from whom we probably differ considerably. The first passage, lifted from the opening pages of Honoré de Balzac's *Old Goriot* (1835)[8], clearly presupposes a reader who is familiar with the Paris of the early nineteen hundreds, who has good taste and a classical education—in short, the narrator assumes the reader is rather like *himself*. Referring to the decorative piece on the table as "one of those" tea sets implies a complicity with the reader ("one of those" being a phrase that "winks" at the reader, implying that the reader and the narrator are on the same wavelength). The fact that the tea set is of the sort that "you" find everywhere reinforces this impression. And the reference to Telemachus assumes that the reader knows (a) the story of Odysseus (Telemachus was his son), (b) the controversial play by this title, written by Fénélon in 1699, and (c) the way the image of Telemachus was appropriated by the *Philosophes* of prerevolutionary France (because some knowledge of the politics is important for understanding the novel). At the very least, the reference to Telemachus, a figure fashionable some fifty or sixty years earlier, in a novel taking place in the early 1830s would signal to the intended reader how *old* the wallpaper is, and the way the narrator condemns the squalor and bad taste of this boarding house sitting room suggests that he is speaking to someone who shares his social class and education.

The second passage above addresses us even more directly: "The first to greet me was *you*, possibly the nicest of all." It comes off as quite a compliment, except that we know the narrator can't really be talking to *us*. Besides, the preceding sentence ("I went . . . to the sitting room to undo my presents") indicates that, at least syntactically, the "you" referred to is a *present*, and one that is probably not a human being. In fact, the lines are the opening from the diary of Anne Frank (*Diary of a Young Girl*, 1952)[9], and the "you" referred to is the diary itself: you, the diary, were the nicest present of all. To whom is Anne Frank writing? To the paper before her? To herself? And to *which* self?—her present self, or the person she anticipated becoming years later, who would, she might (mistakenly) have hoped, look back at the pages written during her youth? In her second entry she confesses that the diary is to serve

---

[8]From Balzac's *Père Goriot* (translated as *Old Goriot*) (Paris: Gallimard-Folio, 1971), 26. My translation.

[9]*Anne Frank: The Diary of a Young Girl*, trans. B. M. Mooyaart-Doubleday (Garden City, N.Y.: Doubleday, 1952), 11.

the role of a friend and confident, and she constructs this ideal reader quite explicitly, even giving it a name: for the next two years every entry in the diary begins with "Dear Kitty."

The third passage is at least as densely packed. Opening with "My dearest life," it immediately identifies itself as a letter; soon after, we can classify it as a love letter, and eventually as a love letter in which the writer begs forgiveness. Although we know that we are not the intended audience of this missive, it would appear relatively unproblematic to characterize the recipient: a beloved person, probably a woman, perhaps a fiancée, who has rebuffed the writer. However, these lines are drawn from Samuel Richardson's epistolary novel, _Clarissa_ (1747)[10], and the letter is penned by the conniving Lovelace, who is attempting to seduce the naïve heroine in a most calculating manner. Although Clarissa, who is the prey he pursues and the woman to whom the letter is addressed, does correspond to the portrait we have sketched, she is not the _only_ intended reader: Lovelace writes simultaneously for his friend and correspondent, Mr. John Belford, to whom he sends copies of his letters to Clarissa, for the former's amusement. The way in which one's intended reader affects what and how one writes is best evidenced by the difference between Lovelace's letters to Clarissa and Belford. The tone is, in the first instance, florid, generous, and simpering; in the second, brash and self-centered. And beyond both of these readers _within_ the novel, there lies the implied readership Richardson aimed for _outside_ it, in eighteenth-century England, which is different yet again.

So, one kind of question we can ask about readers has to do with how the ideal or implied reader has been constructed. Another has to do with how _actual_ readers respond to texts, or how these readers bridge the gap between themselves and their ideal counterparts.

Actual readers present a host of problems. First, they are much less predictable than ideal ones. A narrator has a fair idea of what the ideal reader is up to because, well, she has been creating that reader all along. Actual readers, however, are rarely content simply to play the role that a narrator has prescribed for them. In fact, actual readers _use_ stories in a variety of unintended ways. If, for example, I use a copy of _Waiting for Godot_ to wedge the foot of a wobbly table, I have probably not fulfilled the role of the ideal reader. Or take the more literary example of the passage below, which has been used for rather curious ends. Some readers will recognize the sentence right away, although they may be confused about its provenance. Those readers will be all the more perplexed when they learn that the line comes from a book they may never have read, Richard Henry Dana's _Two Years Before the Mast_ (1840), a tale of a young man's adventures on the open seas, and commonly acknowledged to have served as a source for Melville's _Moby Dick_ (1851):

> As she was to get under way early in the afternoon, I made my appearance on board at twelve o'clock, in full sea rig, with my chest, containing an outfit for a two or three years' voyage, which I had undertaken from a determi-

---

[10]Samuel Richardson, _Clarissa_, ed. Angus Ross (New York: Viking Penguin, 1985), 953.

nation to cure, if possible, by an entire change of life, and by a long absence from books, with plenty of hard work, plain food, and open air, a weakness of the eyes, which had obliged me to give up my studies, and which no medical aid seemed likely to remedy.[11]

The potential confusion arises from the fact that readers who recognize the quote probably do *not* recognize its source: the line has been used for years in eye charts at optometrist's offices. When you stand twenty paces back, one hand cupped over an eye, reading the progressively smaller letters of that sentence, you can be pretty sure that Dana's text ensured his immortality for all the wrong reasons.

Less radically, if I read the opening chapters of *Moby Dick* as a primer to sea mammal anatomy, or as a way to get a sense of Nantucket for my vacation planning, I have engaged the text on *my* terms rather than on its own.

These examples are extreme, but they differ only in degree from the personalization we always practice in reading. Who has not had the experience of putting a book down in utter boredom, only to pick it up some years later and find it fascinating? (Unfortunately, the reverse also occurs, and books that marked our early years may disappoint when we return to them.) In these instances, the *book* hasn't changed; *you* have. And the reasons for which you suddenly connect with (or disconnect from) your reading can be multiple: perhaps you have matured, or have had experiences similar to those described, or have become sensitive to a particular style, or have now visited the country in which the story takes place. In short, books become meaningful for different people at different times, and for different reasons.

Now, even though our *personal* connection with a text is what makes reading electrifying, it is a difficult topic to generalize about. If I undertook an investigation of why Toni Morrison's *Beloved* (1987) moved me deeply, I could well end up with an analysis that is at least half autobiographical, one evoking my own family history, my sense of the operation of memory, my personal experience of guilt. Although *I* might find such an exercise revealing and rewarding, an analysis this personal may not be meaningful for anyone else. In an entertaining essay on interpretation, Umberto Eco asks what we would think if "Jack the Ripper told us that he did what he did on the grounds of his interpretation of the Gospel according to Saint Luke,"[12] and although Eco seems inclined to disallow the Ripper's reading, it would be difficult to assert that such an interpretation is "wrong," at least from the point of view of some reader-response theory; in fact, "rightness" and "wrongness" may cease to apply to our assessment of interpretations. Instead, reading the Bible as a manual on the evisceration of young women might more accurately be described as a *dangerous* interpretation, and one that most readers would not connect

---

[11]Richard Henry Dana, Jr., *Two Years Before the Mast* (New York: Penguin, Signet Classic, 1964), 9.

[12]Umberto Eco, "Interpretation and History," in *Interpretation and Overinterpretation* (Cambridge: Cambridge University Press, 1992), 24.

with or find *satisfying*. Interpretations become useful or significant to the extent readers feel satisfied by them.

To avoid the utter relativism that highly idiosyncratic readings could lead to (and Jack the Ripper has no corner on the market of these readings), critics interested in real readers tend to focus on *communities* of readers, where "community" designates groups of readers with shared experiences or backgrounds. This does not provide a firewall against bizarre interpretation, because sometimes whole communities do indulge in fantastic acts of reading—witness the mass suicide of thirty-nine Heaven's Gate members in 1997 when they read the passing of the Hale-Bopp comet as a second coming. But the idea is that interpretations become increasingly significant when they are shared, and we can learn something about how different *kinds* of readers interact with the texts they read. Do women read Jane Austen's *Persuasion* differently from men? How does Maya Angelou's poetry speak differently to black and white readers? Do urban and suburban youth listen to rap music with the same ear? Does Gabriel Garcia Marquez's *One Hundred Years of Solitude* read the same for those living north of the border?

REWRITING THE ROLE OF READERS

The advent of hyperfiction complicates the role of readers considerably, and reader-response criticism stands a good chance of being able to elucidate the changes. For one thing, we are no longer talking only about how different readers *respond* to a text, but also about how they help to *re-create* it. This does complicate matters further, for it will be hard to talk about a community of readers when the text that forms part of the basis for this community is different for every individual. But a focus on the reader becomes crucial to understanding our new media. For example, an individual reader's decisions could be *recorded* as he clicks through hypertext (remember Vannevar Bush: "The trails do not fade"), so that one could study particular readings, learning how individuals create their idiosyncratic interpretations of texts.

Not everything is rosy, however. Champions of hyperfiction have touted the way stories like "Afternoon" fulfill the promise of much poststructuralist thought. The idea that meaning is multiple, even indeterminate, appears for some critics to find its realization in the way a given word may be hyperlinked to a vast number of different textual spaces. Or, one might argue that the reader is empowered by her handling of the computer mouse: suddenly *she* is in the driving seat, and the author has done little more than equip her with a textual driver's license. But not all readers feel liberated by hypertext. Although it is true that the viewer of a hyperfiction makes choices (do I click here, there, or not at all?), the results of those choices are largely *predetermined*. Moreover, it is difficult or impossible *not* to follow the links provided: in most applications, one cannot browse through or skim a hypertext the way one can a bound volume, making the links and jumps wherever one wishes.

And, although one can argue that in hyperfiction the network of hyperlinks is associative, and thus more akin to the structure of the imagination, it is not *my* imagination that is reproduced: the links I follow will always reflect the logic of the *author's* associations, and the possibilities he has created. As a result, many readers find hyperfictions actually more controlling or manipulative than traditional fiction. This manipulation may be on the part of the author—who has always engineered the possibility of the associations you make—or on the part of the computer itself, whose random function provides you with arbitrary, potentially meaningless associations. In cases in which the reader does not know *who* provides the links—man or machine—the frustration can be great. But *all* narrative is manipulative, and many readers find this manipulation playful and intriguing; indeed, anyone who likes to "lose" him or herself in a book, who likes narrators or poets who play tricks on their readers, is a devotee of manipulation.

Manipulation is not a newcomer to literary studies. It is, in fact, the quintessence of rhetoric, and the art of persuasion (as rhetoric is often defined) consists of nothing less than the studied manipulation of an audience. Hyperfiction manipulates us in new and interesting ways, and the mapping of these manipulations will require a reconsideration, and perhaps even a serious revision, of our understanding of rhetorical devices. In traditional rhetoric, we know many of the gambits played by speech. Metaphor, metonymy, synecdoche, anaphora, chiasmus—the extensive list of terms identifies the various tricks language can pull on readers or listeners. It is easy enough to analyze some of the metaphors at the basis of the digital world around us (the abundance of dog icons and butlerlike "assistants," for example, speak volumes about the faithful servitude we expect from personal computers), but it is less clear how we describe (much less understand) phenomena for which none of our existing definitions seem sufficient. What happens, for instance, when one passage of a text points (via hyperlinks) simultaneously to several others, thereby defying the unilinear tradition of reading; what are the effects when a given word on the screen, prompted by a mouse click, suddenly *morphs* into an animated picture, replete with a sound file?

In short, hypertexts portend a general blurring of traditional categories, which is something reader-response criticism has been particularly sensitive to over the years. At a technical level, this blurring becomes possible because we suddenly have a common denominator among different modes of expression: music, photography, text, sensation—all these can be reduced to bits (not "pieces," but rather the minimal unit of digital information), and we can mix different kinds of bits more or less indiscriminately. Words and images meld, turning into icons, or into objects for which we have no name. In a kind of digital synesthesia, images, sounds, and even tactile sensation (by way of virtual reality) become interlinked. The blurring of the distinctions between readers and writers, and between reality and virtual reality, points in a somewhat fuzzy way to the direction we are headed.

FURTHER READING

Examples of Digital Texts:

Anderson, Laurie. *Puppet Motel* [CD-ROM]. New York: Voyager, 1995.

Joyce, Michael. *Afternoon, A Story* [Diskette]. Cambridge: Eastgate Press, 1987, 1992.

Joyce, Michael. *Twilight, A Symphony* [CD-ROM]. Cambridge: Eastgate Press, 1995.

Joyce, Michael. "Twelve Blue." Available on the World Wide Web at: http://www.eastgate.com/TwelveBlue/Welcome.html

See also this listing of hyperfictions available over the Web:

Shumate, Michael. "Hyperizons." Available on the World Wide Web at: http://www.duke.edu/~mshumate/original.html

About Digital Texts:

Bolter, Jay. *Writing Space: The Computer, Hypertext, and the History of Writing*. Hillsdale, N.J.: Erlbaum, 1991.

Brown University. "Hypertext at Brown." Available on the World Wide Web at: http://www.stg.brown.edu/projects/hypertext/hypertext_ov.html

Bush, Vannevar. "As We May Think." Originally published in *The Atlantic Monthly* 176 (July 1945). Available on the World Wide Web at: http://www.isg.sfu.ca/~duchier/misc/vbush/

Landow, George. *Hypertext: The Convergence of Contemporary Critical Theory and Technology*. Baltimore: The Johns Hopkins University Press, 1992.

Landow, George, ed. *Hyper/Text/Theory*. Baltimore: The Johns Hopkins University Press, 1994.

Landow, George. *Hypertext 2.0*. Baltimore: The Johns Hopkins University Press, 1997.

Voice of the Shuttle Web links on cyber culture: http://humanitas.ucsb.edu/shuttle/cyber.html

Voice of the Shuttle Web links on hypertext: http://humanitas.ucsb.edu/shuttle/techwrit.html#hypertext

About Reader-Response Theory:

Fish, Stanley. "Is There a Text in This Class?" In *Is There a Text in This Class?: The Authority of Interpretive Communities*. Cambridge: Harvard University Press, 1980.

Flynn, Elizabeth, and P. Schweickart, eds. *Gender and Reading: Essays on Readers, Texts, and Contexts*. Baltimore: The Johns Hopkins University Press, 1986.

Lye, John. "Reader-Response: Various Positions." Available on the World Wide Web at: http://www.brocku.ca/english/courses/4F70/rr.html

Prince, Gerald. "Introduction to the Study of the Narratee." In *Reader-Response Criticism: From Formalism to Post-Structuralism*, edited by Jane P. Tompkins. Baltimore: The Johns Hopkins University Press, 1980.

Steig, Michael. *Stories of Reading: Subjectivity and Literary Understanding*. Baltimore: The Johns Hopkins University Press, 1989.

Tompkins, Jane, ed. *Reader-Response Criticism: From Formalism to Post-Structuralism*. Baltimore: The Johns Hopkins University Press, 1980.

8

FOR ECLECTICISM

■ ■ ■

The Role of Theory

When we learn our native tongue, our language is always sufficient to describe our universe; the semiarticulate "duh!" of infants, often accompanied by grimaces or the pointing of fingers, adequately conveys a host of meanings, ranging from "give me that toy" to "look at that cat" to "I want a cookie." As our vocabulary grows we may become more precise, but our language is never more complete.

The same could be said of methods of reading. I learned my first approach to literature in the sixth grade when Mrs. Evans explained that all books fell into one of five thematic categories: Man versus Himself, Man versus Man, Man versus Society, Man versus Monster, Man versus Nature. These themes—however politically incorrect they may appear today—were remarkably sufficient. Mrs. Evans was right; everything *did* fit, even though some of our readings cheated a bit and actually contained more than one of the themes. Nevertheless, by a sort of readerly triage I managed to sort books into types, and I discovered that my level of interest often depended on the category in which a given title figured. (Man versus Monster exerted a powerful draw for a few years.) Of course, after a while the Five Themes Method became rather mechanical, and by the seventh grade we were pushing the envelope a bit further. Each year brought further refinements; soon it became apparent that theme was just one of many aspects to look at in literature, and fiction can speak in many tongues.

The twists and turns of the approaches we have looked at in this volume are intended to expand our vocabulary. But it is not my intent to replace the Five Themes Method with some kind of Five Approaches Theory. For starters, I would not want to suggest that the approaches we have looked at here—primarily structuralism, poststructuralism, psychoanalysis, gender studies, reader response, and cultural studies—are the *only* approaches thriving in the humanities. Moreover, I would not want to give the impression that these approaches are altogether distinct. Although they often express different impulses on the part of readers, they are joined by more than they are separated. Structuralism supplies the underpinning for deconstruction, gender studies and cultural studies are riddled with poststructuralist thought, and psychoanalysis rings hollow without notions of structure and gender. Moreover, all these methods rely heavily on the process of close reading, in which one pays particular attention to textual detail. From one perspective, this methodological overlap among approaches can seem confusing, even dizzying. However, what it really means is that one need not fret unduly about boundaries between schools; no one has to pledge fealty to a particular approach. Indeed, most readers are interested in a variety of topics, and it would only make sense for a certain diversity or eclecticism to develop in their method of reading.

Still, many readers are drawn more to one approach than to others. This does not necessarily mean that structuralism, for example, is "less worthy" than gender studies, or gender studies "less important" than psychoanalysis. Different approaches ask different sets of questions; some questions intrigue us, individually, more than others. And some may prove more or less intriguing depending on the text under study. What this means is not that some texts *must* be read according to a certain approach—that "The Fat Kid," for example, is fundamentally a psychoanalytic story, or that "The Purloined Letter" begs to be deconstructed. If critical approaches are analogous to points of view, to the various angles from which we can look at something, then any approach can be employed to shed light on any text, always illuminating different angles or different aspects of it. *Casablanca*, for example, is just as susceptible to Mrs. Evans's Five Themes Method as it is to structuralism, or to gender studies, or to cultural studies. Of course, certain approaches may have more or less material to work with in a given text, and they may yield more or less interesting results. In short, what makes sparks fly, or lightning strike, is not so much a given text *or* a particular critical approach; more often than not, it is the interaction between the two.

Strict adherence to a theoretical school is neither required nor, probably, desirable. Methods are tools, and one can piece together many of the approaches and questions sketched in the preceding chapters in interesting, coherent ways. But demonstrating mastery of a theory or brandishing the jargon of an approach accomplishes little of interest. So, critical theory remains useful only insofar as it helps to generate subtle, elegant analyses. A critical approach may help you to *arrive* at these analyses, but writers who insist too heavily on a technical terminology, or who apply a method too mechanically, risk eviscerating the texts they are dealing with; moreover, they can alienate their audience. It has been said that it is better to *imply* theory than to *apply* it, and that is not bad advice.

Moreover, approaching texts *methodologically* sounds like a rather dull enterprise. Theory can enrich reading, but it should not be thought of as a road map through the dedalus of fiction, or as a mill that grinds text into meaning. How, then, to proceed? The poet Charles Baudelaire (1821–1867), describing how he soaked up the experience of nineteenth-century Paris, celebrated the virtues of what he called *flânerie*. Often weakly translated as "strolling," *flânerie* suggested to Baudelaire a kind of "attentive wandering" within the city. He portrayed the poet as being constantly on the prowl in the metropolis. Walking with a *studied aimlessness*, he kept an eye out for the surprises the city could provide at every turn. *Flânerie* is, in a sense, the best kind of close reading—one that is attentive without having a destination, one in which the reader is constantly on the prowl. And theory has the potential to heighten one's senses.

THE PLACE OF THEORY

This book sprang from a paradox. Literary study, which was once the foundation of a traditional education, has, at this turn of the century, been pushed toward the margins, decried by some as irrelevant, demonized by others as subversive and dangerous. The scapegoat of this fall from public grace is the same force that has reinvigorated the humanities: theory.

Why is this? Detractors have made their case repeatedly, increasing the volume and intensity of their rhetoric with each attack, rather like an American tourist trying repeatedly to order a coffee from a French waiter. In 1987 an influential book by Allan Bloom, then Professor of Social Thought at the University of Chicago, hit the shelves. In *The Closing of the American Mind* Bloom lamented the degeneration of the American university system, reserving special distress signals for the humanities, the "submerged old Atlantis," where "there is no semblance of order, no serious account of what should and should not belong, or of what its disciplines are trying to accomplish or how."[1] In the central ring of this inferno Bloom places literary study, where "There are endless debates about methods—among Freudian criticism, Marxist criticism, New Criticism, Structuralism and Deconstructionism, and many others, all of which have in common the premise that what Plato or Dante had to say about reality is unimportant."[2] He decries current literary study as a kind of mumbo-jumbo, and he calls for a return to basics, to what he calls "Great Books," comprising a high culture to be shared by all. Bloom's own book partakes of a trend of "criticism-bashing," of books that express a nostalgic longing for a golden age of reading before the current decline. Shelved near Bloom is E. D. Hirsh's volume on *Cultural Literacy* (advocating a universal curriculum in the humanities)[3]; also nearby is David Lehman's *Signs of the Times* (lambasting the particularly "reprehensible" school of deconstruction).[4] Among

---

[1]Allan Bloom, *The Closing of the American Mind: How Higher Education Has Failed Democracy and Impoverished the Souls of Today's Students* (New York: Simon & Schuster, 1987), 371.

[2]*The Closing of the American Mind*, 375.

[3]E. D. Hirsch, *Cultural Literacy: What Every American Needs to Know* (Boston: Houghton Mifflin, 1987).

[4]David Lehman, *Signs of the Times: Deconstruction and the Fall of Paul de Man* (New York: Poseidon Press, 1991).

the latest assaults on the state of the Arts and Humanities is *Telling the Truth*, a volume by Lynne Cheney, the director of the National Endowment for the Arts during the Bush administration, the subtitle of which (*Why Our Culture and Our Country Have Stopped Making Sense—and What We Can Do About It*) pretty clearly articulates Cheney's distaste for the "scandal" of current liberal arts education.[5] In her book Cheney rallies anecdote after anecdote to demonstrate how "politicized" the study of the humanities has become, and she reserves special scorn for what she labels "postmodern" thinkers—figures often associated with current trends in literary and cultural analysis.

If the public has a hard time understanding what one does in the humanities, and if humanists themselves often have difficulty articulating what it is that they do, it is largely because programs in literature, film, history, women's studies, and the like, when compared to the sciences and social sciences, have an extremely high tolerance for ambiguity. Consequently, it's hard to give short, unequivocal answers about much of anything. What does a given book mean? Well, if we look at it *this* way, it could mean *this*; if we read it *that* way, it could mean *that*. What is the significance of such and such historical event? It might be X, or Y, or Z—or many other letters of the alphabet, depending on how we approach it. Uncertainty (nothing is sure) and multiplicity (many answers may be "right" at the same time) are two conditions of operation within the humanities. Although there is a good deal of concern for *evidence* in literary interpretation, nothing approaches the status of scientific or mathematical *proof*; nor is there any disciplinary consensus about what constitutes an appropriate object of study, or about the superiority of a specific method. This flexibility, even plasticity of the humanities can often smack of aimlessness to the outside observer. Thus what is arguably the greatest strength of such study can come across as a disciplinary Achilles' heel.

One can easily see how confusion over these apparently formless studies could lead to a yearning for a return to the basics. These "basics," by dint of the word itself, conjure up notions of sturdiness, solidity, and they appeal because they correspond, often enough, to what we learned in school ourselves. They are known quantities. In literature, in particular, one can understand the allure of a collection of Great Works by Celebrated Authors. Traditional reading lists have often reflected our hunch that certain poems, novels, plays, or even films, have transcended their particular historical moment and cultural situation, and thus hold universal appeal. In the past, although we may have squabbled about the relative merits of authors, and although we occasionally suspected that someone had been inducted into the literary hall of fame by mistake (perhaps we could never stomach Hawthorne, or we found the Russians long-winded), there existed broad consensus about what should be read, and how.

---

[5]Lynne Cheney, *Telling the Truth: Why Our Culture and Our Country Have Stopped Making Sense, and What We Can Do About It* (New York: Simon & Schuster, 1995).

Now, though, we see that on some college syllabi these works of so-called high culture are mingling with (or have been supplanted by) works from gay, chicano, Jewish, and even neo-Nazi literatures. More disturbing to some is that in colleges and universities today people no longer appear to read literature "as Literature"—that is, with a modicum of veneration, focusing on the "texts themselves" rather than turning books into illustrations of literary theory. Such a view is, in my experience, wrong: I see professors teaching books they love, and teaching them with passion. Theory may play a prominent role in many courses (and may be implied in many more), but it is not doled out gratuitously, for its own sake; it is invoked when it can offer insights to what makes a text tick.

Still, the theoretical turn in the humanities, and particularly in literary study, has caused something of a scandal, and it probably hasn't helped that so much of this thought has been imported from foreign soil. America has a reputation for cultural isolationism, and for a wariness of things foreign. As it happens, many of the current trends in the humanities have been spearheaded by European thinkers, which has not helped endear them to the public. When the works of German, Swiss, French, and Russian thinkers in such fields as linguistics, philosophy, and psychoanalysis infiltrated American programs in literature from the 1950s on, academic literary study began to draw attack. Then, as early feminism began to challenge many of our reading habits and prejudices, the battle grew heated.

What the doomsayers all have in common is a distrust for theory, for the very schools of thought I have attempted to introduce in this book. The reasons for their suspicion (a suspicion bordering on paranoia in some instances) are complicated. As I have said, the humanities used to be a settled and somewhat predictable set of disciplines: we had a fairly common understanding of what it meant to study literature, history, and philosophy. These fields were defined by their objects of study—the Russian novel, the French Revolution, the American pragmatists—and *not* by their methods. Method, in fact, was so transparent that it was often taken for granted: you were supposed to know as much about everything as you possibly could, and in the finest detail.

The introduction of method, and especially the proliferation of methods from the sixties to the present day, changed all the rules rather dramatically. The study of literature provides a good example of these changes. The tools for literary study used to be fairly minimal: you could get started if you read and understood English. The technical jargon one used had been around for centuries—sometimes longer—and included principally the terms of classical rhetoric: metaphor, metonymy, allegory, theme, motif, and others. The advent of new critical schools, however, shook everything up, and suddenly there was no common vocabulary or method for students and teachers of literature. Instead, one was expected to learn a whole new discipline. Literary study was no longer just "literary"; it had been grafted onto psychology (psychoanalysis), anthropology (structuralism), philosophy (poststructuralism), or some entirely new discipline, such as gender studies or cultural studies. Each approach came with its own jargon which, arising as it did from disciplines quite different from literature, often seemed frustratingly dense or even deliberately obscure.

Those who have decried the rise of theory seem uncomfortable with the transgressions these new areas of study have committed, especially by crossing over disciplinary boundaries. After all, don't such combinations confuse the literary with the psychological and the historical, with the philosophical and the cultural? Aren't they, in some sense, *monstrous* combinations? But post-structuralism has helped to demystify just such monsters as these, and has demonstrated the hollowness of many hallowed definitions. Literature, it turns out, has always already been a monster of sorts, and the "strictly literary" qualities, whose loss is rued by some, may always have been lacking.

Even more unsettling may be the idea that method, once considered relatively unproblematic, has begun to rival the text itself in importance. It is said that Michelangelo used to take a chisel to a block of marble in order to liberate the statue hiding inside, and this used to be a model for reading: the reader unleashed a meaning locked within the text. Recent movements put less stock in the Michelangelo method. "Literariness," and even meaning, have become less the intrinsic qualities of the text under study, and more the products of the way one reads. The advantage is that the same block of marble can render a potentially infinite number of statues.

Finally, theory has helped to reorganize disciplinary boundaries in the humanities (and even some social sciences), or has at least rendered them more permeable. Because critical approaches straddle disciplines, historians, literary critics, philosophers, and others who used to define their discipline primarily on the basis of the object of study, now share the rudiments of a lingua franca, a common tongue allowing for cross-disciplinary dialogue.

If the humanities have suffered from some bad press, one cannot attribute it to a general disregard for the activities of the academy. Indeed, certain fields have been vaulted to unprecedented visibility. One need only look at national media coverage to see how literary and cultural studies of all sorts live in the shadow of turn-of-the-millennium science. Physics (especially quantum mechanics) and biology (especially the Human Genome Project) appeal to the American imagination the way the dream of the West did a century ago: scientists have become the new pioneers, pushing physical frontiers ever further, progressing steadily toward a new land of technological milk and honey. We track this progress publicly. It is not unusual for the media to report extensively on developments in scientific fields: *Time* and *Newsweek* devote their cover stories to the discovery of quarks and other quirks; the nightly news tracks the publication of such journals as *Nature* and *The New England Journal of Medicine*, regularly announcing breakthroughs in the identification of human genetic code; public radio stations air weekly programs about developments in a variety of scientific fields; *Scientific American*, a highly respected professional journal, is available at local newsstands.

So, when was the last time you heard a news flash about Shakespearean studies, or picked up a copy of *Publications of the Modern Language Association* at your supermarket?

The privileging of the sciences becomes all the more evident when one follows the trail of money. The National Science Foundation alone (the NSF is just one of many funding agencies for research in the sciences) provides over three *billion* dollars in research grants annually, whereas the National Endowment for the Humanities and the National Endowment for the Arts combined (the NEH and the NEA are the only major national agencies for humanities sponsorship) pony up less than two hundred million. Even these comparatively meager funds are now channeled toward projects that bear some kind of entertainment value: recently revised NEH guidelines require that monies go primarily for work deemed to have "broad appeal" to the American public. Research in the hard sciences is rarely subjected to such an explicit popularity contest.

It isn't surprising that the sciences rivet our attention. After all, they promise to offer practical solutions for concrete problems, and quite often, they deliver on that promise. No one wants to argue against developing a cure for cancer or AIDS. Moreover, science touches us in innumerable—and sometimes nearly imperceptible—ways: scientific advances fuel technological developments, which in turn affect the way we build, the way we drive, the way we communicate, the way we make coffee in the morning. When science can offer us a faster computer chip *now*, or can correct an errant gene *tomorrow*, it is hard to see why a book written two, or three, or a thousand years ago should make the headlines *ever*. Science and technology, we often feel, have a more immediate and more important impact on our lives.

Of course, the story of science can be told different ways: we can portray it (as we are wont to do) as a tale of continual progress, of the perfectibility of knowledge, of methods, and of human life; or, it can also be portrayed negatively (this was the point of view of Ted Kazinsky, the Unabomber, for instance) as a wedge that, over the ages, scientists and engineers have driven between humans and nature; or, again, we might show it as an uneven, imperfect adventure, resulting in some gains, some losses, with each generation of research devoting considerable resources to repairing the havoc wrought by the previous generation's discoveries. The point here is not to argue that one version of the story is "truer" than another. Rather, I mean simply to point out that our perception of science is always organized *as a story*. Our whole lives, in fact, are immersed in stories—not just those that we *recognize* as such (tales we read to our kids, books we leave on our night tables, fictions we watch on TV), but also those we *mis*recognize, those we accept, for reasons of convenience, belief, or education, as if they were transparent representations of "the way things are." Yet even these "nonfiction" stories are organized, constructed, and edited to show a certain unity, often a kind of plot: we see this in reports on the TV news, for example, or in our thoughts about the ever-accelerating pace of change in American culture, or in our personal musings about where we are headed in life.

Literary study is not likely to produce medical breakthroughs; nor does it seem on track for providing some "grand unifying theory," as some have said physics is on the brink of achieving. But it *can* help us understand how the notion of "breakthroughs" partakes of science's ability to dramatize itself and hold us spellbound, or how a "unifying theory" appeals because it promises to tell us the "story" of the universe. Such stories are everywhere: our lives are filled with beginnings and endings, small ceremonies, codified interactions. The way we represent these events, to ourselves and others, always involves a certain amount of editing, a skewing by point of view, an embedding in plot. Presumably, then, literary study should not be turned away or kept at a distance, for it touches us in the most intimate and invisible recesses of our lives.

REFERENCES

■■■

AARNE, ANTTI AMATUS. *The Types of the Folktale: A Classification and Bibliography*. Translated by Stith Thompson. Helsinki: Academia Scientarum Fennica, 1961.

ABALONE, HENRY, et al., eds. *The Lesbian and Gay Studies Reader*. New York: Routledge, 1993.

AHRENS, J. "Recovered Memories: True or False? A Look at False Memory Syndrome." *University of Louisville Journal of Family Law* 34, no. 2 (1996): 379–401.

ANDERSON, LAURIE. *Puppet Motel* [CD-ROM]. New York: Voyager, 1995.

BABENER, LIAHNA KLENMAN. "The Shadow's Shadow: The Motif of the Double in Edgar Allan Poe's 'The Purloined Letter'." In *The Purloined Poe*, edited by J. Muller and W. Richardson, 323–334. Baltimore: The Johns Hopkins University Press, 1988.

BAKHTIN, MIKHAIL. *Rabelais and His World*. Translated by Helene Iswolsky. Cambridge: Technology Press of the Massachussets Institute of Technology, 1968.

BALZAC, HONORÉ DE. *Le Père Goriot*. Paris: Gallimard-Folio, 1971.

BARTHES, ROLAND. *Mythologies*. Translated by Annette Lavers. New York: Hill and Wang, 1972.

———. "The Death of the Author." In *Image, Music, Text*, translated by Stephen Heath. New York: Hill and Wang, 1977.

———. "The Reality Effect." In *French Literary Theory Today: A Reader*, edited by Tzvetan Todorov, translated by R. Carter. Cambridge: Cambridge University Press, 1982.

BEARDSLEY, M. C., AND W. K. WHIMSATT. "The Intentional Fallacy." In *On Literary Intention: Critical Essays*, edited by David Newton-de Molina. Edinburgh: University Press, 1976.

BERGER, LOUIS. "Cultural Psychopathology and the 'False Memory Syndrome' Debates: A View from Psychoanalysis." *American Journal of Psychotherapy* 50, no. 2 (Spring 1996): 166–177.

BETTELHEIM, BRUNO. *The Uses of Enchantment*. New York: Knopf , 1976.

BHABHA, HOMI K. "The Other Question: Difference, Discrimination and the Discourse of Colonialism." In *Out There: Marginalization and Contemporary Culture*, edited by Russell Ferguson, M. Sever, T. Minh-La, and C. West. New York: New Museum of Contemporary Art, 1990.

BISKIND, PETER. "Pods, Blobs, and Ideology in American Films of the Fifties." In *Invasion of the Body Snatchers*, edited by Al LaValley. New Brunswick and London: RutgersUniversity Press, 1989, 185–197.

BLOOM, ALLAN. *The Closing of the American Mind: How Higher Education Has Failed Democracy and Impoverished the Souls of Today's Students*. New York: Simon & Schuster, 1987.

BLOOM, AMY. "The Body Lies." *The New Yorker*. July 18, 1994, 38–49.

BOLTER, JAY. *Writing Space: The Computer, Hypertext, and the History of Writing*. Hillsdale, New Jersey: Erlbaum, 1991.

BORGES, JORGE LUIS. *Ficciones*, edited by Anthony Kerrigan. New York: Grove Press, 1963.

Brown University. "Hypertext at Brown." Available on the World Wide Web at: http://www.stg.brown.edu/projects/hypertext/hypertext_ov.html

BUSH, VANNEVAR. "As We May Think." *Atlantic Monthly* 176 (July 1945): 101–108.

BUTLER, JUDITH. *Gender Trouble: Feminism and the Subversion of Identity*. New York: Routledge, 1990.

Casablanca. Dir. Michael Curtiz. Warner, 1942.

CHENEY, LYNNE. *Telling the Truth: Why Our Culture and Our Country Have Stopped Making Sense, and What We Can Do About It*. New York: Simon & Schuster, 1995.

COLETTE, SIDONIE GABRIELLE. "The Hidden Woman," In *The Collected Stories of Colette*, translated by Matthew Ward. New York: Farrar Strauss Giroux, 1984.

CREWS, FREDERICK. "The Revenge of the Repressed." *The New York Review of Books*, Nov. 17 and Dec. 1, 1994.

The Crying Game, Dir. Neil Jordan, 1992.

CULLER, JONATHAN. *Structuralist Poetics: Structuralism, Linguistics, and the Study of Literature*. Ithaca, New York: Cornell University Press, 1975.

CULLER, JONATHAN. *On Deconstruction: Theory and Criticism after Structuralism*. Ithaca, New York: Cornell University Press, 1982.

"Daddy's Little Girl." *Time*. June 4, 1990.

DANA, RICHARD HENRY, JR. *Two Years Before the Mast*. New York: Penguin, Signet Classic, 1964.

DE LAURETIS, TERESA. "Upping the Anti [sic] in Feminist Theory." In *The Cultural Studies Reader*, edited by Simon During. New York: Routledge, 1993.

DELEUZE, GILLES. "Rhizome Versus Trees." In *The Deleuze Reader*, edited by Constantin Boundas. New York: Columbia University Press, 1993, 27–36.

DE MAN, PAUL. *Blindness and Insight: Essays in the Rhetoric of Contemporary Criticism*. New York: Oxford University Press, 1971.

———. *Allegories of Reading: Figural Language in Rousseau, Nietzsche, Rilke, and Proust*. New Haven: Yale University Press, 1979.

DERRIDA, JACQUES. "Differance." In *Speech and Phenomenon*. Evanston: Northwestern University Press, 1973.

———. *Of Grammatology*, translated by Gayatri Chakravorty Spivak. Baltimore: The Johns Hopkins University Press, 1976.

———. "Structure, Sign, and Play in the Discourse of the Human Sciences." In *Writing and Difference*, translated by Alan Bass. Chicago: University of Chicago Press, 1978.

———. "The Purveyor of Truth." In *The Post Card: From Socrates to Freud and Beyond*, translated by Alan Bass. Chicago: University of Chicago Press, 1987.

———. *Truth in Painting*, translated by Geoff Bennington and Ian McLeod. Chicago: University of Chicago Press, 1987.

———. "Signature Event Context." *Limited Inc.*, edited by Samuel Weber. Evanston: Northwestern University Press, 1988, 1–24.

DOUGLAS, SUSAN. *Where the Girls Are: Growing Up Female with the Mass Media*. New York: Times Books, 1994.

DROSNIN, MICHAEL. *The Bible Code*. New York: Simon & Schuster, 1997.

DR. SEUSS. *The Cat in the Hat Comes Back!* New York: Random House, 1958.

"Dubious Memories." *Time*. May 23, 1994.

DURING, SIMON. *The Cultural Studies Reader*. New York: Routledge, 1993.

ECO, UMBERTO. *The Limits of Interpretation*. Bloomington: Indiana University Press, 1990.

———. *The Name of the Rose*. Translated by William Weaver. San Diego: Harcourt Brace, 1994.

———. "*Casablanca*: Cult Movies and Intertextual Collage." In *Philosophy and Film*, edited by Cynthia A. Freeland and Thomas E. Wartenberg. New York: Routledge, 1995.

ECO, UMBERTO, WITH R. RORTY, J. CULLER, C. BROOKE-ROSE. *Interpretation and Overinterpretation*. Edited by Stefan Collini. Cambridge: Cambridge University Press, 1992.

FELMAN, SHOSHANA. "On Reading Poetry: Reflections on the Limits and Possibilities of Psychoanalytic Approaches." In *The Purloined Poe: Lacan, Derrida, and Psychoanalytic Reading*, edited by J. Muller and W. Richardson. Baltimore: The Johns Hopkins University Press, 1988.

———. *What Does a Woman Want?* Baltimore: The Johns Hopkins University Press. 1993.

FISH, STANLEY. "Is There a Text in This Class?" In *Is There a Text in This Class?: The Authority of Interpretive Communities*. Cambridge: Harvard University Press, 1980.

FLYNN, ELIZABETH, AND P. SCHWEICKART, eds. *Gender and Reading: Essays on Readers, Texts, and Contexts*. Baltimore: The Johns Hopkins University Press, 1986.

"Forgetting to Remember." *Newsweek*. February 11, 1991.

FOSTER, HAL, ed. *The Anti-aesthetic: Essays on Postmodern Culture*. Port Townsend, Wash.: Bay Press, 1983.

FOUCAULT, MICHEL. "Qu'est-ce qu'un auteur?" *Bulletin de la Société française de Philosophie* 63 (1969): 73–104.

———. "What Is an Author?" In *Textual Strategies: Perspectives in Post-Structuralist Criticism*, edited by Josué Harari. Ithaca, N.Y.: Cornell University Press, 1979.

———. *The History of Sexuality. Vol. I, An Introduction*. Translated by Robert Hurley. New York: Vintage, 1980.

FRANK, ANNE. *The Diary of a Young Girl*. Translated by B. M. Mooyaart-Doubleday. Garden City, New York: Doubleday, 1952.

FREUD, SIGMUND. "The Unconscious." In *The Standard Edition of the Complete Psychological Works of Sigmund Freud*, translated by James Strachey and A. Freud. Vol. XIV, 159–216. London: Hogarth Press.

———. "Repression." In *The Standard Edition*. Vol. XIV, 141–158.

———. "The Uncanny." In *The Standard Edition*. Vol. XVII, 217–256.

———. *The Interpretation of Dreams*. In *The Standard Edition*. Vol. XIII.

———. *Jokes and Their Relation to the Unconscious*. In *The Standard Edition*. Vol. XIII.

———. "Fragments of an Analysis of a Case of Hysteria." In *The Standard Edition*. Vol. VII, 3–124.

———. *Beyond the Pleasure Principle*, in *The Standard Edition*. Vol. XVIII.

GEERTZ, CLIFFORD. "Thick Description." In *The Interpretation of Cultures: Selected Essays*. New York: Basic Books, 1973.

GENETTE, GÉRARD. "Structuralism and Literary Criticism." In *Figures of Literary Discourse*, translated by Alan Sheridan. New York: Columbia University Press, 1982.

GOODRICH, NORMA LORE. *Charles Duke of Orléans: A Literary Biography*. New York: Macmillan, 1963.

GREENBLATT, STEPHEN. "Towards a Poetics of Culture." In *The Aims of Representation: Subject/Text/History*, edited by Murray Krieger. New York: Columbia University Press, 1987.

———. *Learning to Curse: Essays in Early Modern Culture*. New York: Routledge, 1990.

———. *Marvelous Possessions: The Wonder of the New World*. Chicago: University of Chicago Press, 1991.

HALPERIN, DAVID. "Is There a History of Sexuality?" In *The Lesbian and Gay Studies Reader*, edited by Henry Abelove, M. Barale, and D. Halperin. New York: Routledge, 1993.

HARMETZ, ALJEAN. *Round Up the Usual Suspects: The Making of Casablanca—Bogart, Bergman, and World War II.* New York: Hyperion, 1992.

HARTMANN, GEOFFREY, et al. *Deconstruction and Criticism.* New York: Continuum, 1979.

HIRSCH, E. D. *Cultural Literacy: What Every American Needs to Know.* Boston: Houghton Mifflin, 1987.

Invasion of the Body Snatchers. Dir. Don Siegel. Allied Artists, 1956.

IRIGARAY, LUCE. *This Sex Which Is Not One.* Translated by Catherine Porter and Carolyn Burke. Ithaca: Cornell University Press, 1985.

ISER, WOLFGANG. *The Implied Reader: Patterns of Communication in Prose Fiction from Bunyan to Beckett.* Baltimore: The Johns Hopkins University Press, 1974.

JAKOBSON, ROMAN. "Linguistics and Poetics." In *Style in Language,* edited by Thomas Sebeok. Cambridge: Technology Press of the Massachusetts Institute of Technology, 1960.

JAMES, HENRY. *The Turn of the Screw.* New York: Dover Publications, 1991.

The Johns Hopkins Guide to Literary Theory and Criticism. Edited by Michael Groden and Martin Kreiswirth. Baltimore: Johns Hopkins University Press, 1994.

JOHNSON, BARBARA. "Melville's Fist: The Execution of Billy Budd." In *The Critical Difference.* Baltimore: The Johns Hopkins University Press, 1980.

———. "The Frame of Reference: Poe, Lacan, Derrida." In *The Purloined Poe: Lacan, Derrida, and Psychoanalytic Reading,* edited by J. Muller and W. Richardson. Baltimore: The Johns Hopkins University Press, 1988.

JONSON, BEN. *The Alchemist.* Edited by F. H. Mares. Manchester: Manchester University Press, 1997.

JOYCE, MICHAEL. *Afternoon, A Story* [Diskette]. Cambridge: Eastgate Press, 1987, 1992.

———. *Twilight, A Symphony* [CD-ROM]. Cambridge: Eastgate Press, 1995.

———. "Twelve Blue." Available on the World Wide Web at: http://www.eastgate.com/TwelveBlue/Welcome.html

"Judge Upsets Murder Conviction Focused on 'Repressed Memory'." *The New York Times.* April 5, 1995.

KASCHNITZ, MARIE LUISE. "The Fat Girl." In *Circe's Mountain: Stories by Marie Luise Kaschnitz,* translated by Lisel Mueller. Minneapolis: Milkweed Editions, 1990.

KLAGES, MARY. "Sigmund Freud." Available on the World Wide Web at: http://www.colorado.edu/English/ENGL2012Klages/freud.html

———. "Jacques Lacan." Available on the World Wide Web at: http://www.colorado.edu/English/ENGL2012Klages/lacan.html

———. "Structuralism/Poststructuralism." Available on the World Wide Web at: http://www.colorado.edu/English/ENGL2012Klages/1derrida.html

KOFMAN, SARAH. *The Enigma of Woman: Woman in Freud's Writings.* Translated by Catherine Porter. Ithaca: Cornell University Press, 1985.

KRISTEVA, JULIA. Revolution in Poetic Language. Translated by Margaret Waller. New York: Columbia University Press, 1984.

LACAN, JACQUES. "The Mirror Stage as Formative of the Function of the I." In *Ecrits: A Selection*, translated by Alan Sheridan. New York: Norton, 1977.

———. "The Function and Field of Speech and Language in Psychoanalysis." In *Ecrits: A Selection*, translated by Alan Sheridan. New York: Norton, 1977.

———. "On a Question Preliminary to any Possible Treatment of Psychosis." In *Ecrits: A Selection*, translated by Alan Sheridan. New York: Norton, 1977.

———. "The Agency of the Letter in the Unconscious, Or Reason since Freud." In *Ecrits: A Selection*, translated by Alan Sheridan. New York: Norton, 1977.

———. "Desire and the Interpretation of Desire in Hamlet." In *Literature and Psychoanalysis: The Question of Reading Otherwise*, edited by Shoshana Felman et al. Baltimore: The Johns Hopkins University Press, 1980.

———. "Seminar on 'The Purloined Letter'." In *The Purloined Poe: Lacan, Derrida, and Psychoanalytic Reading*, edited J. Muller and W. Richardson. Baltimore: The Johns Hopkins University Press, 1988, 28–54.

LANDOW, GEORGE. Hypertext: The Convergence of Contemporary Critical Theory and Technology. Baltimore: The Johns Hopkins University Press, 1992. (Revised as *Hypertext 2.0* in 1997).

LANDOW, GEORGE, ed. Hyper/Text/Theory. Baltimore: The Johns Hopkins University Press, 1994.

LEHMAN, DAVID. Signs of the Times: Deconstruction and the Fall of Paul de Man. New York: Poseidon Press, 1991.

LEITCH, THOMAS. "The Rhetoric of the Remake." *Literature Film Quarterly* 18, no. 3 (1990): 138–148.

LEVER, MAURICE. Donatien Alphonse François, marquis de Sade. Paris: Fayard, 1991.

LÉVI-STRAUSS, CLAUDE. The Raw and the Cooked. Translated by John and Doreen Weightman. New York: Harper & Row, 1970.

LIU, ALAN, ed. Voice of the Shuttle Website on Literary Theory [Website]. Pages include:

On cultural studies: http://humanitas.ucsb.edu/shuttle/cultural.html

On cyber culture: http://humanitas.ucsb.edu/shuttle/cyber.html

On hypertext fiction: http://humanitas.ucsb.edu/shuttle/techwrit.html#hypertext

On deconstruction: http://humanitas.ucsb.edu/shuttle/theory.html#deconstruction

On postcolonial studies: http://humanitas.ucsb.edu/shuttle/cultural.html#postcolonial

On feminism and women's studies: http://humanitas.ucsb.edu/shuttle/gender.html#women

On gender studies: http://humanitas.ucsb.edu/shuttle/gender.html

On gay-lesbian and queer studies: http://humanitas.ucsb.edu/shuttle/gender.html#queer

On reader response theory: http://humanitas.ucsb.edu/shuttle/theory.html# reader-response

On postmodernism: http://humanitas.ucsb.edu/shuttle/theory.html#postmodern

On structuralism: http://humanitas.ucsb.edu/shuttle/theory.html#structuralism

On psychology and psychoanalysis: http://humanitas.ucsb.edu/shuttle/theory. html#psycho

On semiotics and signs: http://humanitas.ucsb.edu/shuttle/theory.html#semiotic

LOFTUS, ELIZABETH, AND K. KETCHAM. *The Myth of Repressed Memory*. New York: St. Martin's Press, 1994.

LYE, JOHN. "Some Elements of Structuralism and its Application to Literary Theory." Available on the World Wide Web at: http://www.brocku.ca/english/ courses/4F70/struct.html

———. "Reader-Response: Various Positions." Available on the World Wide Web at: http://www.brocku.ca/english/courses/4F70/rr.html

MILGRAM, STANLEY. "Behavioral Study of Obedience." *Journal of Abnormal and Social Psychology* 67 (1963): 371–378.

MILLER, J. HILLIS. "The Critic as Host." *Critical Inquiry* 3 (1977): 439–447.

MITCHELL, JULIET. "Femininity, Narrative, and Psychoanalysis." In *Women: The Longest Revolution. Essays on Feminism, Literature and Psychoanalysis*. New York: Vintage, 1974.

MITCHELL, STEPHEN, AND MARGARET BLACK. *Freud and Beyond*. New York: Basic Books, 1995.

MORRIS, MEAGHAN. "Things To Do with Shopping Centres." In *The Cultural Studies Reader*, edited by S. During. New York: Routlege, 1993: 295–319.

MOULTHROP, STUART. "Rhizome and Resistance: Hypertext and the Dreams of a New Culture." In *Hyper/Text/Theory*, edited by George Landow. Baltimore: The Johns Hopkins University Press, 1994, 299–319.

MULLER, JOHN, AND W. RICHARDSON, eds. *The Purloined Poe: Lacan, Derrida, and Psychoanalytic Reading*. Baltimore: The Johns Hopkins University Press, 1988.

MULVEY, LAURA. "Visual Pleasure and Narrative Cinema." In *Visual and Other Pleasures*. Bloomington: Indiana University Press, 1989.

"Oedipal Wrecks." *World Press Review* 41 (October 1994): 30–31.

PEIRCE, CHARLES SANDERS. *Peirce on Signs: Writings on Semiotics*. Edited by James Hoopes. Chapel Hill: University of North Carolina Press, 1991.

PIPHER, MARY. *Reviving Ophelia: Saving the Selves of Adolescent Girls*. New York: Putnam, 1994.

POE, EDGAR ALLAN. *The Complete Works of Edgar Allan Poe*. Edited by James A. Harrison New York: AMS Press, 1965.

PRINCE, GERALD. "Introduction to the Study of the Narratee." In *Reader-Response Criticism: From Formalism to Post-Structuralism*, edited by Jane P. Tompkins. Baltimore: The Johns Hopkins University Press, 1980.

PROPP, VLADIMIR. *Morphology of the Folktale.* Austin: University of Texas Press, 1968.

QUENEAU, RAYMOND. *Cent Mille Milliards de Poèmes.* Paris: Gallimard, 1961. (Not available in English.)

RICHARDSON, SAMUEL. *Clarissa.* Edited by Angus Ross. New York: Viking Penguin, 1985.

ROGIN, MICHAEL PAUL. "Kiss Me Deadly: Communism, Motherhood, and the Cold War Movies." In *Invasion of the Body Snatchers,* edited by Al LaValley. New Brunswick and London: Rutgers University Press, 1989.

RORTY, RICHARD. "From Ironist Theory to Private Allusions: Derrida." In *Contingency, Irony, and Solidarity.* Cambridge: Cambridge University Press, 1989.

SAUSSURE, FERDINAND DE. *Course in General Linguistics.* Edited by Charles Bally and Albert Sechehayein in collaboration with Albert Reidlinger, translated by Wade Baskin. London: Fontana, 1974.

SEDGWICK, EVE KOSOFSKY. *Epistemology of the Closet.* Berkeley: University of California Press, 1990.

SHKLOVSKY, VICTOR. "Art as Technique." In *Russian Formalist Criticism: Four Essays,* edited and translated by Lee Lemon and M. Reis. Lincoln: University of Nebraska Press, 1965.

SHOWALTER, ELAINE, ed. *The New Feminist Criticism: Essays on Women, Literature, and Theory.* New York: Pantheon, 1985.

———. "Feminist Criticism in the Wilderness." *Critical Inquiry* 8, no. 2 (Winter 1981): 179–205.

———. "Feminism and Literature." In *Literary Theory Today,* edited by Peter Collier and Helga Geyer-Ryan. Ithaca: Cornell University Press, 1990.

Shumate, Michael. "Hyperizons." Available on the World Wide Web at: http://www.duke.edu/kmshumate/original.html

SIDEL, RUTH. *Keeping Women and Children Last.* New York: Penguin, 1996.

SIEGEL, JEFF. *The Casablanca Companion: The Movie and More.* Dallas: Taylor Publishing, 1992.

SPIVAK, GAYATRI CHAKRAVORTY. "Post-Structuralism, Marginality, Postcoloniality and Value." In *Literary Theory Today,* edited by Peter Collier. Ithaca: Cornell University Press, 1990.

STEIG, MICHAEL. *Stories of Reading: Subjectivity and Literary Understanding.* Baltimore: The Johns Hopkins University Press, 1989.

STEVENSON, ROBERT LOUIS. *Robert Louis Stevenson: The Complete Shorter Fiction.* Edited by Peter Stoneley. New York: Carroll and Graf, 1991.

STOPPARD, TOM. *Travesties.* New York: Grove Press, 1975.

TANNEN, DEBORAH. *That's Not What I Meant!: How Conversation Style Makes or Breaks Your Relations with Others.* New York: Morrow, 1986.

———. *Women and Men in Conversation.* New York: Morrow, 1990.

TATAR, MARIA. *Off with Their Heads: Fairy Tales and the Culture of Childhood.* Princeton, New Jersey: Princeton University Press, 1992.

TERR, LENORE. *Unchained Memories*. New York: Basic Books, 1994.

TOMPKINS, JANE, ed. *Reader-Response Criticism: From Formalism to Post-Structuralism*. Baltimore: The Johns Hopkins University Press, 1980.

VEESER, H. ARAM, ed. *The New Historicism Reader*. New York: Routledge, 1994.

Voltaire's Philosophical Dictionary. New York: Knopf, 1924.

"Was it Real or Memories?" *Newsweek*. March 4, 1994.

WILLIAMS, RAYMOND. "Advertising: The Magic System." In *The Cultural Studies Reader*, edited by Simon During. New York: Routledge, 1993.

WITTIG, MONIQUE. "The Trojan Horse." In *The Straight Mind*. Boston: Beacon Press, 1992, 68–77.

WRIGHT, ELIZABETH. *Psychoanalytic Criticism: Theory in Practice*. London and New York: Methuen, 1984.

ZIPES, JACK. *Don't Bet on the Prince: Contemporary Feminist Fairy Tales in North America and England*. New York: Routledge, 1989.

ZUMTHOR, PAUL. *Langue, Texte, Enigme*. Paris: Editions du Seuil, 1975.

INDEX

■ ■ ■